Airport Spotting Guides
World
Airports

Second Edition

Second Edition 2020

ISBN 978 1 9996470 8 7

British Library Cataloguing-in-Publication Data
A catalogue record for this book is available from the British Library.

Published by Destinworld Publishing Ltd.
www.destinworld.com

Cover design by John Wright
All photographs © Matthew Falcus

CONTENTS

v

INTRODUCTION

Thank you for purchasing this guide to spotting at the world's best airports. Hopefully it will unlock opportunities to enjoy your hobby logging and photographing aircraft, and prove useful in both planning your trips and the airports you'll visit, and as a reference guide while on the road looking for good places to watch aircraft action.

The book includes all of the world's major airports for commercial aviation – namely airliners and biz jets, listed by country. Whilst a lot of the airports also have general aviation and military activity, this is not strictly a guide to military or light aircraft airfields.

For those new to spotting, there are plenty of great airports around the world to try out, and most have at least one good spot for viewing from. The world's busiest airports are usually found in major cities. Depending on your interests or the places you'll travel to, other very interesting airports can be found in more unusual places, like deserts or smaller cities.

Where possible I've tried to include other useful bits of information about the airports listed, including nearby aviation museums where the past is brough to life or historic aircraft are preserved. You'll also find tips on spotting hotels which are listed because they have rooms with views of the aircraft or runways at that airport – a useful place to continue spotting after dark or in poor weather!

Notes on Using This Guide

As always, the information provided is for use at your own risk. We do not take any responsibility for your actions when visiting the airports listed here, or using the information provided. Maps are our own interpretations, and are not meant to be used for navigation.

You should always ensure you have permission to spot aircraft from private property, and the advice we'd always stand by is that informing airport police or security officers of your intentions is a good thing. Most will be perfectly happy to allow you to continue, or to suggest a better place to stand.

Information provided in this book is always subject to going out of date; airports develop, roads and rights of way change, and perhaps most common of all, the airline operators and aircraft types being used will change. We have done everything to ensure the information provided in this book is correct at the time of publication, but must warn that it can go out of date.

Keep up with changes in the world of airports and spotting at **www.airportspotting.com**

PLANE SPOTTING INSPIRATION

Top 20 Spotting Locations

1. St Maarten Maho Beach
2. Tokyo Haneda Observation Decks
3. Zurich Observation Decks
4. London Heathrow Myrtle Avenue
5. Sydney Sheps Mound
6. Atlanta Hartsfield-Jackson Renaissance Concourse Hotel
7. Frankfurt Autobahn Viewing Platform
8. Los Angeles International Imperial Hill
9. Bangkok Suvarnabhumi Observation Area
10. Madrid Barajas Mound
11. Amsterdam Schiphol Polderbaan
12. Singapore Changi Viewing Areas
13. Phuket Nai Yang Beach
14. Dallas Ft. Worth Founders Plaza
15. Osaka Kansai Sky View Observation Hall
16. Washington Reagan National Gravelly Point
17. Dusseldorf Observation Deck
18. Las Vegas McCarran Sunset Road
19. Osaka Itami Sky Park
20. Tokyo Narita Observation Decks

Ten Best Aviation Museums

1. National Air & Space Museums, Washington DC
2. Museum of Flight, Seattle, WA
3. Oleg Antonov State Aviation Museum, Kiev, Ukraine
4. Duxford Imperial War Museum, Cambridge, UK
5. Pima Air & Space Museum, Tucson, AZ
6. Chinese Aviation Museum Datangshan, Beijing China
7. Qantas Founders Museum, Longreach, Australia
8. Aeroscopia, Toulouse, France
9. Aviodrome Themepark, Lelystad, Netherlands
10. Museum of Air & Space, Le Bourget, Paris, France

Ten Best Spotting Hotels

These hotels are among the best in the world for spotting aircraft, based on their views, quality of aircraft movements, facilities and the opinions of other spotters.

1. Renaissance London Heathrow Hotel, United Kingdom
2. Renaissance Concourse Hotel Atlanta Hartsfield-Jackson, USA
3. TWA Hotel, New York JFK, USA
4. Cordis Beijing Capital, China
5. Royal Boutique Hotel Corfu, Greece
6. Embassy Suites South Los Angeles LAX South, USA
7. Crowne Plaza Singapore Changi, Singapore
8. Rydges Sydney Airport Hotel, Australia
9. Regal Airport Hotel, Hong Kong
10. Grand Inn Come, Bangkok Suvarnabhumi, Thailand

ANTIGUA AND BARBUDA

ANTIGUA V C BIRD INTERNATIONAL

ANU | TAPA

A fairly busy airport in the Caribbean with a single runway and small terminal. It handles a lot of inter-island traffic with LIAT, as well as large airliners from Europe, the USA and Canada.

If you have a car there are spots to watch arrivals and departures at either end of the runway. Try the side of the Sir George Walter Hwy for runway 07, or Burma Road for 25. The latter runs around the western side of the airport where light aircraft park on a disused runway.

ARGENTINA

Buenos Aires Aeroparque Jorge Newbery

AEP | SABE

This is the secondary airport at Buenos Aires, but busier than the primary Ministro Pistarini. Aeroparque is in the north eastern part of the city, alongside the sea. It is the city's domestic airport, with airlines like Aerolineas Argentinas, Austral, Andes Lineas Aereas, JetSmart Argentina and LATAM coming and going all day. The airport is also a military base, and home to the government's transport aircraft.

Many people watch aircraft here from the car park alongside the terminal, which overlooks the taxiway and runway. A grassed area at the end of runway 13 is also good for photography. With both areas it is not wise to be alone or to display too much expensive equipment openly.

Buenos Aires Ministro Pistarini / Ezeiza

EZE | SAEZ

The main airport in Argentina, Ministro Pistarini handles long-haul international flights, as well as some domestic routes. It is home to Aerolineas Argentinas and its maintenance area, and also a hub for Gol and LATAM Argentina. The airport also handles a decent amount of cargo flights.

The two runways (and a disused one) are arranged in a RAF-style triangle pattern, with the terminal complex on the north western side, and the maintenance area in the north east.

There are very few spotting opportunities here, but you can see aircraft movements and many stands from within the terminal departure areas. The busiest time of day is often after dark.

With a car, the roads passing the ends of runway 11/29 can be used for spotting and photographing arrivals.

Buenos Aires Morón Airport and Air Base

SADM

Formerly the main airport of Buenos Aires, Morón is now a military base. It is of interest to the spotter because of the National Aeronautical Museum and its interesting aircraft on site.

MUSEUM

Museo Nacional de Aeronáutica

Av Eva Perón al 2700, Morón - CP (B1708FEZ) | +54 4697 6964 | www.fuerzaaerea.mil.ar/historia/museo_salas.html

Set up to showcase the history of the Argentine Air Force, this museum is also home to various transport aircraft including BAC One Elevens, de Havilland Dove, McDonnell Douglas MD-81, Bristol Freighter and Vickers Viking.

Ushuaia – Malvinas Argentinas International

USH | SAWH

The world's southernmost international airport, Ushuaia is the gateway to the Antarctic. The current airport was opened in 1997 on a spit of land to the south of the city. The smaller airport that it replaced is still evident a short distance to the north, and operates sightseeing and aero club flights. It has a preserved DC-3 outside.

The new airport is small but has a runway capable of handling the largest airliners. Often Aerolineas Argentinas will send widebody aircraft on the Buenos Aires route during heavy tourist periods. Aside from domestic flights, airlines such as Gol and TAM link Ushuaia to Brazil. State-owned airline LADE also operate into the airport regularly with their interesting fleet. The airport is busiest when cruise ships are scheduled to pass through.

Spotting is possible either side of the terminal through the fence, with gaps big enough for cameras. There's also an elevated bank to the east of the terminal which offers a good photographic spot looking over the parking apron.

AUSTRALIA

Adelaide

ADL | YPAD

Adelaide is a moderately busy airport with two runways and a terminal which was redeveloped in 2005. Qantas and its feeder partners are the biggest operators here, along with Virgin Australia and a handful of international carriers from Asia and the Middle East. A number of smaller carriers operate from the General Aviation Terminal.

It's fairly easy to find places to spot at Adelaide. A drive around the service roads near the terminal will yield many aircraft parked outside hangars and the general aviation area. For morning arrivals a good spot is at the end of Richmond Road, alongside the runway 23 threshold (the terminal is visible from here too). At the 05 end of the runway is the official viewing point, with parking, off the Tapleys Hill Road is great for watching aircraft on the runway and taxiways, and photography on the afternoon. There are many other spots around the roads to explore.

Brisbane

BNE | YBBN

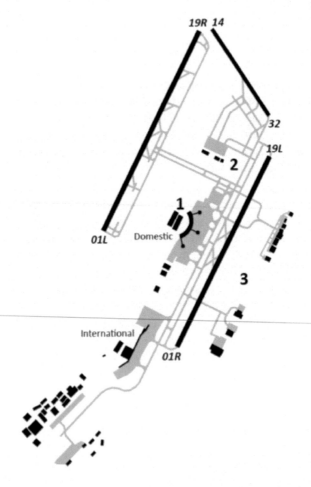

Brisbane Airport is the largest and busiest in Queensland, on Australia's eastern coast. It is the third busiest in Australia and served by the main operators in the country, along with plenty of overseas airlines. Qantas sends their Airbus A330 fleet here for maintenance. Jetstar Airways, Qantas/Qantas Link, Tigerair Australia and Virgin Australia all have bases here. The original airport site to the south west is now the cargo and general aviation area, whilst maintenance is done on the opposite side of the main runway to the two terminals. The new runway 01L/19R opened in 2020.

Just outside the International Terminal is a hangar housing the preserved Southern Cross aircraft, which was the first to fly across the Pacific (with Charles Kingsford Smith at the helm).

Spotting Locations

1. Domestic Terminal & Car Park
Within the domestic terminal you are able to visit all gate areas and spot/take photographs through the windows. You must pass through security screening to do this, but do not require a boarding pass. An alternative is the top level of the car park outside the domestic terminal. From here you have panoramic views of the main runway and part of the gates and taxiways.

2. Viewing Platform
A small parking area and raised concrete slab makes this a nice official spot for watching aircraft on the main and secondary runways, as well as taxying to and from the terminals. You won't miss much here, although the fence makes it a little difficult to take unobstructed photographs. To reach the spot, follow Dryanda Rd under the new taxiways, then turn right onto Acacia St and follow to the end. If the viewing area is closed, you can still spot from the access road.

3. Fire Station
On the opposite side of the airfield, this is a good spot to see what's in the maintenance hangars and also to photograph aircraft on the main runway with the Brisbane skyline as a backdrop. To get there, head towards the city from the terminals and take a left onto Lomandra Dr. At the end turn left onto Myrtletown Rd. Turn left onto Pandanus Ave, and then left again onto Baeckea St. Park in the car park.

Canberra

CBR | YSCB

Canberra is not a particularly busy airport, but has a decent domestic network served by Qantas and Virgin Australia, and their regional partners. One particular note of interest is that RAAF Fairnbairn shares the airport, with its own facility north east of the runways. The Australian government's VIP transport fleet is based here.

You can view inside the terminal by passing through security (you don't need a boarding pass), or alternatively outside at either end of the terminal. The RAAF aircraft can be seen from the terminal if they are parked outside.

Longreach

LRE | YLRE

This remote spot in the north east of Australia isn't busy with movements, which consist only of Qantas and Regional Express feeder flights. But its aviation museum is a major draw for enthusiasts. Longreach is a very historic airport, being the place where Qantas was founded, and also where aviators Charles Kingsford Smith and Amy Johnson visited on various tours.

MUSEUM

Qantas Founders Museum

Sir Hudson Fysh Drive, Longreach, QLD 4730 | +61 7 4658 3737 | www.qfom.com.au

Establish to preserve the heritage of Australia's national airline and its founding years, this museum is a big draw for its aircraft collection which includes a Boeing 707, 747-200, Catalina and Douglas DC-3 amongst others.

Melbourne Avalon

AVV | YMAV

Situated around 30 miles south-west of Melbourne city centre, Avalon is the city's second-busiest airport. It has a single runway and flights operated by AirAsiaX, Citilink and Jetstar Airways. Qantas also send their aircraft here for heavy maintenance. The Australian International Airshow is held at Avalon every two years.

Aircraft parked at the terminal and approaching the runway can easily be seen from the car park and Airport Drive. Alternatively, to see aircraft at the Qantas hangars head east on Beach Road, then turn right onto Pousties Road.

Look out for the former Qantas Boeing 747-300 that once wore the special Nalanji Dreaming livery. It is used as a ground trainer at Avalon.

Melbourne Essendon

MEB | YMEN

This was formerly Melbourne's first international airport, opened in the 1920s. It is located 4 miles from the current Melbourne International Airport. Today it is still an important gateway for business and light aircraft, and offers some regional flights operated by commuter carriers.

If you have a car, take a tour of the small roads leading in either direction from the terminal which lead past the many hangars and log whatever you can see. Occasional views across the airfield can be had

Melbourne Tullamarine

MEL | YMML

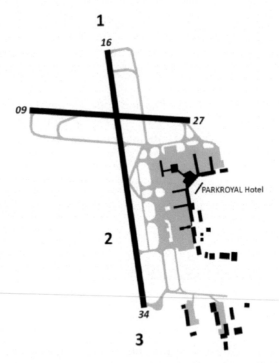

Melbourne is Australia's second-busiest airport and a major hub for Qantas, Jetstar Airways, Regional Express, Tigerair Australia and Virgin Australia. Many airlines from Asia, North America and the Middle East also fly in daily.

There are four passenger terminals on the eastern side of the airport, plus a cargo terminal, with two runways. Tigerair and Qantas have maintenance facilities to the south.

Spotting Locations

1. Northern Viewing Area
Where Oaklands Road joins route C743 there is a small parking area for spotters off the roundabout. At this spot you are just underneath the final approach path to runway 16 and good for photos if you wander along the road in either direction depending on the sun. It is a bit distant to see much of the rest of the airport.

2. Operations Road Viewing Area
Another designated viewing area is on Operations Road along the airport's western perimeter. You are alongside runway 16/34 here, and have views across to the terminals. It is a bit distant, and you'll need a ladder to get any useful shots.

3. Southern Perimeter
Alongside Operations Road on the southern perimeter is a good spot for photographing arrivals on runway 34, with parking by the side of the road. You will also see aircraft taxying for take-off. Plenty of spotters congregate at this location.

Spotting Hotel

PARKROYAL Airport Hotel Arrival Drive, Melbourne Airport, Melbourne, VIC 3045 | +61 3 8347 2000 | www.parkroyalhotels. com You can walk directly into this hotel from the terminals via a covered walkway. Rooms can be a bit pricey, but some have excellent views over the airport. Ask for those in the ranges 800-825 and 900-925. You can also get views from the ends of the corridors.

Perth

PER | YPPH

Perth is the busiest airport in Western Australia and a major hub for domestic travel as well as links throughout Asia and to Africa and the Middle East. A nice mix of airlines serve the airport, though naturally Australian carriers dominate. Also, due to the amount of mining operations in this part of Australia, Perth Airport handles large numbers of charter flights to remote airfields supporting these activities. Principal operators are Alliance Airlines, Qantas, Skippers Aviation and Virgin Australia.

AUSTRALIA

Perth has four terminals - two on either side of the airport, which are almost 8 miles apart by road. It is planned to ultimately have all terminals on the eastern side of the airport.

Spotting Locations

1. Terminal 1 Viewing Deck
Atop the International Terminal, on the eastern side of the airport, is the official viewing deck. The views are perfect for any aircraft using that terminal, and you can see all movements on the runways. However, you are some distance from aircraft using the western terminals.

3. Public Viewing Area
Off Dunreath Drive the airport has constructed a viewing platform alongside the runway 03 threshold which is free to enter and gets you close to the action. The area is open 6.30am to 7pm (October to March) and 7.30am to 5.30pm (April to September). The location is too far to see aircraft parked at the terminals, or using the smaller runway 06/24.

2. Executive Area
On the domestic side of the airport, if you arrive via the Great Eastern Highway, exit onto Fauntleroy Ave, and then turn 2nd left onto Bungana Ave. Along here you'll find with views over the parking areas for business jets and FBO's, and some distant views of the runways and domestic terminal.

Sydney Bankstown

BWU | YSBK

Sydney's second airport, at Bankstown, is largely a general aviation hub 14 miles east of downtown and Kingsford Smith Airport. Despite only having a couple of airline routes from Toll Aviation, Bankstown is presently the fourth busiest airport in the country, so worth a visit if you're not just into airliners. There are often smaller airliners and bizjets present. Spotting is best if you have a car and can drive around the perimeter logging what you see through the fence as there are lots of parking areas and hangars.

Sydney Kingsford Smith

SYD | YSSY

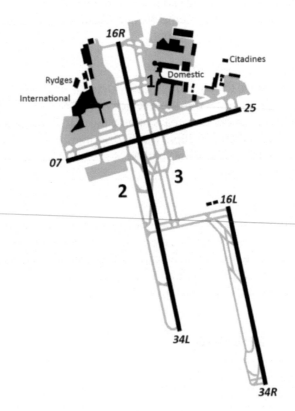

Australia's busiest airport, Sydney Kingsford Smith is very busy and often very sunny, making it a photographer's paradise. It is located in the suburb of Mascot and alongside Botany Bay.

Sydney is the main base of Qantas, with most of their fleet passing through every week, and also a sizeable maintenance base.

The airport has three main terminals – two on the eastern side, and the International Terminal on the western side, plus a freight area. There are three runways.

Aside from Australian carriers, Sydney is served by many airlines from across Asia, New Zealand, the Pacific, North and South America.

Spotting Locations

1. Domestic Terminals
One of the better views of the action at Sydney is from the domestic terminals gate areas. You will need to pass through security screening, but don't need a boarding pass. The windows at the end of the pier look out over the domestic gates, runways, and the distant international terminal. So you won't miss many movements, and photography - although through glass - is acceptable.

2. Beach
A very popular spot, the beach sits close to the International Terminal's aprons, and alongside runway 16R/34L. From the pleasant surroundings you can watch and photograph aircraft taxying and using the runway, and take some nice photographs. Some movements will be obscured, and you can't really see the terminals. To reach the spot you'll need a car or taxi. Exit General Holmes Drive after passing underneath the runway, signposted Airport View/Cooks River. Park in the car park and walk to the beach.

3. Shep's Tower Mound
A new official spotting location at Sydney located alongside runway 16R/34L, but with all runways and some taxiways visible. The location has parking and raised areas to give you unobstructed photography opportunities above the fenceline. Its all-round views make it good throughout the day. To reach the spot follow Ross Smith Ave from the domestic terminal area (behind the DHL buildings) all the way to the end.

Spotting Hotels

Citadines Connect Sydney Airport 121 Baxter Road, Mascot, 2020 NSW, Australia | +61 2 8303 8888 | www.citadines.com A fairly new hotel on Baxter Road, behind the Domestic Terminal and maintenance area, and close to the biz jet parking areas. It was called the Felix Hotel when first opened, but has since changed. Smart and stylish, with a travel theme throughout. 70 of the 150 rooms face the airport, and have different prices based on class. Views are good of movements and nearer areas, but International Terminal out of sight.

Rydges Sydney Airport Hotel 8 Arrival Ct, Sydney Airport, NSW 2020 | +61 2 9313 2500 | www.rydges.com A good replacement for the closed International Terminal observation deck. Located just behind the terminal, the Rydges has seized the opportunity presented by spotters by providing day access to its panoramic terrace for a fee. You can see and photograph movements around the terminals and runway 16R/34L. Higher rooms facing the same direction have a similar view, and the hotel offers spotters packages which include the best views, food and drink allowance, information sheet, free Wi-Fi and a pair of binoculars!

AUSTRIA

Innsbruck

INN | LOWI

Nestled deep in a valley in the Alps, Innsbruck Airport is busier
in the winter months. Despite its short runway and precision
approach, you may often find large airliners on the ramp. At other
times of the year it mainly sees commuter and some low-cost
flights from the likes of Austrian Airlines, British Airways, easyJet
and Transavia. Executive and general aviation aircraft are also
common here.

The best spotting and photography location is the terrace upstairs
in the terminal. Another good spot, where you can catch those
spectacular shots with the mountains as a backdrop, at the end
of runway 08. It's easier to drive west along the main B171 road
along the northern side of the airport and leave just after the
roundabout where there is a car park. Then walk along Hans-
Flockinger-Promenade to the end of the runway.

Salzburg W A Mozart

SZG | LOWS

Like other airports in Austria, Salzburg is busiest in the winter
when the ski season is in full swing, but also well connected by
low-cost and leisure airlines at other times of the year.

Salzburg is a small airport close to the city, with a single runway.
The terminal and executive parking ramps are on the western
side, with another smaller FBO on the eastern side. The official
viewing area in the terminal is a good option, open 9am-10pm,
but there are other good spots. Walking south from the terminal
you'll usually see a resident DC-3, and a little further on is a

mound for spotters which is great for photographs on the runway and taxiway.

To the north, cross over the busy main road and head along Kröbenfeldstrasse. It leads past the perimeter fence to the end of runway 15 with good opportunities for photographs.

Vienna International

VIE | LOWW

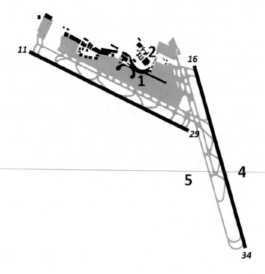

Today Vienna Airport is the main hub in Austria, handling primarily scheduled traffic to the main business and leisure destinations around Europe, North America, the Middle East and Asia. Austrian Airlines and its subsidiaries are based here, as well as easyJet, Eurowings, Laudamotion, LEVEL and Wizz Air. Other interesting carriers are Air Algerie, Air China, EVA Air, Hainan Airlines, and Qatar Airways.

The airport has three terminals, however Terminal 2 is currently closed. All are located along the northern portion of the site, with a maintenance area and FBO apron to the north-west, and busy cargo hub to the north which handles many big carriers like Asiana Cargo, Cargolux, FedEx Express, Korean Air Cargo, Turkish Airlines Cargo and UPS Airlines.

Vienna has two runways – 11/29 and 16/34 – which are used in all directions. The airport has some good spotting opportunities, but can be frustrating due to the lack of easy access to locations.

Spotting Locations

1. Terminal
The viewing terrace on top of the terminal is signposted and easy to find. You must pass through a security check and pay an entrance fee. Most movements around the terminals and on runway 16 can be seen and photographed, and it's a good overall position.

2. Car Parks P3 and P4
The top level of the multi-storey car parks 3 and 4 are a favourite location for spotters. Both runways can be seen, but 16/34 is a little distant. You will also see a remote parking area alongside this car park which is hard to see from anywhere else. However, the terminal partly obscures the view.

3. VISITAIR Airport Tour
An airside tour is available from the VISITAIR Centre adjacent to Car Park 4, which takes in the maintenance, general aviation, executive and passenger aprons. A security check is required. Tickets cost €9 for adults, less for children/concessions. The tour departs on the hour from 9am to 6pm, and lasts 50 minutes. Reservations required, on +43 1 7007 22150 or visitaircenter@ viennaairport.com

4. Spotter Hill
Located on the eastern side of the airport, alongside runway 16/34. This is an official viewing location and provides an elevated position above the fence which is great for photographs –

particularly on a morning. To reach the location head east from the terminals along 9/Hainburger Strasse into Fischamend village. In the centre, turn right onto Klein-Neusiedler Strasse and continue south. Just before the village of Klein-Neusiedl there is a car park on your right. Then you must walk along the path to reach the hill. You can follow the perimeter track south from here to find other locations.

5. Runway Viewing Positions
Additional positions along the southern perimeter of the fence are great for photographs, but require quite a lot of walking. From the car park at position 4, drive on towards Schwadorf. At the edge of the town there is an industrial area where you can park. Then, walk down the street and cross the road to head down a track next to a dance school. Follow this for 1.5km, then turn right and walk till you reach the perimeter fence. From here on you can find a position which works – further on you'll reach the point where both runways and parts of the terminal are visible.

Spotting Hotel

NH Vienna Airport Hotel Einfahrtsstrasse 3, Wien Flughafen 1300 | +43 1 7015 10 | www.nh-hotels.com The best hotel at Vienna Airport for views of movements. Odd-numbered rooms on the third floor will give views over the apron. Some other higher rooms have views over the 11/29 runway. The hotel is one of the more affordable at the airport, and it is a short walk from the terminal.

BAHAMAS

Nassau Lynden Pindling International

NAS | MYNN

This is the largest and busiest airport in the Bahamas. It has two runways and a terminal with two large concourses of gates, plus a smaller commuter pier. Principal operators are Bahamasair, Delta, JetBlue, SkyBahamas and a number of smaller regional operators.

There are few places to spot here, although views are possible inside the terminal. Security personnel have been known to ask spotters to stop or move on when seen. Roads run past either end of the main runway 14/32 (head for Geography Park at 14, or Coral Harbor Rd for 32), where you can take good pictures of arrivals. Note that regional airliners often use the smaller cross runway.

BAHRAIN

Bahrain International

BAH | OBBI

Bahrain is one of the smaller, yet older of the Gulf region's hub airports. It hasn't grown as much as the likes of Dubai and Doha, but has ambitions to and may be replaced by a brand new airport in the future. Nevertheless it handles an interesting mix of airlines, and is home to Gulf Air. It also offers more spotting opportunities than airports such as Dubai. Remember, however, that spotting is not often understood in this region.

The airport has a single runway with the passenger terminal and most aircraft parking aprons on its south side. Muharraq Air Base is also located at the site.

A small park alongside the water at the southern end of the main runway, called Galali Garden, is a good place to watch arrivals at the airport. You can also log aircraft if you have a car and drive along the northern boundary of the airport.

BARBADOS

Grantley Adams International

BGI | TBPB

A relatively busy airport serving the island of Barbados and its capital, Bridgetown. It has a single runway and terminal, which was upgraded recently to handle the growth in flights being experienced. It is one of the main bases for the intra-Caribbean carrier LIAT, and sees a good number of scheduled and holiday flights from Europe and North America, often associated with the cruise trade, with anything up to Boeing 747-400 size flying in.

Spotting is possible on the south side of the airport, where a road runs towards the flying club. You can park up and walk towards the fence to find a good spot where all movements can be seen.

BELARUS

Minsk National

MSQ | UMMS

The main international airport for Belarus, is situated to the east of the city. It has a pair of parallel runways and a central terminal. An area to the south of the terminal is where maintenance and cargo operations are handled, and often has a selection of Ilyushin IL-76s, Antonov An-12s and various relics from days gone by.

It's possible to spot aircraft at the northern part of the ramp from the roads outside the terminal. There's also a nice collection of preserved Russian airliners next to the car park which represent the aviation of Belarus in the past. Once airside a sweep of the gates gives a view of most aircraft, although blinds sometimes obscure the view.

BELGIUM

Brussels Airport

BRU | EBBR

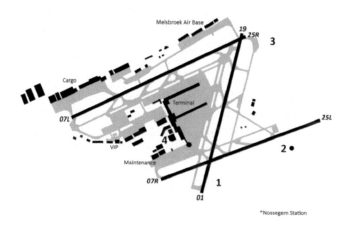

Brussels Airlines is the dominant carrier here, along with TUI fly Belgium and the likes of Ryanair and Vueling. Most of Europe's carriers visit and, while traffic to the USA has suffered some setbacks in recent years, long-haul services to Asia, Africa and the Middle East have enjoyed growth. As a result, you can see some interesting carriers here.

Cargo has also traditionally played a major role at Brussels National (as this airport is usually known). DHL has a base here, and plenty of other cargo airlines use the facilities.

The airport has three runways – two parallel, and one cross runway in the 01/19 direction. The majority of arrivals are on 25L and departures on 25R (apart from cargo aircraft which usually land on 25R).

The single terminal in the centre of the airport has two long piers. Older piers and administration buildings have now been demolished, and a connector building constructed to link what was a remote pier.

Melsbroek Air Base occupies a site in the north-east corner of the airport. Because of the city's connections on the world stage, this base often plays host to unusual VIP and government movements, as well as the Belgian Government's fleet. If you're driving past along N21/Haachtsesteenweg, look out for a few preserved aircraft in the base (not accessible). The cargo areas are to the west and north-west of the terminal, whilst Brussels Airlines has hangars to the south-west.

Recently Brussels Airport has undertaken to construct two dedicated viewing areas to watch aircraft, and regularly reaches out to the enthusiast community to offer airside visits and communicate what is going on at the airport – a very welcome thing!

Spotting Locations

1. Spotter Platform 01/19 One of the two new sites constructed by the airport. It includes a small park and raised platform to elevate you above the fence line. This platform overlooks the intersection of runways 01/19 and 07R/25L, and also has views across to part of the terminal. It's good for shots of aircraft on these runways – especially 01 arrivals. You'll find it near Nossegem, where there is free parking at the football club canteen followed by a 7-minute walk. Otherwise it's a 20-minute walk from Nossegem train station.

2. Spotter Platform 25L/07R
The other new platform. This replaces the most popular unofficial spotting location previously used by spotters and gives them a dedicated raised platform to view over the fence. It's perfect for 25L arrivals (the most common direction), with distant views towards the terminal. There is free parking at the transit centre (just off N227 near the tunnel under the runway). Alternatively it's

a 15-minute walk from Nossegem train station. A footpath follows the fence line toward the end of runway 25L if you want approach shots.

3. Steenokkerzeel Cemetery
A popular spot for catching arrivals on runway 25R is the car park for the cemetery in Steenokkerzeel. You'll find it off Coenenstraat in the village. Please remember to show respect when using this area as people are often visiting graves.

4. P1 Parking
The top floor multi-storey car park outside the terminals has sweeping views across the airport and to all three runways. Look for 'Front Park P1'. This location is better for logging movements rather than photography as the buildings can sometimes get in the way.

Spotting Hotel
Sheraton Brussels Airport
Brussels National Airport, Brussels 1930 | +32 27 10 80 00 | www. sheraton.com This is the best hotel option for spotting aircraft at Brussels Airport. Although expensive, rooms have views over parts of the aprons. It is a short walk from the terminal and multi-storey car park location. Photography is not possible from the rooms because of the shutters, however.

Brussels South Charleroi

CRL | EBCI

Located almost 30 miles south of Brussels, Charleroi Airport was renamed with the arrival of Ryanair in 1997. It has then grown into one of the airline's biggest European hubs, and has attracted other low-cost airlines such as Wizz Air. TUI fly Belgium has a base here, and other charter carriers fly in seasonally.

The airport has a single runway to the north-east, with hangars, FBOs and training operators to the south-west. There is also a retired Boeing 727 used as a ground trainer just north of the runway 07 threshold, and visible from aircraft or by driving along Rue Santos-Dumont south-west from the terminal area.

Inside the terminal, a new indoor observation area opened in 2019. It has seating and large windows to watch the action through.

Walk west outside the terminal at departures level to the bus stop and you'll find good views of the apron and runway from above the fenceline.

If you have a car, a good spot on the south side of the runway is in the village of Ransart, just off the N568/Rue Ransart. In the centre is a car park, with a little lane running north towards the airport. You can see movements here and photograph anything in the air.

Liège Airport

LGG | EBLG

Despite being only a modest sized regional airport, Liege has positioned itself as one of Europe's leading cargo airports. It is a hub for ASL Airlines Belgium, and is also served by many other worldwide cargo airlines. Passenger flying is mostly seasonal charters to the sun by TUI fly Belgium.

To make the most of seeing cargo aircraft it's best to visit at night. Most movements are during the early hours, with departures starting at 4am. If you visit during the day you may still see a number of aircraft parked on the ramp, and the occasional movement.

If you drive into the airport complex, head south-west along Rue de l'Aeroport and you will come to a spot with views over the parking apron where you can stop quickly to log/photograph aircraft on the ground, but don't loiter.

You can continue along this road toward the end of runways 04L/R. There is a large open area which is blocked for cars, but has good views. For evening arrival shots, you can continue along the road and turn right at the roundabout along Rue du Bihet. Find somewhere to park and stand by the fence.

Finally, if arrivals are from the north, drive past the Park Inn hotel near the terminal, cross the roundabout onto Rue Valise, and then turn left onto Chaussee de Liege. Find somewhere to park near the village of Bierset and climb onto the hill on your left. It has views over part of the airport and runways.

Ostend-Bruges International

OST | EBOS

Ostend is a quiet regional and general aviation airport. It handles plenty of cargo aircraft, as well as holiday flights. You can see the main ramp from the restaurant inside the terminal and the fence either side. There is also a spot near the crash gate on the south side at the threshold of runway 08 which is good for landing shots. You can reach it off N324/Kalkaartweg.

Look out for the retired Boeing 727 parked at Ostend Air College near the Restaurant Runway 26-08.

BRAZIL

Belo Horizonte Tancredo Neves

CNF | SBCF

Also known as Confins International Airport, this is the main gateway to Belo Horizonte It is a hub for Azul and LATAM Brasil, and Gol, has a maintenance base in one corner of the airport. The terminal has an observation deck on the top floor which has good views of movements.

Brasília Presidente Juscelino Kubitschek International

BSB | SBBR

One of Brazil's busiest airports, which is also an air force base. It is a hub for LATAM and Gol, and also sees a number of cargo flights. Another draw to the enthusiast is the presence of the VIP aircraft operated by the Brazil Government.

Passengers using the domestic terminal can easily read off aircraft from the gates, but unfortunately the excellent viewing area in the terminal has been closed for a while. Some opportunities exist, such as near the petrol station at the entrance to the airport which is good for watching and photographing aircraft arriving on the northern runway. To reach it, turn right after exiting the terminal. You can also see through the fence to parked biz jets and other aircraft.

Florianópolis Hercílio Luz International

FLN | SBFL

A moderately busy regional airport served by most Brazilian carriers, and with some international flights. There is a viewing area inside the terminal.

Rio de Janeiro Galeão

GIG | SBGL

This airport has two runways and two terminals. Galeão is a main hub to LATAM and Gol Transportes Aereos. It is also served by major international carriers from Europe, North America and the Middle East. The airport is also a busy cargo hub, with numerous domestic and international carriers flying in each day.

The main spotting location is the large area of windows in Terminal 1. It is located on a higher floor and has good views over the parking areas, general aviation ramp and part of both runways, so you should see all aircraft movements from here. Head to the southern part of the second floor behind the banks and ATM machines.

The storage area near the maintenance hangars at Galeão have a number of retired aircraft parked outside, such as Boeing 727s and 737s. These can often be seen on departure.

Rio de Janeiro Santos Dumont

SDU | SBRJ

Santos Dumont has two short parallel runways, a single terminal, and an area for business aircraft. The airport operates between 6am and 11pm. Its downtown location makes it a busy hub for executive aircraft, and also for domestic flights by airlines such as Azul, Gol Transportes Aereos and LATAM. There is also a military presence at the airport, so be careful when pointing binoculars and cameras around the perimeter.

The best spotting location is within the terminal where there is a large window on the upper level (go far right overlooking the aircraft apron and runways in the distance. Despite there once being an observation deck, it is now obstructed by gates.

An alternative location outside the terminal is close to the southern end of the runways, on Avenida Almirante Silvio Noronha. Turn left outside the terminal and walk past the college. It takes about 20 minutes to get here, and photography is best in the afternoon.

São Paulo Congonhas

CGH | SBSP

Situated 5 miles from downtown Sao Paulo, Congonhas sits atop a plateau surrounded by the urban sprawl. It has a single terminal, two runways, and is Brazil's third busiest airport in terms of passengers, and second busiest in terms of aircraft movements. So there's plenty to see!

Congonhas only handles domestic flights, but is quite popular with executive aircraft. The principal airlines are Azul, Brava Linhas Aereas, Gol and LATAM.

Avenue Washington Luiz is a good spotting location at Congonhas as it has a walkway alongside which parallels the runway. You can walk here from the terminal if you turn right. However, it can be unsafe to be here alone or for long.

Another good spot if runway 17R is in use is to continue along Avenue Washington Luiz to where it joins Avenue Bandeirantes. Aircraft will pass above you at close quarters.

Spotting Hotel

Ibis Hotel Congonhas R. Baronesa de Bela Vista, 801 – Vila Congonhas, Sao Paulo 04612-002 | +55 11 5097 3737 | www.ibis.com A good value spotting hotel at Congonhas Airport. It is situated next to the terminal, and rooms on higher floors have a great view of all movements.

São Paulo Guarulhos

GRU | SBGR

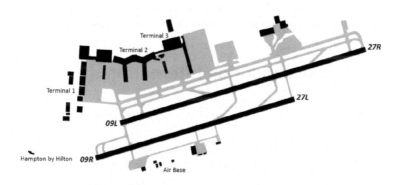

Guarulhos is the largest airport in South America, and a busy international gateway to Brazil. It is located in the north of the city and has two parallel runways and four terminal sections. The airport is a main hub for Azul, LATAM Brasil and Gol Transportes Aereos, and is served by many international carriers.

Inside the terminal there are two areas where you can see aircraft, at either ends of the building through large windows, but you will miss some movements.

The Hampton Hotel to the west of the airport is a popular place for spotting, as it has a terrace which is perfect for landing shots. However, sometimes this is closed, or requires to you pay for day access if you're not a guest. It is best to e-mail the hotel a few days prior to your arrival to request access. It is situated at the westerly end of the runways.

Upstairs in Terminal 2 (ASA D) there is a panoramic area behind glass with seats, phone charging and nearby refreshments/toilets. You can take good pictures, but the glass can be dirty.

Spotting Hotel

Hampton by Hilton Guarulhos R. Pedro de Tolêdo, 1000 – Jardim Santa Lidia, Guarulhos | +55 11 3411 7000 | www.hilton.com Formerly the well-known Hotel Matiz, this place is great for spotting with great views of arrivals on the parallel runways 09L/R. Aircraft can be read off from rooms facing the approach paths.

São Paulo Viracopos International

VCP | SBKP

Viracopos is a growing airport which was upgraded for the 2014 World Cup and 2016 Summer Olympics. It is a large base for Azul Brazilian Airlines, and also has some international services. It is the main cargo airport for the São Paulo region with worldwide links and many freighters to see. Airlines include Atlas Air, Cargolux, Emirates SkyCargo, Ethiopian Cargo, LATAM Cargo, Lufthansa Cargo, Qatar Airways Cargo and UPS Airlines.

There are two good spots for photographing aircraft approaching runway 33 alongside the Santos Dumont highway, but you need a car to get here. Alternatively, the food court inside the terminal is a good place to watch aircraft movements.

CANADA

Calgary International

YYC | CYYC

Calgary is the main base for WestJet and its Encore subsidiary. It is also a hub for Air Canada and its regional partners. Most airlines from America and a few European carriers fly in, plus lots of smaller carriers serving remote communities. A freight hub is situated on the western side of the airport.

The airport has a pair of parallel runways and two cross runways. The terminal, in the northern part of the airport, has various concourses including a new international facility.

It is difficult to find a good place to spot at Calgary, although there are plenty of locations where you can make a quick visit – especially if you have a car. Often security will move on spotters who loiter too long, particularly on top of the multi-storey car parks, which offer some views of aircraft around the terminals.

There are a couple of official viewing locations at the end of runway 35L. You will need a car to get there. Head for McKnight Blvd NE, which passes the southern end of the airport. The spot is called Edward H LaBorde Viewing Area and is on Aviation Pl. It has a large car park and you'll see aircraft approaching the runway at close quarters. Other movements and the terminals are quite distant.

Following the road north you'll pass behind the executive aircraft ramp. Another parking area can be used for spotting, but the views aren't as good.

One of the best locations if you have a car is on 21st Street NE, which is amongst the cargo buildings directly opposite the passenger terminal across the taxiways. From the fence at the end of the road you are very close to aircraft, and can see movements on both parallel runways. Photography is through the fence, however.

Near this spot are the cargo ramps and the WestJet maintenance hangars, so you may see aircraft parked in various places.

Spotting Hotel

Marriott In-Terminal Hotel Calgary Airport 2008 Airport Rd NE, Calgary, AB T2E 3B9 | +1 403 717 0522 | www.marriott.com A good option for spotting. Located above the terminal, the hotel has many rooms with views over the gate areas and taxiways. Photography and logging aircraft is possible.

Edmonton International

YEG | CYEG

Edmonton is a medium international airport with two runways and a single terminal building. As well as being a hub for Air Canada and WestJet, it also acts a hub for many smaller carriers which link the city with smaller communities in the north of the country. It is therefore an interesting place for the enthusiast to see airliners and cargo aircraft not often seen elsewhere in Canada.

An official viewing area is at the Chamber of Commerce car park off 50 St to the south east of the airport. This is directly underneath the approach to runway 30, and quite distant from the rest of the airport, but nevertheless good for photography. There is a retail area alongside and various food outlets.

Another option is to take the Niksu/Hwy 19 exit from Hwy 2 and follow the service road towards the cargo and business aircraft ramps. You can see movements on runway 20 from here, as well as some aircraft parked on these ramps.

Halifax Stanfield International

YHZ | CYHZ

Halifax has two runways, one of which is among the longest in Canada. The terminal building has gates for larger jets in the centre, with smaller piers for commuter aircraft at either end. Spreading alongside the runway from the terminal are a number of smaller aprons and hangars operated by various fixed base operators. Driving or walking along Barnes Drive should allow you to see some of the aircraft parked here.

The passenger terminal has an Observation Room on the third floor which overlooks the central gates and the runways beyond. The room is free to enter, but photography is through glass. There is also a large window with views of aircraft on the main level.

Hamilton John C Munro International

YHM | CYHM

Home of Canadian Warplane Heritage Museum, this is not a busy airport but worth a look around if you are visiting the museum. Passenger flights are mainly seasonal, with Swoop having a focus hub here. Cargo airlines are quite common. Exploring the roads leading to the general cargo area and the KF Aerospace area should uncover any parked cargo aircraft.

MUSEUM

Canadian Warplane Heritage Museum

9280 Airport Road, Mount Hope, ON L0R 1W0 | +1 905 679 4183 | www.warplane.com Canada's most notable aviation museum. It is home to one of only two airworthy Avro Lancaster aircraft in the world, as well as a number of other notable historic aircraft in flying condition. Keep an eye on the website for upcoming events. Open daily from 9am-5pm. Adults $16; cheaper for concessions, and under 5's go free.

Montréal Pierre Elliott Trudeau

YUL | CYUL

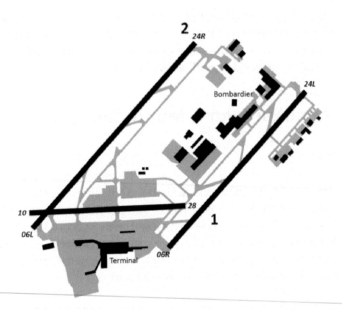

A large gateway for Quebec and French-speaking Canada. This airport is the headquarters of Air Canada, Air Canada Express, Air Canada Rouge, and a hub for Air Transat and Sunwing Airlines. It is on the route map of most airlines from the USA, and many from Europe. There are lots of flights heading to remote communities in the north.

The airport has two large parallel runways and a smaller cross runway which is not really used. The large passenger terminal complex occupies the southern part of the site. The northern and central areas are filled with maintenance hangars and bases used by Air Canada, Bombardier, and Air Inuit.

Spotting Locations

1. Jacques-de-Lesseps Park
The only official spotting location at the airport is a small park along the south eastern boundary, off Avenue Jenkins (postcode H9P 2W6). It looks out over runway 06R/24L and across to the terminal in the distance. You should be able to see all movements from here, and can take photographs from the grandstand seating.

2. Runway 24R
A small patch of land in the northern corner of the airport is good for photographing arrivals on runway 24. It is found on the corner of Chemin St-François and Rue Percival-Reid, just off the main Trans Canada Highway. It is accessible by Autoroutes 13 and 40 and STM bus 175 Griffith/St-François from the Du Collège metro station too.

Spotting Hotels

Montreal Airport Marriott In-Terminal Hotel 800 Pl Leigh-Capreol, Dorval, QC H4Y 0A4 | +1 514 636 6700 | www.marriott.com Built over the terminal building, this hotel has rooms with views over the gates and taxiways. Photography is possible of nearer aircraft.

Sheraton Montreal Airport 555 Boulevard McMillan, Montréal, QC H9P 1B7 | +1 514 631 2411 | www.sheraton.com This is not a tall hotel, but many of the rooms face towards the adjacent threshold of runway 06R, which makes it good for monitoring aircraft movements.

Ottawa Macdonald-Cartier International

YOW | CYOW

The second busiest airport in Ontario, Ottawa is a hub for Air Canada and Porter Airlines. It mainly handles domestic routes, and flights across the USA, but also sees seasonal services to the Caribbean and Europe.

Ottawa has a single passenger terminal at the centre of the two main runways. A smaller runway is situated to the north west for use by general aviation. A cargo terminal is at the north east corner of the airport.

Heading past the cargo buildings and hotels to the east of the passenger terminal, along Alert Road, is a good spot to park up on the gravel and watch and photograph arrivals and departures on runway 25.

Continuing along Alert Road until it reaches a dead end, you'll be able to see activity on runway 14/32.

Toronto City Billy Bishop

YTZ | CYTZ

Probably Canada's most unique airport. Named after the Canadian World War I flying ace, Billy Bishop is the downtown airport situated on an island in Lake Ontario, in front of Toronto's iconic skyline.

The airport was first developed in the 1930s. However, in the 1990s it was expanded, with a new terminal to handle regional turboprops. When Porter Airlines commenced operations in 2006, Billy Bishop Airport started to grow once again. Today it handles almost 3 million passengers per year, with many general aviation aircraft movements in addition to Porter and Air Canada Express flights.

Aircraft can be seen from the airport car park and inside the terminal if you are flying. If you are visiting the observation level of the CN Tower, you also have an elevated view of the airport.

Toronto Downsview

CYZD

This airport is owned by Bombardier Aerospace for production and testing of its aircraft. It has a large factory on site, and you can often see production aircraft parked around the airfield.

Hanover Road leads to the Bombardier facility, passing the main runway with various views through the fence. You can also see movements from a car park off Carl Hall Road near the northern end of the airfield, and a car park off Transit Road at the southern end.

Toronto Pearson International

YYZ | CYYZ

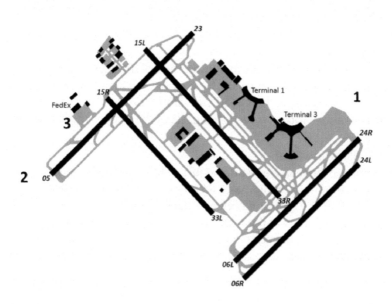

Toronto Pearson International is the largest and busiest gateway to Canada. It has five runways and two main terminals. In the middle of the field are large areas of hangars and aprons used for maintenance and cargo. The airport is the headquarters of Air Canada and WestJet, and these two carriers make up most of the movements, along with carriers like Air Transat and Sunwing. The variety of international carriers is quite good and covers a wide range of airlines from around the world and United States.

There are no official locations for spotting at Toronto, but a number of locations offer opportunities for logging and photography around the airport perimeter. Given that there are five runways, it is difficult to cover everything.

Spotting Locations

1. Park 'n' Fly
To the north east of the airport is the Park 'n' Fly parking lot. It is located off Carlingview Rd. This is a good place to watch and photograph arrivals onto runway 24R. You can walk up and down this road to find the best angle and position.

2. Dixie Rd
Dixie Rd runs past the south western side of the airport, passing close to the end of runway 05. Near where the road crosses Derry Rd you can park up, then head back along the road for some great arrivals shots. You can't see other parts of the airport from here.

3. FedEx Crash Gate
Continue north up Derry Rd and just before the FedEx cargo centre, turn right on Bramalea Rd which leads to a crash gate. Don't block the gate and park well back. From here you can see aircraft parked at the FedEx ramp, as well as movements on runway 05/23. You might need a ladder to photograph over the fence.

Spotting Hotels

Sheraton Gateway Hotel in Toronto Airport Terminal 3, Toronto Airport, On L5P 1C4 | +1 905 672 7000 | www.marriott.com A good hotel connected to the terminals with excellent views across the ramp and some of the runways. Terminal 1 is not visible, however most aircraft will taxi into view. Ask for a high level (floors 6, 7 or 8) odd-numbered room facing the airport.

ALT Airport Hotel Toronto 6080 Viscount Road, Mississauga, ON L4V 0A1 | +1 905 362 4337 | www.althotels.com Another option close to the terminals, a high level room facing the airport should give a decent view of aircraft movements. It is a little more distant than other hotels, but still possible to read off aircraft.

Vancouver Boundary Bay

YDT | CZBB

Second busiest general aviation airport in Canada. It has two active runways, and another used as aircraft parking. Aircraft also park on ramps and inside hangars along the northern boundary. The roads leading to the airport have some views, and access to hangars may be possible.

Vancouver Harbour Flight Centre

CXH | CYHC

A busy sea plane base on the edge of Vancouver Harbour in downtown, close to the port and cruise ship terminal. You can watch the action from the neighbouring Harbour Green Park, and it is within walking distance of Downtown. The main operators are Harbour Air, Kenmore Air and Salt Spring Air.

Vancouver International

YVR | CYVR

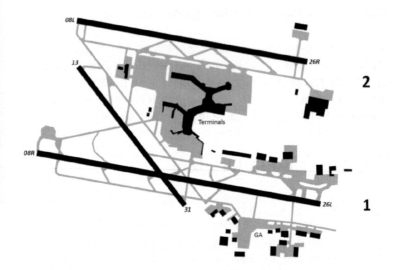

Canada's main west coast gateway, and the second busiest in the country, is Vancouver International. It has one main terminal with multiple concourses, and a second terminal in use as a float plane base. The airport has three runways, although the parallel 08L/26R and 08R/26L are the most commonly used.

Vancouver is a hub for Air Canada and WestJet, and is on the network of carriers which link the remote north of Canada. You'll also see plenty of international carriers from Asia, Europa and the United States.

An extensive cargo area is located on the eastern side of the airport, whilst biz jets and local carriers use the original terminal area to the south of the airport (where the sea plane base is).

Spotting Locations

1. Larry Berg Flight Path Park
An official location, on the corner of Russ Baker Way and Airport Road, around half a mile from the end of runway 26L. There are information boards and seats provided, and a small car park. It is a good location for photography of aircraft landing on this runway.

2. Runway 26R
A similar view to the first location, but for runway 26R, is possible off Grauer Road. This is not an official location, but has parking and is right underneath the flightpath.

Spotting Hotel

Fairmont Vancouver Airport 3111 Grant McConachie Way, Richmond, BC V7B 0A6 | +1 604 207 5200 | www.fairmont.com
Located in the northern side of the terminal. Ask for a higher room facing the airport and you'll have views of some of the parking gates and movements. Some rooms even have telescopes! The bar and restaurant areas also have good views.

Yellowknife

YZF | CYZF

Yellowknife in Northwest Territories has gained worldwide fame because of the media and old aircraft enthusiast coverage of Buffalo Airways – one of the last operators of classic old piston props such as the Douglas DC-4, DC-6, Curtiss C-46 and Lockheed Electra. The airline is based at Yellowknife and operates freight and other charter flights regularly from its own hangar.

In addition to Buffalo Airways, Yellowknife sees regular flights from Air Canada Express, Air North, Air Tindi, Canadian North, Northwestern Air and WestJet Encore, alongside various local and freight operators.

Driving or walking along Bristol Avenue from the terminal area will lead past the different ramps and hangars where you will see some of the stored and active Buffalo aircraft, plus other based operators. Buffalo Airways are used to enthusiasts coming to see their aircraft and are usually accommodating, but try to arrange something in advance to avoid disappointment.

CHILE

El Tepual International

PMC | SCTE

One of Chile's busiest airports, situated at Puerto Montt in the south of the country. It only serves domestic destinations through JetSmart, LATAM Chile and Sky Airline. A busy road passes close to the end of runway 17, with a rental car park to where all movements can be seen.

Santiago Comodoro Arturo Merino Benítez International

SCL | SCEL

Serving the capital, this airport has two parallel runways in a north-south orientation. The passenger terminal is in the southern section, with the LATAM and Sky Airline maintenance bases in the middle, and a military and government air base to the north.

Movements are dominated by JetSmart, LATAM, Sky Airline flights and military traffic. International carriers include Aermexico, Aerolineas Argentinas, Air Canada, American, British Airways, Delta, Emirates, Iberia, KLM, Level, Qantas and United.

It is not advisable to go exploring alone around Santiago airport as there have been reports of robberies by spotters.

The best views can be had near the control tower. To reach this area you'll need to drive away from the terminal and follow the Diego Barros Ortiz Highway up the western side of the airport, then into the north central area (follow under the taxiway) and find the fence. Here you have views of the aircraft coming and going to the terminals on the taxiways.

If you have transport and are not alone, it's possible to drive around the perimeter alongside and passing the ends of both runways. At the northern end, you can follow the road into the centre of the site, passing the air force base and leading to the maintenance area.

CHINA

Beijing Capital International

PEK | ZBAA

1   Cordis Hotel

Beijing Capital is the principal airport for the city, and has been steadily expanded and modernised. It is today a large hub where domestic and international flights meet, and it is currently the world's second-busiest airport. It has three parallel runways, and a very large International Terminal to the east. The older domestic terminals and areas for maintenance and Chinese Air Force operations are to the north and west.

Capital is one of the better airports for spotting at in China, which is useful considering the sheer number of aircraft that pass through. It also has a good hotel for spotting.

Beijing Daxing recently opened to ease pressure, which has resulted in some airlines and flights relocating away from Capital. It also resulted in Nanyuan Airport closing.

Many enthusiasts come to Beijing for the famous Datan Shan aviation museum, which is a short distance north of Capital Airport and well worth the visit for any airliner fans.

Spotting Locations

1. Viewing Mound
This dedicated area is situated under the final approach to runway 36R. It is elevated, with views over the western side of the airfield, Terminal 3, and the nearby executive apron. Photography is good from this spot, which is reached by walking along the twisting path from the terminal. Alternatively, you can reach the spot by road.

2. Domestic Terminals
Inside the Domestic Terminal you're free to roam around and enjoy the views from the windows. Photography is acceptable from here, and you can see across to the International Terminal. You should see all movements from this terminal.

3. Runways 18L/R
Walking about a mile north of the Domestic Terminals 1 and 2 takes you under the taxiways to an area between the runways 18L/R thresholds (albeit quite a distance apart). From here you can move about to monitor aircraft on these runways. You can also see aircraft parked on the remote and China Post Service stands.

Spotting Hotel

Cordis Beijing Capital Airport 1 Yijing Road, Terminal 3, Capital International Airport, Beijing 100621 | +86 10 6457 5555 | www. cordishotels.com The best spotting hotel at Beijing Capital is the Cordis (formerly the Langham Place). It is situated close to Terminal 3 and has rooms facing the runways, city skyline, or the lake. Rooms facing the runway look over the approach to runway 01, whilst those facing the lake will have views of aircraft approaching runway 36R, with 36L in the distance. Windows in the corridor offer views of aircraft on opposite runways. When aircraft are landing from the north the views are not as good. The hotel is a 10-15 minute walk from spotting location 1.

MUSEUM

China Aviation Museum (Datangshan)

Xiaotangshan, Chan Ping County, Beijing | +86 10 6178 4882
Linked via a very long taxiway to Beijing Shahehzen airfield around 15 miles north east of Capital Airport. This excellent museum is a place all enthusiasts should visit once. It is home to a large number of airliner, transport and military aircraft in various states (many are fully preserved). These include HS121 Tridents, Ilyushin IL-18, Douglas DC-8, Vickers Viscount, many Lisunov Li-2's, MiG's, Shenyang F-5's and Ilyushin IL-10's. Over 200 aircraft can be found here. The museum is open Tuesday to Sunday from 8am to 5.30pm. Entrance is 40 Yuan for adults. Bus 912 runs from Andingmen Station to the gate of the museum, but a taxi from your hotel is often best.

Beijing Daxing International

PKX | ZBAD

Opened in late 2019, Daxing International is the new showpiece airport for China, situated 46km south of Beijing. Built to ease pressure on Beijing's other airports amid spiralling passenger numbers and airline demand, this facility will ultimately feature 7 runways (including a military facility linked to the airport).

Daxing has a unique star-shaped passenger terminal designed to allow the maximum number of aircraft stands while keeping walking distances to the gates to a minimum for passengers. Airlines already operating include Air China, Beijing Capital, China Eastern, Hebei Airlines, Juneyao, and XiamenAir. China United moved its entire operation to Daxing as the older Beijing Nanyuan airport was closed when the new airport opened.

Spotters have not yet explored Daxing sufficiently to find the go-to locations, but it is known that there are views from most gate areas within the terminal.

At the time of writing the area around Daxing has not yet been developed. Therefore, for those with a car there are many opportunities for photographing aircraft on approach by exploring the minor roads and tracks around the perimeter.

Guangzhou Baiyun International

CAN | ZGGG

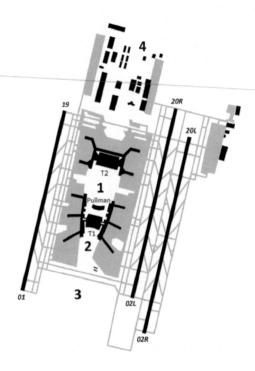

Guangzhou Baiyun International is China's third-busiest airport and a major hub in the south of the country. There are three parallel runways and a large central terminal complex with the six-pier Terminal 1, and even larger Terminal 2, which opened in April 2018, as a home to the based China Southern Airlines and its partners.

Since 2008 the airport has also been the Asia-Pacific hub for FedEx Express and handles hundreds of flights per week from the dedicated cargo complex on the northern part of the airport. Many other cargo airlines also visit.

Guangzhou is not an easy airport for spotters. The Pullman Hotel is a good option.

It's worth taking a trip to the nearby technical institute (4) on the northern perimeter of the airport, which is home to a variety of historic airliners used as instructional airframes, including Tridents, MD-80s, IL-14s and Y-7s. Try to arrange a visit in advance if you want access to take pictures.

Spotting Locations

1. Terminals
Airside in the terminals there are plenty of windows through which parked aircraft and movements can be observed. However, the number of aircraft that can be seen is limited to whichever side of the terminal you are in.

2. Car Park A1
You can see aircraft departing from this car park situated close to Terminal 1. Security have been known to move spotters on from here, however.

3. Cross Taxiway
South of the terminal a taxiway crosses between both sides of the airport. Cross 8th Road runs parallel to this with some good views

of aircraft taxying by. It is within walking distance of the hotels to the south of the airport.

Spotting Hotel

Pullman Hotel Guangzhou Baiyun Airport, 510470 | +86 20 3606 8866 | www.pullmanhotels.com Club rooms on the higher floors of this hotel have good views of the runways, which is especially useful if aircraft are landing towards you. If the opposite direction is in use you will see aircraft departing past you. Some parking aprons are also visible.

Shanghai Hongqiao International

SHA | ZSSS

Hongqiao was Shanghai's main airport until 1999 when the new Pudong Airport to the east of the city opened. Despite this, Hongqiao remains in the top ten busiest airports in China and is very convenient for the city centre. It is mainly a domestic airport, although some international flights operate to neighbouring Asian countries. It is the home base of China Eastern Airlines.

The airport layout involves a pair of north-south parallel runways with passenger terminal areas on the western side, and cargo, corporate and maintenance areas on the eastern side.

For spotters, it is good to spend time at both Shanghai airports to make sure you catch aircraft that don't operate from both.

At Hongqiao, Terminal 2's observation deck is no longer open, but there is a café area alongside its entrance with some views over the airport.

The windows in the domestic Terminal 1 are great for viewing traffic and photographing aircraft parked close to you. You will not see much at the distant Terminal 2 from here, but aircraft on the runway are visible if you pick your spot.

Another option is to alight the Metro (line 2) one stop before the airport (Songhong Road), then walk to the west along Tianshan W Road, you'll come to a position under the approach to runway 18L/R after about 15 minutes' walk. Position yourself with regards to the sun and the runway in use for good approach shots.

Spotting Hotel

Boyue Shanghai Hongqiao Airport (Air China) Hotel No.181, Shen Da San Road, Hongqiao Airport, Shanghain 200335 | +86 21 2236 6666 | www.zhboyuehotel.com Situated in Terminal 2, if you get an Executive Airport View room on floors 9 and above you have excellent views of movements. Rooms 1101-1119 and 1201-1223 have good views. You'll see aircraft parked at both of the terminals, plus runway movements and the executive ramp. You can take good photographs from these rooms.

Travel Between Shanghai Airports

Shanghai Metro Line 2 travels between the two airports in under two hours. Alternatively there is a bus service.

Shanghai Pudong International

PVG | ZSPD

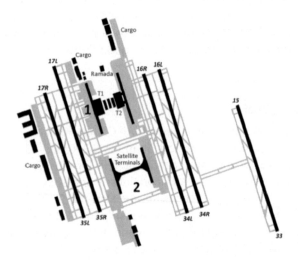

Situated around 20 miles east of the city, Shanghai Pudong is one of Asia's busiest hubs. The airport has five parallel runways and two passenger terminals in the centre; it is also a large cargo hub with various ramps on the north, south and western side of the airport dedicated to this.

Unfortunately, Pudong wasn't built with the enthusiast in mind. No dedicated viewing facilities are provided, and very few views through terminal windows are possible without passing through security. What's more, the roads around the airport do not offer many views. Because of this, many spotters have better luck by booking a room in one of the airport hotels which overlook the action.

The majority of movements at Pudong are international. Therefore, if you want to see domestic airlines whilst in Shanghai, you should visit Hongqiao Airport.

Buses run to Hongqiao Airport from Pudong on a regular basis from outside domestic arrivals. It is useful to visit both airports as many aircraft in the fleets of the bigger carriers do not visit both.

Spotting Locations

1. International Terminal
There are windows in the terminal with some views of aircraft on the international side of the airport. Head up to departures level and walk to the end alongside the coffee shop. Be discrete as some security officers like to move spotters on.

2. Southerly Arrivals
If aircraft are arriving on the 35L/R runways, you can walk south from the terminal along the road and find a spot which has views. Photography isn't very good from this area, but at least you can log most arrivals.

Spotting Hotels

Dazhong Merrylin 'Ease' Hotel Pudong Airport 6001 Yingbin Avenue, Pudong New Area, Shanghai 201202 | +86 21 3879 9999 | www.dazhongairporthotel.com This hotel is located in the centre of the airport. It is reasonably priced and has a direct link to Terminal 2 and train station. Rooms on higher floors facing south have views over the taxiways and runways. Night movements will need flight tracking websites or SBS. Rooms 8801, 8802 and 8806 are reportedly good.

Shenzhen Bao'an International

SZX | ZGSZ

A part of the hugely important concentration of population in the south of China which includes Hong Kong, Macau and Guangzhou, Shenzhen Bao'an International has grown significantly over recent years.

The airport has two runways, and in 2013 opened a large, modern terminal in the central area to replace the three older facilities. The former passenger terminals on the north side are now used by corporate jets.

Shenzhen is China's fifth busiest airport, and since the area is a large centre for manufacturing, the airport handles a lot of cargo flights (it is a UPS Airlines hub) in addition to the large range of passenger airlines with flights across China and the rest of the Far East.

It is possible to take a ferry direct from Bao'an Airport to Hong Kong Airport.

The top floor of the multi-storey car park has some useful views, but security are known to question people using cameras and binoculars in this area. The Sunway Hotel (see later) is a good option for spotting here.

Spotting Hotel

Sunway Hotel Shenzhen Bao'an Airport | +86 755 2730 0888 | www.sunwayhotelsz.com Located outside the original terminals A and B. Even-numbered rooms on the top floor from 1012-1032 offer the best views of the airport, but are quite distant from the action. Most movements can be seen, but the biz jet ramps can't be seen. This is probably the easiest place to spot at Shenzhen if you aren't in the departures lounge, and hotel staff are aware of the needs of spotters. The hotel also offers a 'Spotters Package' if you contact them directly.

CHINA

Tianjin Binhai International

TSN | ZBTJ

Tianjin, in north east China, is an interesting airport for spotters as home to a final assembly line for the Airbus A320 family aircraft. The airport is also the home base of Okay Airways and Tianjin Airlines.

Other carriers include Air China, Asiana, EVA Air, Japan Airlines, Korean Air, Lion Air, NokScoot, Thai Lion Air and Tibet Airlines, among the usual Chinese carriers. There is also a significant cargo operation, which operates from the western side of the airport, as well as a large corporate apron where biz jet aircraft park.

Viewing is possible from the departures level outside the terminal, where some aircraft on the cargo and corporate areas can be seen. The Airbus site in the south-east corner is not visible. Views are good airside, too.

In the south-west corner is a technical school with a number of retired airliners from China's past. These can be seen from a distance, or by employing a taxi driver to explore the side streets in the area.

Tianjin Binhai International Hotel on Xi'er Road situated on the main entrance road leading to the terminal has rooms facing the airport on higher floors which have a good view of most movements, although you have runways on either side. It's not possible to see the biz jet ramps from the hotel.

Wuhan Tianhe International

WUH | ZHHH

Wuhan is a large hub for Air China, China Eastern, China Southern, Hainan Airlines and XiamenAir. Recent upgrades include a second runway and large terminal building which replaced the three previous terminals.

Views from the terminals are best for spotting if you walk behind the check-in desks to the large windows. There is also a large cargo terminal to the north, near the runway 22R threshold.

There are views from the terminal in the landside area where aircraft taxying to and from the runways can be seen.

Xi'an Xianyang International

XIY | ZLXY

Xi'an Xianyang is a large airport in the north west of China. It handles a large list of both passenger and cargo airlines and is one of the top ten busiest airports in the country. It is a hub airport for China Eastern Airlines, Hainan Airlines and Joy Air.

Two terminals are located alongside the northern runway, whilst the third and cargo apron are alongside the southern apron. The windows in the departure lounges of Terminal 1 and 2 are tall and clean, offering plenty of views of the apron and runway beyond.

There is also a footbridge between the terminals which is good for spotting, and is within reach of WiFi.

Try the Aviation Hotel, situated opposite the passenger terminal, where rooms on floors 8 and 9 are reportedly the best, and you can easily spot aircraft movements even after dark.

COLOMBIA

Bogotá El Dorado International

BOG | SKBO

This is one of South America's busiest and most interesting airports, but it can be frustrating for spotting. It is one of the few places where you can still occasionally catch some classic types like the Boeing 727 and Douglas DC-3 in regular operation, albeit not in a passenger role.

Bogota is the home base for Avianca, Aerosucre, Copa, LATAM Colombia, Satena, EasyFly and VivaColombia. The airport also has a military and police presence and lots of cargo flights.

There are two parallel runways. Terminal 1 is the main facility for passengers, which is home to Avianca and most other airlines. The old Puenta Aereo terminal is now used for domestic flights by EasyFly and Satena.

Spotting is possible from within both passenger terminals. Try not to be obvious with the use of cameras and binoculars as security will likely question you.

There is a footbridge crossing the wide main road leading to the airport terminals which also has some elevated views of the maintenance areas at the airport. Other spots exist at the end of runway 31R and 13R, but it's best if you have a car.

Spotting Hotel

Movich Buró 26 Calle 26 #102-20, Bogotá | +57 1 5215050 | www.movichhotels.com A good option for spotting at Bogota, the Movich hotel is situated alongside the busy access road leading to the terminals. Close behind it are some of the maintenance and storage areas where interesting aircraft can often be seen. A room facing north on the top floor (you may need to pay extra for this as it's the Executive Floor) has views over the northerly runway. Aircraft using the other runway are visible from outside the hotel.

Cartagena Rafael Núñez International

CTG | SKCG

A busy little airport on the Caribbean coast of Colombia which handles a mix of domestic and international flights, particularly to the USA. It has a single runway and a small terminal which unfortunately has slatted shutters on the departure lounge windows and an external walkway which makes viewing a little difficult. Nevertheless, the ramp is quite compact with most executive aircraft parked close to airliners and easy to read off (some do park on the opposite side of the runway). A small Navy ramp is out of sight alongside the runway, too.

Around the terminal there are no obvious views of the aircraft, but on the road passing the northern end of the runway (and the beach next to it) you'll see aircraft just as they depart or land.

CYPRUS

Larnaca International

LCA | LCLK

Larnaca is the busiest airport in Cyprus, handling both scheduled and holiday flights throughout the year. It was developed following the split in Cyprus in 1974 when Nicosia Airport was taken out of action. Today it is home to the island's national airlines – Cyprus Airways and Tus Airways. It has some unusual and interesting movements from airlines of the Middle East, Russia and former Soviet Countries, as well as the usual airlines from northern Europe.

The airport has a single runway and a modern passenger terminal at the south western end which replaced older facilities. A remote ramp at the north eastern end of the runway is where cargo, general aviation and executive aircraft park up.

Spotting Locations

1. Mackenzie Beach
The most popular spotting location, particularly if runway 22 is in use, is Mackenzie Beach. It is a good place to relax with good opportunities to photography of landing aircraft.

2. Eastern Apron View
When driving along the main B4 road passing behind the airport from the passenger terminal towards Mackenzie Beach, look out for a hill on your right just after a roundabout. This has a view over the ramp used by cargo and general aviation. With a good lens you can photograph aircraft here, but don't stay long at this position as you will be moved on.

Spotting Hotel

Flamingo Beach Hotel 152 Piale Pasha Avenue, Larnaca | +357 24 828208 | flamingohotelcyprus.com A popular resort hotel on Mackenzie Beach, to the north east of Larnaca Airport. This beach is great for spotting and photographing arrivals, and rooms in the hotel looking towards the approach are perfect (301 and 401 reportedly the best). The hotel also has a rooftop area which is good for watching aircraft.

CZECH REPUBLIC

Prague Václav Havel Airport

PRG | LKPR

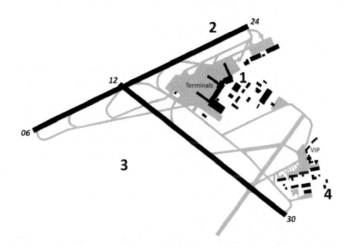

Following a boom in traffic in the early 2000s, Prague Airport went through a small amount of decline before numbers started to rise again in 2013. It now handles almost 17 million passengers per year through a mix of based carriers like CSA, Smartwings, Travel Service and Ryanair, plus airlines from all over Europe and further afield. In recent times airlines from the Far East have been capitalising on the tourist demand to the city, offering an interesting mix to the traffic.

The airport has two runways and three passenger terminals, plus a VIP terminal and two cargo centres. The latter are located on the southern section of the airport (the original site), while the passenger terminals are to the north, at the intersection of the two runways.

Spotting opportunities are quite good, and there's a strong local community who keep the hobby alive in cooperation with the airport.

Spotting Locations

1. Terminal Car Parks
There are views over parts of the terminal parking aprons and runways from the top floors of the car parks, however glass makes photography difficult.

2. Northern Viewing Mound
An official spot provided by the airport, this is still a great place to watch and photograph aircraft. It is located alongside the runway 24 threshold, which makes it perfect for landing shots. To reach the mound, head north from the terminals on the D7 motorway. Leave at exit 3 (Tuchoměřice / Kněževes). Turn right to go under the motorway bridge, then turn left immediately (you'll see a sign for Prague Airport). At the roundabout turn left. There is parking available.

3. Central Viewing Mound
On the south side of the point where the two runways cross is a raised viewing mound. Here you can see all movements and parts of the terminal, and get great photos of takeoffs and landings. To reach the mound is tricky and requires a car. Head south on the motorway from the terminals and exit at Hostivice. Drive through the village and turn right onto Cihlářská. Follow this road under the railway line and then across the motorway. Turn right at the end, then left. Before you come to the fence, turn left again and you'll reach the mound.

4. Shopping Centre
Useful for seeing some of the aircraft parked around the hangars and aprons at the southern end of the airport, as well as using runway 30. This shopping centre is off the main motorway heading south, signposted Terminal 3 and Prague Centrum. Turn left onto K Letišti and left again on Fajtlova. Head for the car park on the roof.

Spotting Hotel

Courtyard by Marriott Aviatická 1092/8, 161 00 Praha | +420 236 077 077 | www.marriott.com Located in the car park behind the terminal complex. Top floors rooms are high enough to see aircraft movements on the runways and taxiways, although the terminal buildings can get in the way and the position is a little distant for photographs.

DENMARK

Aarhus Airport

AAR | EKAH

Aarhus is a former military base now used as a regional airport. It has two runways, and a passenger terminal and parking area to the north. Regular carriers include Danish Air Transport, SUN-AIR, easyJet, Ryanair and Scandiavian Airlines.

Just east of the terminal alongside the road is a layby where you can park and watch any movements on the runways. You can also see the general aviation apron from the terminal car park.

Billund Airport

BLL | EKBI

Billund is an airport handling around 3.5 million passengers per year. Located in the centre of mainland Denmark, it is a popular place for inbound tourists thanks to nearby LEGOLAND and LEGO headquarters, and also sees plenty of outbound tourism during the summer season with airlines like Jet Time, Norwegian, and Thomas Cook Scandinavia.

The passenger terminal area is to the north of the runway. SUN-AIR is based here, and other important carriers include Ryanair, Scandinavian Airlines and Wizz Air, among many other European airlines. Billund is also a busy cargo hub served by ASL Airlines and DHL, using facilities to the south of the runway. To its east is an area of maintenance hangars used by SUN-AIR, SAS, and Nordic Aviation Capital – a leasing company based at the airport which often has some of its fleet parked up pending new leases or maintenance.

If you have a car, leave it in the airport car park and walk along the access road in front of the Zleep Hotel. Continue south past the end of runway 09 and find a spot to watch movements. Photography is good if aircraft are landing on 09.

There are also views of the maintenance areas through the fence on the south side. Drive past the entrance to LEGOLAND.

Copenhagen Airport

CPH | EKCH

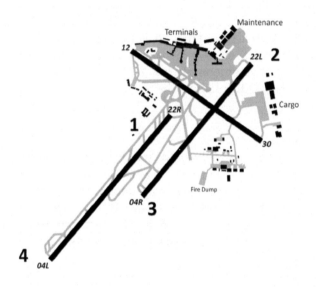

Copenhagen is one of Europe's oldest airports. It is a hub for Scandinavian Airlines and Norwegian.

Aside from these, Copenhagen is on the route network of airlines from across Europe, North America, Asia and the Middle East.

Perched at the southern end of the city on a peninsula, Copenhagen Airport has three runways and is surrounded by residential areas and the coast. It has two terminals along the northern side, with various piers and remote parking areas.

Next to the terminals is an area of maintenance hangars, and a number of cargo airlines use facilities on the eastern side of the airport. Further south are more maintenance hangars, and a compound used for training which includes some Bombardier CRJs and a Douglas DC-8.

Spotting Locations

1. Flyvergrillen
By far the most popular spotting location at Copenhagen is the Flyvergrillen alongside Runway 04L/22R. This is a café and burger bar which has a dirt mound alongside offering views of movements on the runways and taxiways. It is acceptable for photography on afternoons. To reach the spot you can drive and park there, or take Bus 35 from the terminals. It takes 30 minutes to walk.

2. Runway 22L
From Terminal 3, walk to the right. At the roundabout with McDonalds, turn right and walk past the SAS hangars. Follow the path/road past the end of the runway until you reach a suitable spot between the P15 and P17 car parks. This location is good for photographs of aircraft on short finals on afternoons. You will also be able to log some aircraft at all terminals and the cargo area.

3. Runway 04R
A good spot can be reached by car when aircraft are using Runway 04R. Follow the road away from the terminals and past the Flyvergrillen spot. Eventually, join Englandsvej southbound and go through the tunnel under the airport. After emerging at the other side, take the first left on to Nordre Kinkelgade. Follow this to the left through the small village, and eventually you will come to the spot alongside the fence. A stepladder is required for

good shots. Aircraft at the terminals are too far away to accurately read off.

4. Runway 04L
Again, from the Flyvergrillen, turn on to Tømmerupvej until you reach the end of the runway. There is room to park a few cars on the grass, and then find a good spot for photographing arrivals.

Spotting Hotel

Clarion Hotel Copenhagen Airport Ellehammersvej 20, Copenhagen 2770 | +45 32 501 501 | www.nordicchoicehotels. dk The Clarion (formerly the Hilton) is linked to the terminal via a covered walkway. Most rooms ending in 31-35 from the 10th floor up offer views, with photography possible.

ESTONIA

Tallinn Airport

TLL | EETN

The main airport serving the capital of Tallinn is only a short distance from the centre of the historic city. It has a modern terminal at the western end, with an east-west runway, and substantial cargo area to the east of the terminal. The latter is served by ASL, DHL, FedEx and UPS, and some aircraft park up during the day. airBaltic, LOT Polish Airlines, SmartLynx and Ryanair are the dominant passenger carriers.

Upstairs in the terminal is a restaurant with views over the parking apron. It has an outdoor terrace to make things easier, and photography is possible here.

South of the terminal you can walk along footpaths for a view through the fence, as well as views of any arrivals on runway 08. You can also drive in this direction and turn right for PEETRI kula. Just on your right is some open ground to park on.

ETHIOPIA

Addis Ababa Bole International

ADD | HAAB

This busy and crowded airport recently underwent expansion and upgrades to reflect the stature of Ethiopian Airlines and its growing hub and spoke network. However, plans are afoot to create a brand new airport for the city in the coming decades.

As well as Ethiopian, airlines from across Africa and some European and Middle Eastern carriers fly in regularly. There are some stored and derelict airliners to look out for.

Airside gate areas have good views of aircraft on the passenger apron and runways beyond. There are no obvious spotting locations outside the airport and care should be taken when exploring.

FINLAND

Helsinki Airport

HEL | EFHK

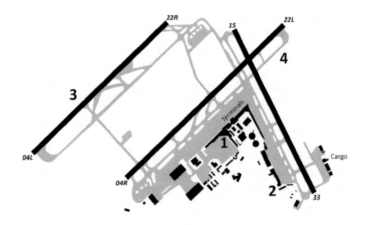

This airport at Vantaa was opened in 1952 for the Helsinki Olympics. It replaced the older facility at Malmi, which today is used as the city's general aviation airport. It is a busy hub for Finnair and handles flights from around the world. In addition to this, a healthy cargo operation takes place at the airport. Thanks to Finnair's links to Asia, many travellers pass through Helsinki in transit.

The airport has three runways and two terminals. Maintenance and cargo facilities stretch in either direction from the terminal, and are also located on the opposite side of runway 33.

The weather can often put a dampener on spending time at Helsinki, but long hours of sunlight in the summer months also prove advantageous. When the weather is against you, the café in the International Terminal provides a warm location with excellent views.

Whilst most of Europe's airlines visit Helsinki, its proximity to former Soviet and Baltic States means there's always something of interest passing through. Runway 22L is the most commonly used for movements due to the prevalent winds and noise abatement procedures, however runways can regularly be switched or used in parallel.

Spotting Locations

1. Scenic Terrace
Situated on top of a building next to Terminal 2, this official spot was opened in April 2013 to replace the old viewing area. It is open from 7am to 10pm daily and has elevated views over the gates and two main runways. There is an indoor part with snack machines.
There is also a terrace in the airside area of the terminal, located upstairs at Exit 2B in the centre of Terminal 2.

2. Business Terminal
A short walk south from Terminal 1 along Rahtitie leads to a fence with views across the remote parking ramp where executive aircraft can usually be found. You will also have views of runway 33 if it is in use. Walk past the cargo buildings to get there.

3. Runway 04L/22R
Exit the terminal area along Lentoasemantie and turn right at the traffic lights. Around 3km later, turn and drive along Katriinantie, then look for a layby on your right which has a barrier blocking most of it. You can park here, and there is a hill alongside with paths worn out by spotters who come here for good views of runway 04L/22R.

4. Runway 22L
On the north side of the airport is a hill next to runway 22L, which is most commonly used for arrivals. To get there drive east from the terminals on Ilmakehä and turn left towards Tuusula/Tusby/Cargo II. You'll eventually pass under the 45 motorway. Turn north at the petrol station and follow Tusbyvägen. Turn right after passing under the bridge, towards Tuusula/Tusby. After passing

over the motorway, you'll now by on Koivukylänväylä. Where the road turns sharply left, turn right onto the smaller Simosentie road. At the t-junction turn right again and find somewhere to park after about 500m. You can walk from here to the hill.

Spotting Hotel
Hilton Helsinki Airport
Lentäjänkuja 1, 01530 Vantaa | +358 9 73220 | www.hilton.com
The hotel is located directly behind the airport's main terminal complex and is a couple of floors higher than the terminal buildings. There are only outward facing rooms on two sides of the hotel, facing northeast and southwest (the rest face an inner courtyard). For spotting purposes, you will need rooms facing southwest; rooms facing northeast have views blocked by an adjacent building. The top two floors are best, with rooms on the southwest side overlooking final approach to runways 04L/R and many of the terminal stands.

Helsinki Malmi Airport

HEM | EFHF

Malmi is the original Helsinki Airport, and it has a well-preserved pre-war terminal building and an aviation museum. It is the city's general aviation airport, and the second busiest in Finland. Ramp access can occasionally be granted, otherwise views are possible from the terminal area. Many attempts have been made to close Malmi, but it is likely to remain operational until the 2020s.

MUSEUM

Finnish Aviation Museum

Karhumäentie 12, 01530 Vantaa, Finland | +358 98 70 08 70
| www.suomenilumuseo.fi This popular museum at Helsinki
Airport houses over 70 historic aircraft linked in some way to
Finnish aviation history. Included are a Convair 440, DC-2 and
a DC-3. It is open daily from 10am to 8pm (10am-5pm Sat &
Sun).

FRANCE

Beauvais Tillé Airport

BVA | LFOB

An airport with a focus on low cost operators situated around 50 miles north of Paris, an often referred to as Paris Beauvais. It has two runways and handles around 3.5 million passengers per year. Movements are dominated by Ryanair and Wizz Air, with others such as Blue Air and Laudamotion adding some extra spice. Not really worth a trip in its own right, if you are flying from the airport you can get views from the road leading to the terminal over the end of runway 12. Alternatively, there are a few spots along the footpath running alongside the perimeter fence down the length of the runway.

Bordeaux Mérignac

BOD | LFBD

A fairly busy airport in south-west France with two runways and central terminal area. A cargo terminal is to the east, which DHL uses. The main airlines at Bordeaux are Air France, easyJet, Volotea, and Ryanair. The airport is also home to a military base, with some French Air Force traffic operating from ramps on the southern part of the airfield.

The northern part of the airport is a large maintenance base and technical school, and you'll often see Airbus airliners parked up. In addition, there are two preserved Dassault Mercures, a Douglas DC-3, Airbus A300 and a Sud Aviation Caravelle in this area. Other airliners come and go for maintenance.

There aren't many opportunities to spot at the terminal unless you're flying. To view the storage and maintenance ramps, it's possible to drive to an area of waste ground nearby. From the terminal head north, then west along the D213 around the rear of the hangars along the northern perimeter. Then turn left at the next roundabout (signposted Institut du Maintenance Aeronautique), and follow to the end. You'll also see aircraft on the 05/23 runway from here, and can follow the perimeter track past the stored Dassault Mercure. Additionally, the D106 passes the end of runway 29, with some views across to the cargo ramp.

EuroAirport Basel Mulhouse Freiburg

MLH/BSL/EAP | LFSB/LSZM

This regional airport is located just inside France, but shares its facility with Basel in Switzerland and Freiburg in Germany. It is a hub for easyJet Switzerland and served by most European carriers, as well as a number of major cargo airlines. Biz jets are fairly common, especially during the World Economic Forum in January. A large FBO with parking and hangars for executive aircraft is to the south of the airport, alongside runway 33, with another on the eastern side near runway 26.

There is an official viewing platform near the runway 16 end which can be walked to from the terminal in 25 minutes, or driven much quicker. Head through the road tunnel under the runway and the platform, known as Belvedere, is on your right.

There is a spot to the south which is good for runway 33 arrivals, which also has a view over the executive ramp. Head south from the terminal on the motorway and exit for Hésigne/Lörrach (Germany). Turn left at the junction for Hésigne and at the roundabout take the second exit, followed by the third exit at the next one. You'll pass the end of the runway and see a place to park by the side of the road.

Lyon–Saint-Exupéry

LYS | LFLL

Lyon is a fairly busy airport in the south of France. It has two parallel runways in a north-south direction, with the two passenger terminal on the western side. The airport is a focus city for Air France, easyJet and Transavia France. Other interesting airlines include Emirates and Air Algérie. Because of the proximity of the Alps, the airport has many seasonal flights in the winter months. Emirates, DHL, FedEx and UPS all provide cargo flights.

To the south of the passenger and cargo terminals look out for a former Air Transat Lockheed L1011 TriStar, C-FTNA, which was damaged by hail in 2001 and has remained here ever since. It is now used for events by the airport.

A raised viewing area is good for spotting. From the terminal, follow the D517 through the car parks and north towards Pusignan. Eventually the road will turn right at a roundabout and cross the railway line before sweeping left. A small road on the right appears shortly afterwards. Take this, and then turn right again down a track which leads to a raised area of ground. You can see all movements from here, especially if using the northerly runways. The fence can obstruct photographs.

Marseille Provence Airport

MRS | LFML

One of the busiest airports in France, and one of two major airports on the south coast. Marseille is a focus for Air France and its partners, and also for Ryanair which offers plenty of low-cost links. Other major European airlines are also regulars, and there is a Eurocopter facility at the airport. Cargo flights are common, with ASL and DHL the busiest.

On the western side of the airport, directly across from the terminals, you may see a retired Dassault Mercure and Sud Aviation Caravelle. You can get closer to these aircraft if you have a car by following Route de la Plage from nearby Marignane.

There is a raised area close to the end of runway 31R which can be reached by car or on foot. Turn right out of the terminal and follow the perimeter for about 20 minutes. If driving, follow the D20 motorway south and exit for Marignane. You can park by the side of the road shortly after leaving the motorway. This spot is close to the military part of the airport, so beware of sensitivities.

Alternatively you can turn left out of the terminal and walk round for a view of the cargo and biz jet ramps.

Nantes Atlantique Airport

NTE | LFRS

Nantes is a busy airport in north-western France and a hub for easyJet Transavia France and Volotea. Airbus produce parts here. It has a large terminal on the eastern side of the runway, flanked to the north by an executive and general aviation ramp, and the south by a cargo terminal (DHL uses it). Just on the southern edge of the airport, along Route de Fremiou, is a preserved Lockheed Constellation which is open to the public on Saturdays (9am-5pm).

The Constellation is actually a good place to watch and photograph movements. Other good spots include the fence south of the terminal where Rue Clement Adler runs past, and the road which passes the northern end of the airport (Rue de la Croix Rouge). To reach it, head north from the terminal and turn left after the car parks.

Nice Côte d'Azur Airport

NCE | LFMN

FRANCE

This is the busiest airport in France outside Paris, catering for the busy Côte d'Azur which is a magnet for tourism. The airport has direct long-haul links with airlines such as Air Canada Rouge, Air Transat, Delta, Emirates and Qatar Airways. Meanwhile, most European and North African scheduled and low-cost carriers fly here. Nice is a hub for Air France and easyJet.

The proximity of the airport and its two parallel runways to the city means aircraft often make a spectacular curved departure to avoid overflying the beach which lies at the northern end of the airport. Therefore, most movements can be seen from the city, however other viewing locations are hard to come by.

You can walk to the busy executive aircraft parking areas north-east of the terminal, with views through the green mesh fence possible, but photography difficult.

Other areas for viewing aircraft are possible from around the entrance roads to the two terminals. Terminal 2 has a landside café with views.

Spotting Hotels

Campanile Hotel 459-461 promenade des Anglais L'Arénas, 06200 Nice | +33 493 21 20 20 | www.campanile.com Situated opposite Terminal 1 at the airport. Ask for a room on floor 5 facing the airport and you'll have views of aircraft movements and the runways. Not great for photography.

Hotel Premiere Classe 385 Prom. des Anglais, 06200 Nice | +33 4 93 71 72 13 | www.premiereclasse.com High floor rooms facing the airport look down over the biz jet parking apron and the runways 22L/R thresholds, so you can see most movements easily.

Palm trees on the road and wire mesh fence get in the way of photographs.

Paris Charles de Gaulle

CDG | LFPG

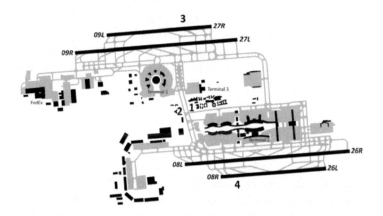

Charles de Gaulle, also known as Roissy, is the busiest airport in France and one of the busiest in Europe. It is the main operating base for Air France, and a hub for easyJet, Norwegian and Vueling. It handles flights from every corner of the globe, and is a major cargo hub for FedEx Express.

Terminal 1 is now fairly outdated with a curious design. Nevertheless, it still handles much of the non-Air France traffic at the airport. Air France, its partners and easyJet use Terminal 2 which stretches along the eastern side of the airport. The central Terminal 3 is used by low-cost and charter airlines. Large cargo facilities can be found to the west of both terminal areas, as well as Air France maintenance facilities.

Charles de Gaulle has four parallel runways – two to the north and two to the south; traffic can use any section regardless of which terminal it is destined for. Look out for a preserved Air France Concorde aircraft near Terminal 3.

Authorities have placed a ban on aircraft photography at Charles de Gaulle and Le Bourget airports, and can be less than welcoming to spotters, however it is possible to write and apply for a permit. Take the permit and letter with you to show to authorities if they question you.

To apply for a three-year permit for photography at Paris (covering Charles de Gaulle and Le Bourget), you will need to send some documents and a letter. Details available here: www. prefecturedepolice.interieur.gouv.fr/Demarches/Professionnel/ Transports/Aeroports-Paris-Charles-de-Gaulle-Paris-Orly-et-Paris-Le-Bourget/Spotters

Spotting Locations

1. Central Terminal Area
What was once the go-to location at Charles de Gaulle has now been ruined by new building construction. Therefore this spot is only good for watching aircraft using the taxiway between the north and south areas, and not for photography. The spot is located alongside the Hilton hotel and train station between all three terminals, and easily reached by foot.

2. Motorway Bridge
A little to the west of the first spot, and closer to Terminal 1 is the motorway bridge. Follow the road underneath the taxiways to reach it. From here aircraft can be seen taxiing. It is fine for photography, but there are no views of Terminal 2.

3. North Side
A road runs along part of the northern runway 09L/27R. To reach it drive east through the Terminal 2 area and you'll eventually reach the N1104 road. Head north around the airport until you come to a roundabout. Take the first exit onto Route de l'Arpenteur. Find a safe place to park alongside the road and enjoy the view of the runway (bring a ladder if you have one).

4. South Side

Again, following the road through the Terminal 2 area, when you reach the N1104 this time head south. Take the exit for the D84/Jully/Tremblay and Zone Cargo. At the roundabout take the first exit and follow the D84 along the length of the runway. Near the 08R end there is a small parking area and bike path, with a bridge over the TGV line. From here you have good views of arrivals on 08R or departures on 26L.

Spotting Hotels

Hilton Paris Charles de Gaulle
Roissypôle, Rue de Rome, Tremblay-en-France 95708 | +33 1 49 19 77 77 | www.hilton.com Situated between the two terminal areas. Rooms on the fourth floor or higher offer views of the taxiways and some aprons – particularly rooms ending in 01 and 29. Windows next to the elevators also give views over the holding points.

Ibis Hotel
Roissy Aéroport Cedex
Roissypôle, Roissy 95701 | +33 1 49 19 19 19 | www.ibis.com A more affordable option is the large Ibis hotel. North facing rooms have views over Terminal 3 and northern runways, and south facing have views over Terminal 2. The hotel is also located next to the Mound spotting location.

Paris Le Bourget

LBG | LFPB

Only a ten-minute drive, or 30 minute bus journey (line 350 or 351) from Charles de Gaulle, Le Bourget is an excellent airport to visit when in Paris. It handles many of the city's executive jet traffic, and is also famous for the bi-annual Paris Air Salon. There are no scheduled services here now, but the original terminal building is still present.

If you haven't visited, the Musée de l'air et de l'espace is worth coming to the airport for (see later). It has a huge collection of aircraft relating to French aviation history, including many prototypes. Large preserved airliners are parked outside on the ramp to explore. The aircraft not currently on display are kept in a compound on the western perimeter of the airport and not really visible from the museum.

As with Charles de Gaulle, photography is not allowed without a permit.

Spotting Locations

1. Central Road
To log the many bizjets and props, walk or drive along the main road (Avenue de l'Europe) running from the terminal/museum between the long row of hangars, taking time to stop in between each one to log what is parked in front. This is best done on a weekday, and sometimes you will be moved on. At the end, past the main ramp and terminal area, is the Dassault maintenance area which usually has some interesting visitors parked outside.

2. North Side
With a car, drive north from the airport entrance and turn left onto the D317. Exit on to the D370 towards Gonesse. When you reach the second roundabout, turn left towards Bonneuil-en-France. At the centre of this village, turn left onto Rue du Pont Yblon and park when you reach the gate and the cemetery. Continue walking past the gate until you reach the airport fence. From here you have a good view of runway movements, and a distant view across the airport parking aprons.

3. Dugny Store
Whilst occasional open days are held, the storage location for the museum's aircraft is usually only visible over the fence next to the cemetery in Dugny. From the terminal/museum drive past the exposition site and follow signs for Dugny, along the D50 and then the D114. At the roundabout in the town, take the first exit along Rue Normandie Niemen, and then left on to Rue Maurice

Bokanowski. Turn right at the next round about and the cemetery is on your immediate right, with parking.

MUSEUM

Musée de l'air et de l'espace

93352 Le Bourget | +33 1 49 92 70 62 | www.museeairespace. fr The fantastic Paris Air and Space Museum. Open daily except Monday from 10am to 6pm (5pm in winter). Exhibits include two Concordes, a Boeing 747-100, Airbus A380, Dassault Mercure, Douglas DC-8 and many historic French aircraft. The museum is free, but tickets must be bought to enter certain aircraft.

Paris Orly

ORY | LFPO

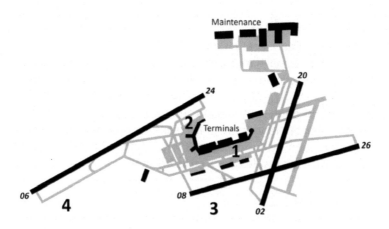

Orly is the second busiest airport in both Paris and France and very much worth a visit as most of Air France's domestic network operates from here, as well as a number of long haul flights, plus airlines like Air Caraibes, Air Corsica, Corsair International and French Bee. Many other scheduled, charter and low-cost airlines use Orly which also wouldn't be seen at Charles de Gaulle. Air Algerie and Royal Air Maroc have many daily flights.

Orly has two terminals – West and South. There is an official viewing location in the South Terminal which is adequate for viewing most movements. However, many photographers choose to move to various spots around the perimeter for better results.

The airport is easily linked to Paris and Charles de Gaulle by the road, bus and RER train network.

Whilst aircraft photography here is permitted, it may be wise to have your permit letter for Charles de Gaulle and Le Bourget with you to present to authorities if questioned.

Look out for a retired Airbus A300 on the eastern perimeter, a Sud Aviacion Caravelle among the fire training area to the west, and a Concorde prototype at the Museum Delta to the south of the airport (visible from the viewing terrace).

Spotting Locations

1. South Terminal Observation Deck
The South Terminal has an outdoor observation area which can be reached from within the terminal. This is a good location for logging most of the airport's movements, and photography is possible (although south-facing and through glass). The deck is free to enter, opening from 6am in summer and 10am in winter, and often open as a smoking area through the night. If you find it closed, windows inside offer a reduced view.

2. West Terminal
Upstairs in the West Terminal are a number of windows around the food court which allow views over the aircraft gates.

3. Runway 08
Take the N7 motorway underneath the airport from the South Terminal. At the second crossroads (past the museum) turn

right. Then at the large roundabout, take the third exit – Avenue d'Alsace-Lorraine. At the end, there are places to view aircraft lining up on the runway around Rue des Mimosas. Photography is possible.

4. Runway 06
Take the A106 away from the terminals towards Paris. Leave the motorway at Rungis and head along Rue Notre Dame. Turn left at the roundabout on to Rue de la Gare, which turns into the D167A. This eventually runs along the northern perimeter and around the end of runway 06. Turn left onto Rue des Mares Juliennes and park up. There are places to spot along the road, as well as along the cycle path which leads to a raised dyke.

Travel Between Paris Airports
The easiest way to travel between Charles de Gaulle and Orly airports is on the RER train (get off at Antony station for Orly and take the light rail to the terminal).

Le Bourget is also reachable by RER. The airport and museum is a short distance on bus line 350.

Tarbes–Lourdes–Pyrénées Airport

LDE | LFBT

This airport is located on the road between Lourdes and Tarbes. It is not busy for airline traffic, with only Brussels Airlines, Air France and Ryanair offering schedules. However, the airport sees a lot of seasonal flights, and Catholic pilgrimage flights.

The main draw for enthusiasts is the collection of stored aircraft on the opposite side of the runway to the terminal. These range from smaller airliners to large widebodies such as Boeing 777s and Airbus A340s. Many are ultimately scrapped, however Airbus will also occasionally place their demonstrator and development aircraft in short term storage here.

It is possible to see most of the stored aircraft from the car park outside the terminal. However, it is also possible to get closer by driving north from the terminal and then towards Ossun. Following side roads towards the stored aircraft you can get some views across the field, however later in the summer the crops can be tall and obscure the view.

Also explore the roads south from the terminal as more airliners are stored by the side of the taxiway.

Toulouse Blagnac

TLS | LFBO

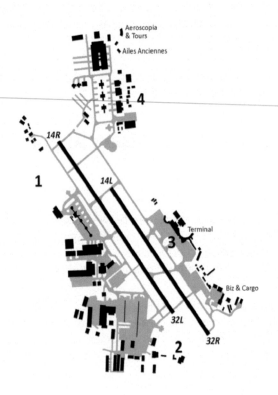

The main draw of visiting Toulouse is the Airbus and ATR factories which churn out new aircraft destined for the far corners of the globe at an impressive rate. Their facilities sprawl over much of the airport site.

Airbus produces the A319, A320, A330, A350 and A380 here, in conjunction with its other facility in Hamburg. Many of these aircraft are unlikely to be seen again in European skies for many years, if ever, and so it is incredibly tempting for the spotter to come and see them.

Airbus and ATR movements can be relied upon most weekdays, with test flights of the latest aircraft off the production line operating regularly. Additionally, the recent airframes to emerge from the giant hangars can usually be seen in plentiful supply around the various aprons and maintenance areas around the airfield.

The north of the site is where the A380 production line is (along with the Aeroscopia museum and starting point for tours). The western side are where the other production halls are, plus the delivery centre.

Many visitors choose to take a tour of the Airbus factory, which must be booked in advance (see www.manatour.fr). This gives the opportunity to see aircraft on the production line. Photography is not allowed, but logging and binoculars are fine.

Aside from manufacturing, Toulouse has a growing number of passenger links. Air France and easyJet are busiest, but you'll see airlines from all over Europe here. Just south of the modern terminal building is the general aviation, cargo and executive aprons.

Spotting Locations

1. Spotting Hill
A large hill exists on the western side of the airport which overlooks all movements on the runways, particularly in the 14L/R direction. Photography and logging are possible here. To reach the spot, head north from the terminal building on the motorway, but leave at the first exit and drive along D1 under the Airbus taxiways. At the end of the airport, turn left at the next two roundabouts and on to Avenue Latécoere. Look for a restaurant named Le Vingtième Avenue and park here. Then walk up the narrow road on the right. At the top of the hill turn right and then right again onto the rough ground. Be careful when the ground is muddy.

2. Car Park
On the southern perimeter amongst the Airbus side of the airport is a car park from which arrivals on runways 32L/R can be logged and photographed easily, and some of the Airbus ramps can be partially seen. From the main A624 motorway passing along the southern perimeter, take exit 2. Turn right at the roundabout where the Airbus entrance is and follow Chemin de la Crabe to a small roundabout. The second exit leads into the car park.

3. Airport Café
Inside the terminal building is a café on the second floor, with a walkway alongside the windows. It has views over the runways, taxiways, gates and the distant Airbus ramps. Photography is easy here, but restricted to aircraft closer to you and through glass.

4. Northern Site
Aircraft are often parked outside the hangars behind the northern Airbus site. From the museum and tour entrance, drive or walk south past the Ailes Anciennes Museum. Keep following the road, noting any aircraft you can see through the fence on your right.

MUSEUM

Aeroscopia Museum

Allée André Turcat, 31700 Blagnac | +33 5 34 39 42 00 |
musee-aeroscopia.fr Opened recently in a new hangar, this
museum includes many aircraft from the previous museum
here. Highlights include an Airbus A300B, Super Guppy, two
Concordes, Sud Aviation Caravelle 12, and lots of military and
light aircraft. The museum is open every day from 9am to
6pm. Adult admission is €11.50, concessions €9.50, and those
under six go free.

GERMANY

Berlin Schönefeld Airport (Berlin Brandenburg)

SXF | EDDB

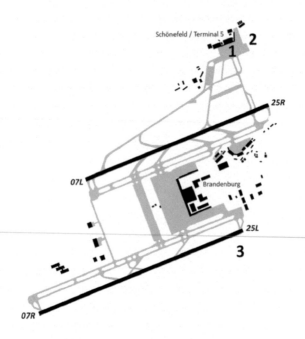

Schönefeld is currently Berlin's second busiest airport. However, it is being developed into the new Brandenburg Airport which has been delayed for many years and is expected to open in late 2020. The new terminal and runway are to the south of the present site, whilst Schönefeld's main runway will also be used. When Brandenburg opens, the existing Schönefeld terminal will become Brandenburg's Terminal 5, handling some low-cost and charter flights.

At present Schönefeld is served by many low cost airlines –
particularly easyJet and Ryanair. It has four terminals all linked
side-by-side to the north, and a fairly small parking apron.
Additional parking for executive aircraft is on the south side of the
runway on the Brandenburg site.

Tegel Airport will close in November 2020 when Brandenburg
opens. Its existing airline traffic (including easyJet and Eurowings
bases) will transfer to the new airport.

Spotting Locations

1. Viewing Terrace
There is a viewing terrace in the main terminal which faces
south. You can see all movements and take photographs, but
photography is into the sun for most of the day. There is a €2
entrance fee.

2. Brandenburg Viewing Terrace
The new airport's terminal has an observation deck on top which
has views over the apron. It is outdoors, but there are glass
screens in around the terrace. Views of the runways are difficult.

2. Apron View
To the side of the main parking apron is the road Jurgen-
Schumann-Allee, which is reached by walking east from the
terminal and turning right onto Waltersdorer Chaussee. The
disused section of the road overlooks the terminal area through
the fence and can be better for photographs if you have a ladder.

3. Runway 25L
This spot is great for watching and photographing arrivals for
runway 25L. While this runway is used for the current Schönefeld
Airport, it will come into its own once Brandenburg Airport
opens. To reach the spot head south from the airport on the
113 motorway. Take exit 8 and follow the road south through
Waltersdorf (you'll pass an IKEA store on your left). Take a right
onto the L402 road to Kiekebusch and pass through the village.

Where the road bends left, turn right immediately onto a track and follow it all the way to the fence.

Cologne Bonn Airport

CGN | EDDK

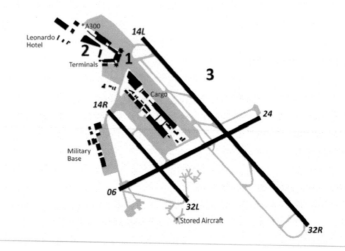

The major draw of Cologne/Bonn for many enthusiasts is the busy UPS hub which has been based here since 1986. In addition to this the airport is one of Germany's busiest, serving a large catchment area which stretches into Luxembourg, Belgium and the Netherlands.

Many of the airport's passenger flights are operated by low-cost airlines, including easyJet, Ryanair, Wizz Air, Eurowings and TUI fly which have bases here.

The airport has two terminals. Terminal 1 handles Lufthansa, Star Alliance and Eurowings movements, whilst all others use Terminal 2. Elsewhere, the large cargo terminal, maintenance area, and German Air Force ramp can be found between the two parallel runways.

Most cargo movements operate at night, which can mean that catching everything of interest is difficult. But there is usually a good selection operating or parked up during the day.

Another note to enthusiasts is the storage area at Cologne/Bonn which has held a number of decaying aircraft for many years, as well as a few temporary residents. This is far off to the south next to the threshold of runway 32L and difficult to see unless you're on a departing aircraft. Also, just near the terminal alongside the entrance road is the preserved Airbus A300 formerly used for by Zero-G.

FBOs and the base of the German Government's transport fleet is on the western side of the airport. This area should be avoided.

Spotting Locations

1. Terminal Observation Platform
The official terrace is provided within Terminal 1 between areas B and C on the fifth floor. The terrace covers views over the apron and northern runway operations, and can usually be relied upon for logging some aircraft at the cargo terminal. Photography is generally good when the windows are clean (or climb to the higher level which is above the glass). The terrace is open daily from 5am to midnight (except in poor weather) and is free.

2. Terminal 2 Car Park
The top level of the Terminal 2 Car Park is another spot with views over the passenger terminal aprons. It can also help with identifying some of the cargo aircraft, and gives limited views of the stored aircraft at the far end of the airfield.

3. Perimeter Road
For those with a car (it is also possible to walk), take the road motorway leading away from the terminal, but immediately take the first exit and turn right, and right at the lights on to Alte Kölner Strasse. Follow this road for a few miles as it loosely follows the perimeter through the forest. Look for areas to park along the

way. Various footpaths lead to the fence from here, giving views across Runway 14L/32R to the passenger and cargo terminals. The road also leads to a spot at the end of runway 24.

Spotting Hotel

Leonardo Hotel Cologne-Bonn Airport
Waldstrasse 255, Cologne 51147 | +49 2203 5610 | www.leonardo-hotels.com Conveniently located for the airport and motorway. Rooms can be expensive at times. The hotel is not ideally suited for viewing, although some upper rooms may offer views of the passenger apron and aircraft on finals to runway 14L/R.

Düsseldorf Airport

DUS | EDDL

Always a popular airport because of the excellent viewing facilities and interesting mix of aircraft, Düsseldorf is also easy to get to by full fare and low-cost airlines from across Europe.

The airport has a single terminal with three piers. An executive terminal and remote parking can be found to the west, whilst a cargo terminal, maintenance hangars and commuter parking ramp stretch off to the north east.

There's a good variety of airlines serving Dusseldorf, with many of Germany's charter and leisure carriers providing a good number of movements. A number of eastern European airlines also serve the airport, and long haul routes are offered by All Nippon Airways, Delta, Emirates, Etihad, and Lufthansa.

The best spotting location is the observation deck located above the B pier. It allows visitors to get close to the action, with aircraft parking all around you, and the runways in the near distance. Access is signposted, via the third floor of the terminal. It is open daily from 9am to 6pm (8pm between 26 March and 29 October).

Entrance costs €2.20 for adults, €1.50 concessions, and €1 for children.

With the railway station observation deck closed, an alternative is the footpath to the east of the airport which is great for landing shots of aircraft on runway 23L. To get there, take the monorail to the train station, then walk across the bridge to the car park. Follow the footpath straight ahead to the Lichtenbroicher Baggersee lake, then walk north until you reach the fence. You can also park for free at the station if you have a car.

Spotting Hotel

Sheraton Airport Hotel
Terminal-Ring 4, 40474 Düsseldorf | +49 21 14 1730 | www. sheraton.com The most convenient hotel at Düsseldorf Airport, and connected to the terminal via a walkway. Rooms on higher floors with numbers ending in 10 will give views of the domestic ramp and distant taxiway.

Frankfurt Airport

FRA | EDDF

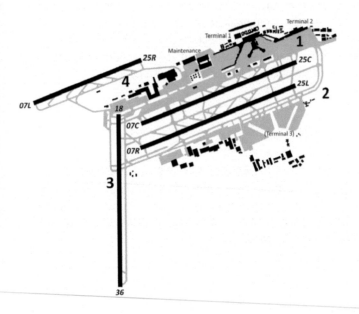

Frankfurt is Germany's busiest airport, and one of the busiest in Europe. It has been a favourite with aircraft enthusiasts for many years, particularly due to the exotic mix of airliners from the all around the world.

The airport has two passenger terminals linked by a connector passage. Terminal 1 is larger, and home to Lufthansa and Star Alliance partners. A new terminal is under construction on the south side of the airport, where Lufthansa will relocate once opened.

There are three parallel runways at Frankfurt, with one located slightly north and west of the rest of the site. Another runway is aligned north-south at the western side of the airport. It is only used for departures in the 18 direction.

As well as most of the Lufthansa and Condor fleets, Frankfurt is served by all major airlines from around the world. Cargo airlines are very prominent, using facilities on the south side.

Lufthansa's maintenance base is to the west of Terminal 1, but is only visible from on board a taxying aircraft.

Spotting Locations

1. Terminal 2 Visitors' Terrace
The terrace on Terminal 2 is the easiest location to get to. It gives close-up views of the action around part of this terminal, and the nearby runways and commuter ramp. It can be difficult to see movements at parts of Terminal 1 and runways 18/36 and 07L/25R from here. There are holes in the fence for camera lenses. Open daily. Adults €3.

2. Autobahn Viewing Platform
This is the best spot for runway 25L/C arrivals. From Terminal 2, it is possible to walk past the end of runways 25L/C along a designated footpath (takes 20 minutes). At ground level outside the terminal, follow Hugo-Eckener-Ring past the catering and office buildings. The footpath starts to the left of the terminal when facing it. Eventually it rises to meet a bridge crossing the Autobahn 5 where the platform is located.
To reach the location by car, drive towards Darmstadt on the A5 and exit for Zeppelinheim. After passing over the autobahn, take the first left into the forest and find the car park, then walk towards the airport.
Finally, you can also take the S-Bahn to Zeppelinheim and walk to the viewing platform through the forest.
At this location excellent photographs of aircraft on short finals can be taken, and many movements logged with good binoculars. A little further on is the Berlin Airlift Memorial, with a preserved C-47 and C-54 on display.

3. Runway 18 Viewing Area
A viewing area (with a small car park) is good for photographing departures on Runway 18, and also aircraft on short finals for Runways 07C/R. Some aircraft on the taxiways and cargo ramps can be logged from here. To reach it, drive west along Airportring (follow signs initially for Lufthansa Cargo). The road will eventually turn south and you'll come to a car park on your right before the road goes through a tunnel. It takes an hour to walk here from the terminals.

4. Runway 07L/25R Viewing Platform
The newer runway 07L/25R is used primarily for arrivals. It is situated to the north-west of the airport. A viewing platform was constructed alongside which gives elevated views over the fence of aircraft on the runway and taxiway. To get there drive west along Airportring following signs initially for Kelsterbach/Rüsselsheim. Turn right onto Okrifelter Strasse after the taxiway bridge, and then turn right into the car park. It takes 30 minutes to walk here from the terminals.

5. Airside Bus Tour
It is possible to take a bus tour of the airside facilities, including various ramps and the maintenance area. Tours start at the Frankfurt Airport Centre in the bridge between terminals 1 and 2. There are a variety of tour lengths and times available, and each has a different cost. See the airport website www.frankfurt-airport.com for more information and to book.

Spotting Hotel
Hilton Garden Inn
Am Flughafen, The Square – East, 60549 Frankfurt | +49 69 45 00 25 00 | www.hilton.com Situated near the terminals, above the railway station, this hotel also has TV screens in the lobbies with aircraft registrations (including the freighters) and some rooms with views of movements. There is an upgrade cost to book one of the quoted 'airport view' rooms. Useful to have flight tracking websites or equipment.

Frankfurt Hahn

HHN | EDFH

Hahn is a an alternative gateway to Frankfurt and Luxembourg for low cost carriers Ryanair and Wizz Air, as well as a cargo airport. Despite its name, it is around 75 miles from Frankfurt city.

You can catch aircraft parked on the general aviation and biz jet apron to the south of the terminal parking apron. Reach it by walking south from the terminal to the parking area near the GA terminal.

The most famous location for spotters is a hill overlooking the 03 end of the runway and the taxiway linking it, on the same side as the terminal. It's possible to walk 20 minutes from the terminal. If driving, turn left onto Flugplatzstrasse instead of continuing on to the terminal. Turn right towards Winterdienst and park when you reach the fence. The hill is on your right after a short walk towards the terminal.

Hamburg Airport

HAM | EDDH

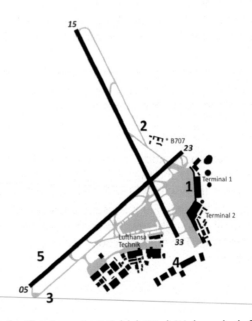

The main airport for Hamburg is at Fuhlsbüttel. It's busy hub for Condor, Eurowings and Ryanair, and is served by most European airlines, plus others from Africa and the Middle East. There are lots of seasonal charters to the sun in the summer, and Lufthansa Technik has a maintenance base here.

The airport has two runways, with two terminals on the eastern side of the site. Something to look out for is a preserved Lufthansa Boeing 707-400, D-ABOD, close to the threshold of runway 23 (and visible from the terminal access road ramp). A large central apron between the terminals and Lufthansa Technik hangars is used for biz jets, commuter aircraft and cargo aircraft.

Spotting Locations

1. Terminal Observation Decks
Both terminals have observation decks to watch aircraft movements. They are signposted and accessed from the respective departure levels in each terminal where you must ascend two more levels. Photography is through glass, but you won't miss any movements.

2. Coffee to Fly
Alongside runway 15/33 is a hut selling coffee and other refreshments with an elevated position, space to park and great views of aircraft movements. By car you can reach it by heading away from the terminals on Flughafenstrasse, turning left onto Langenhorner Chaussee, then left onto Witterkopsweg. This turns into Holkoppel, which leads to the spot. It would take 30 minutes to walk here from the terminal via a more direct footpath.

3. Runway 05 Arrivals
A walking route follows most of the airport perimeter. It curves around the end of runway 05, so you can pick your spot depending on light conditions if aircraft are landing on this runway. With a ladder you may see some aircraft at the Lufthansa Technik facility.

Hamburg Finkenwerder

XFW | EDHI

Finkenwerder Airport is located in the south west part of the city, alongside the River Elbe. It is primarily used as a manufacturing and outfitting site by Airbus, in addition to their Toulouse facility in France. The plant is the third largest aircraft manufacturing facility in the world. Airbus A319 and A321 models are manufactured here, as well as sections of the A380 fuselage and wings. Some models are also brought here to have their interiors fitted and final paint schemes applied ready for delivery.

Finkenwerder doesn't have any commercial flights, but regularly handles freighters of all sizes in addition to the A300-600ST "Belugas" operated by Airbus. In addition to this, there are daily worker transport flights on behalf of Airbus, and many executive jet movements in relation to their activities.

Naturally many aircraft enthusiasts visit Finkenwerder to log new airframes, many of which will shortly be flying in far flung corners of the world and not seen again in Europe. A number of spots around the airport offer views and opportunities for photography. It is advised to park your car in one of the two lots near the delivery centre and walk to the spotting locations. Bus line 150 from Altona station will deliver you close by if you alight at Am Rosengarten.

The most famous spotting location at Finkenwerder is a hill for visitors to watch aircraft close to the centre point of the airfield and runway. The hill is located off Neßdeich and has a car park. It offers elevated views of aircraft on the runway and nearby taxiways, and is the best all-round place for spotting here.

The old dike running the length of the runway also gives good views of aircraft landing and departing. It is good for photographs until late afternoon, and most aircraft parked in the open can be logged from here. From a position near the eastern entrance to the Airbus facility you can climb up onto the dike for good views of aircraft. It's not easy to park nearby, however.

Tours of the Finkenwerder Airbus plant can be taken, but photography is not permitted (logging is fine). See www.globe-tours.de for more information.

Hannover Airport

HAJ | EDDV

Germany's ninth busiest airport. Hannover has three parallel runways (one is a tiny strip for light aircraft) and a terminal with three concourses. Many European carriers fly in here, with Condor, Eurowings and TUI fly Deutschland the most common. You may also see airliners parked outside the maintenance hangars to the east of the terminal.

Spotting is best from the top level of the P1 Parking garage outside the terminal. Some of the gates and taxiways can be seen, as can the northern runway. Car park P7 also has some good views.

There is also a spotting hill on the southern perimeter, overlooking runway 09R/27L. To reach it, head east from the terminal and turn right onto Münchner Straße before the Autobahn. Follow this road through the factories, and park by the side of the road just before it turns left and becomes Schwabenstraße. Cross the road and walk down the track next to the factory to reach the hill.

Leipzig/Halle Airport

LEJ | EDDP

Most spotters come to Lepzig to watch the cargo movements, which are dominated by DHL and its partner carriers and cover all aircraft sizes up to Boeing 747-8.

The airport has two parallel east-west runways. The passenger terminal, access roads and railway station are between the runways, as is the AMTEs aircraft maintenance hangar and ramp which is often working on large aircraft such as the Boeing 747 or Antonov An-124. There is an Ilyushin IL-18, DM-STA preserved near the passenger terminal.

The vast cargo site is on the southern boundary stretching the length of runway 08R/26L. Most cargo movements are at night, so spotting in the summer months can enable you to get pictures of these aircraft when it is lighter later.

The easiest place to spot at Leipzig is the viewing terrace atop the yellow administration building next to the terminal. It is open 24 hours a day, making it ideal for catching those night time movements (if a little chilly in winter!). It costs €2 and you can see much of the airfield.

The multi-storey car park next to the terminal has six levels. Head to one of the upper floors for a view of runway 08L/26R and aircraft on nearby aprons, taxiways and the maintenance apron.

Munich Airport

MUC | EDDM

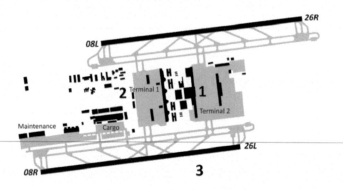

Munich is Germany's second busiest airport, and an important hub for Lufthansa and its partners. It has two terminals in between a pair of parallel runways. A third runway is in the planning stages.

Airline traffic includes many European scheduled and leisure airlines, plus long haul links from Asia, North America and the Middle East.

As with most German airports, facilities provided for watching aircraft are of excellent quality and very popular with spotters and locals alike. The small collection of preserved historic airliners near the terminal area adds interest to visiting enthusiasts.

Spotting Locations

1. Terminal 2 Terrace

Atop Terminal 2 is a good place to log aircraft, and photography is also possible, although glass surrounds the deck. Sadly many movements at Terminal 1 are not visible from here, although aircraft can usually be seen on the runways. Terminal 2 is used by Lufthansa and its Star Alliance partners. Good binoculars are required to read off aircraft on the business ramp to the left. This location is the most popular choice, although many prefer to take a log of Terminal 1 aircraft from the Mound before moving here. Access the Terrace via the Skywalk. It is open 8am-10pm daily.

2. Viewing Hill (The Mound, or *Besucherhügel*)

The second official viewing location is the Mound, located between the runways alongside the roads leading to the central terminal area. As the name suggests, this is an elevated position with views over the ramps and runways over two levels. It is open daily and has a €1 charge (and also a car park charge if you drive). Also at the spot is an aviation shop and a few preserved historic aircraft, including a DC-3, Junkers Ju-52, and Lockheed Constellation. It is possible to walk to the Mound, however the S-Bahn train service stops here one station before the terminal. Airport Tours are available a few times daily from the Mound which take you on a coach ride around both aprons and runways, and give you a behind-the-scenes view of various aspects of the airport. A tour lasts 50 minutes and can be booked through the airport website for a fee, or at the Mound itself.

3. Southern Perimeter Track

A track runs the length of runway 08R/26L on the southern boundary of the airport. There are positions all along which are good for spotting and photography on this runway. At the mid-point of the runway is an elevated hill which takes you above the fence for better shots. There is limited parking available here. To reach the spot, head east from Terminal 2 along Erdinger Allee. Cross the first roundabout, then exit towards Schwaig after 2km. Turn right onto Lohstraße and keep going, over the roundabout, until you see the Holiday Inn Express on your left. Turn right along

Helbergmooser Str and follow this along the perimeter until you find the position you want.

Nuremberg Airport

NUE | EDDN

Nuremberg is a hub for the low-cost airlines Eurowings, and Ryanair, with plenty of flights by Wizz Air, too. Aside from this there are good links with other scheduled European airlines as well as seasonal charters.

The airport has a single runway and terminal on the south side, with FBO facilities alongside. There is an observation terrace atop the terminal with good views of movements, albeit through glass.

Alternatives are the grass area alongside the control tower, or the top of the car park. Both have views of aircraft movements.

Stuttgart Airport

STR | EDDS

Stuttgart is a fairly large airport handling over 10 million passengers per year. The main operators here are Condor, Eurowings, Lauda, SunExpress and TUI fly Deutschland. Other mainline, low-cost and charter airlines serve the airport daily, including Delta Air Lines from Atlanta. DHL Aviation provides cargo services.

The airport has a single runway, 07/25. The three passenger terminals (combined into one building) are to the north-west, whilst the cargo terminal, maintenance hangars and a small air force base are to the south. General aviation aircraft park to the north-east.

Upstairs in Terminal 3 is an observation deck with good views over the main apron and runway. It is open from 8am-9pm (9am-7pm in winter) and has some preserved aircraft resident.

There is also a small spotting area with limited parking on the south side, off Nord-West-Umfahrung just after it emerges from the tunnel. Look for the supermarket and retail area, which has more parking. The viewing area is alongside, with views onto the runway.

Weeze Airport

NRN | EDLV

Known previously as both Niederrhein Airport and Düsseldorf Weeze, this is a small airport close to Duisburg on the Germany-Netherland border. Ryanair has a focus here and is the only passenger carrier at present.

The airport has a single runway and small terminal, and very little traffic. The parking apron is visible from the terminal car park.

GREECE

Athens Eleftherios Venizelos International

ATH | LGAV

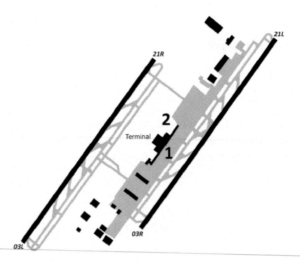

Opened in 2001 and replacing the original Hellenikon Airport in the city centre, Eleftherios Venizelos International is around 12 miles east of the city.

The airport features two long parallel runways and a single main terminal building, with a satellite building to handle extra aircraft. It is the busiest airport in Greece, and a hub for Olympic Air, Aegean Airlines and some other carriers. Most major airlines in Europe and the Middle East serve the airport, including some low-cost carriers. Some airlines from North America and the Far East also send aircraft daily.

At either side of the terminal building are ramps for commuter aircraft, cargo, business and private aircraft, and maintenance.

Spotting Locations

1. McDonalds Restaurant
On the 4th floor of the terminal, this location has plenty of seating and large windows give views over the gates, taxiways and eastern runway. Photography is possible, but not always recommended. Most movements will be seen from here.

2. Departures Level
Walking outside the terminal at Departures level, turn right and you'll find an area with views over the other runway. There are shaded seats here to enjoy the view, although photography is fairly difficult. Walking a little further to the end of the pedestrian area gives some views over the executive jet ramp.

Spotting Hotel

Sofitel Athens Airport
Athens Airport, Attiki Odos, Spata-Artemida 190 04 | +30 21 0354 4000 | www.sofitel.com This hotel is right outside the airport terminal. Ask for a high room facing the airport and you won't miss many movements, which can be read off with binoculars. Photography is not really possible.

Corfu International

CFU | LGKR

Like most Greek airports, Corfu is busiest in the summer months and sees charter and leisure airlines from the rest of Europe arrive, including some from Russia. The busiest days are Friday to Monday. The airport has one runway which juts out into the bay. At the northern end is the terminal and parking apron, with a smaller apron on the opposite side used for light aircraft and firefighting aircraft.

Spotting Locations

1. Royal Boutique Hotel

Most spotters at Corfu head for the Royal Boutique Hotel (see later), which has a bar and terrace overlooking the end of runway 35. You can catch all aircraft movements here, and take good photographs with a standard zoom lens. The bar opens to non-guests at 9.30am, however there are other spots nearby if the hotel is not accessible.

2. Kanoni Dam

Another good spot is on the dam which crosses the southern end of the bay underneath the approach to runway 35. At the southern end is a beach and café which are also good for photography.

3. Runway 17

Walking north from the terminal you'll reach the road which passes the end of runway 17. It is so close that traffic is stopped when an aircraft is about to land. You can find a spot to photograph arrivals, or through the fence, but there are no places to park.

Spotting Hotel

Royal Boutique Hotel
Palaiopolis 110, 49100 Kanoni | +30 2661 035342 | www.hotelroyal.gr A hotel with views of the action from an elevated position if you get a lagoon-facing room. Watch the aircraft from your balcony, with views down to the parking apron, or enjoy similar views from the public bar.

Heraklion International

HER | LGIR

A joint civil-military airport on Crete which gets very busy in the summer with charter flights. Because of this is also a military base spotters should be very discrete with cameras and binoculars.

The airport has one main east-west runway, with a shorter cross runway. At the eastern end is the sea, whilst to the west is the city and port of Heraklion.

There are some views inside the terminal in the café area, and from the roads either side of the terminal. If arrivals are from the east, it is best to position yourself on Karteros Beach which is very close to the end of runway 27 and should allow you to observe aircraft without drawing attention to yourself.

A new airport is due to be built to replace this site.

Rhodes International

RHO | LGRP

The third-busiest airport in Greece, Rhodes serves the island of the same name which is a busy tourist destination particularly in the summer months. Traffic is dominated by holiday flights, and is largely seasonal.

The airport hugs the north shore of the island and has a single runway (07/25) and terminal buildings on the south side.

Drive or walk east from the terminal along the Epar Od road. You'll come to some car rental offices next to the perimeter fence at the runway threshold and can watch or photograph aircraft arriving and lining up through the fence (or over if you can elevate yourself).

At the end of runway 07 is a café/restaurant called Airportview. You can reach it by driving west from the terminal, through the village (Paradeisi). The restaurant is signposted, and if you go in to enjoy a snack and a seat, you'll have views of aircraft arriving and lining up on 07 with good light for photographs.

Skiathos International

JSI | LGSK

This is not the busiest of Greek airports, with a small parking apron. However, many spotters love the location; it is often dubbed the 'St Maarten of Europe' with a road passing so close to the threshold that cars must stop and pedestrians duck when aircraft arrive.

Most movements are in the summer, with seasonal charters and low-cost flights from leisure airlines across Europe.

If landings are from the south, the Paraliakos road from Skiathos town leads past the end of the runway and you can usually see tourists and spotters congregating.

If landings are from the opposite direction, the pleasant Xanemos Beach is a great place to watch aircraft passing low overhead.

Zakynthos International

ZTH | LGZA

Not as busy as neighbouring island of Corfu, Zakynthos is nevertheless a decent summer resort airport with flights from airlines across Europe, as well as domestic links. It has a single runway (16/34) and terminal on the eastern side.

You can discretely see aircraft parked on the apron from either side of the terminal. Roads pass either end of the runway at a short distance; you can risk parking up and/or walking along to find a vantage point depending on which direction arrivals are from, which will result in good photographs.

Kalamaki Beach to the south is a good place to relax and watch aircraft pass low overhead. There are various hotels here which have some spotting opportunities.

HONDURAS

Tegucigalpa Toncontín International

TGU | MHTG

A horrendous airport for the nervous flyer, but incredible for the enthusiast. Toncontín International has a single runway and is positioned amongst mountains in the south of the city. It requires aircraft to make a precise, sweeping approach to line up with the runway and pass perilously close to cliffs and roads. Numerous accidents have happened here.

On the eastern side of the airfield are numerous old propliner wrecks, as well as a nice aviation museum with some interesting exhibits. It is possible to spot from here.

To get the classic close-up action of aircraft on approach, head along the road leading uphill to the south of the museum and find a good spot away from the buildings.

To the north of the passenger terminal there is an open area with views of movements.

The airport is served by local airlines, plus American, Avianca and United.

MUSEUM

Museo del Aire de Honduras

Atras del Club de Oficiales de la Fuerza Aérea Hondureña, Teguciguicigalpa | +504 2233 4692 A nice outdoor collection of historic aircraft relating to the Honduras Air Force. Larger exhibits include Douglas DC-3 and DC-6 aircraft. Open Thursday-Friday from 8am to 12pm and Saturday-Sunday from 10am to 5pm.

HONG KONG

Hong Kong Chek Lap Kok International

HKG | VHHH

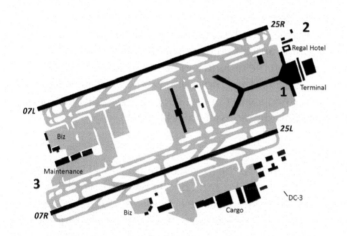

Hong Kong's current airport is to the west of the city, built on reclaimed land to replace the famous Kai Tak airport in 1998. The new airport is much more spacious and modern and has two runways and a large central terminal complex. This will be added to with an additional terminal and runway in the coming years.

To complement the terminal, which is on the eastern side of the airport, there are sizeable maintenance areas to the west, and cargo apron located on the southern side of the airport. A centre for business jet is also on the southern side.

Hong Kong is always busy and a pleasure to spot at, with an official spotting location and good spotting hotels. Traffic is dominated by Cathay Pacific and Asian carriers, operating mainly wide-body airliners.

The airport is the world's busiest for cargo, with freighters taking up a good portion of movements.

Spotting Locations

1. Sky Deck
This official location is on top of Terminal 2 is the Sky Deck. It is accessed via the Aviation Discovery Centre, and you require a ticket to enter (bought from the cinema entrance, priced HKD15). This is a good location for an overall view of movements, and you won't really miss anything going on at the airport. It is good for photographing arrivals on runway 25R until late afternoon, although aircraft on the ground can be too distant. The deck is open weekdays from 11am-10pm, and weekends from 9.30am-10pm. There are no facilities on the deck, but you can head back downstairs for refreshment and toilet facilities.

2. Alternative 25R
An alternative location to the Sky Deck for runway 25R arrivals is the corner of Cheong Yip Rd and Cheong Wing Rd, which is still close enough to the terminal to be convenient, but free to use and not restricted by opening times. It is great for photographs of arriving aircraft. To reach it, leave the terminal and walk north past the taxi rank. Be careful as there is a security post nearby.

3. Maintenance Areas
At the extreme western side of the airport, there are a number locations near the maintenance hangars which are great for watching and photographing arrivals and departures. You can also log aircraft parked in this area. It is a long walk from the terminals, so take a car or the S52 bus (destination Aircraft Maintenance Area) from Tung Chung. The S1 bus runs from the terminal to Tung Chung. Look out for a preserved Douglas DC-3 which you will pass on the bus.

Spotting Hotels

Regal Airport Hotel
9 Cheong Tat Road, Hong Kong International Airport, Hong Kong
| +825 2276 8888 | www.regalhotel.com This hotel is linked to the
terminal building and some rooms have excellent views of aircraft,
especially on runway 25R. Be sure to ask for a room with views of
the airport, and higher up if possible (1140, 1142, 1146, 1148 are
all good). The hotel is expensive, but is comfortable and has the
benefit of the views and a restaurant which also overlooks the
aprons and runways.

Marriott Skycity Hotel
1 SkyCity Road East, Hong Kong International Airport, Lantau
Hong Kong | +852 3969 1888 | www.marriott.com Rooms in this
hotel offer fantastic views, and it's only a short walk from the
terminal and the Skydeck viewing area. Even numbered rooms
high up offer views of short finals to runway 07R, and some views
of the cargo ramp. Flight tracking software will be needed at
night.

HUNGARY

Budapest Ferenc Liszt International

BUD | LHBP

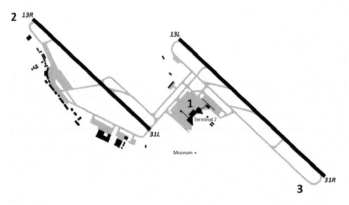

Budapest Airport has reinvented itself since the demise of Malev. It is now a hub for low-cost airlines like Ryanair and Wizz Air, and sees a good selection of European carriers, plus long-haul links from North America and the Middle East.

The airport has a pair of parallel runways, with the passenger terminal in the middle (alongside the Aero Park collection of preserved airliners).

On the western side of the airport is the original terminal (now closed) as well as military and cargo ramps, and maintenance facilities which often have airliners undergoing work.

A couple of retired airliners are used by the fire service for training, visible opposite the terminal. One aircraft, Tupolev Tu-154 HA-LCA, has recently been painted in historic Malev colours and can often be seen in different positions around the airport.

Spotting Locations

1. Terminal 2A Observation Terrace

On the northern side of Terminal 2A, accessed via the mezzanine departure hall (level 3) pre-security, this outdoor deck has views over the northern stands and runway 13L/31R. It is open from sunrise to sunset and has a 500Ft admission fee. It is better in the mornings due to the sun position.

There is another observation area post-security with similar views.

2. Spotter Hill

An official spot, located down by the side of runway 13R. The spotter hill is popular with locals. You'll need a car to get here as it's a long walk from the terminal, or alternately take airport bus 200E to "Szemeretelep Vasutallomas". You will be able to photograph aircraft landing and lining up, and can see some traffic using the other runway at a distance. By car, drive past the old terminal 1 towards Budapest (keep right) and turn right onto Igló utca. Follow it to the end.

3. Spotterdomb

For runway 31R arrivals and departures, this location is great in good weather. It is located close to the town of Vecses, and you'll need a car as it's too far to walk. Head along the M4 towards Szolnok and turn off at Vecses/Ecser and turn left on Uj Ecseri and towards the town. Then turn right onto Ecseri ut and follow to the end. You'll be able to find a gap among the trees to watch and photograph aircraft, and there are some benches to sit at.

Aeropark Budapest

Budapest Airport | +36 20 617 4141 | www.aeropark.hu A fantastic collection of Soviet airliners related to national airline Malev and the Hungarian Air Force. The aircraft can be seen outdoors alongside Terminal 2 at the airport, but it's worth paying the entrance fee to see them up close. They include a TU-134, TU-154, IL-14, Yak 40 and two IL-18s.

ICELAND

Keflavik International

KEF | BIKF

Iceland's main international airport and the home base of
Icelandair. Traffic is not particularly busy, but comes in banks
throughout the day as aircraft arrive and depart from Europe
and North America. Many of the airlines here operate seasonally,
making winter a quieter time. The airport also sees some
ferry traffic, aircraft testing (making use of regular crosswind
conditions), and military movements.

The airport has two runways at right angles to each other. The
passenger terminal is at the northern point of the site, with cargo
and maintenance facilities alongside. Military and testing facilities
are located further south and are difficult to see.

Spotting is possible either side of the airport terminal, and also
from the windows inside the pier.

Reykjavik Airport

RKV | BIRK

The city's original airport is now surrounded by the city, and only
a short walk from downtown. It has two runways, and most airline
traffic is by domestic operators which link all remote airports
around the country with the capital.

Reykjavik is a popular stop over for ferry pilots taking light aircraft
and biz jets across the North Atlantic. As such, this often provides
something of interest to see, with aircraft usually parked on the

eastern perimeter. In this area you'll also find general aviation hangars.

Spotting is possible at the side of the passenger terminal on the north side of the airport and also by walking or driving along the Nauthólsvegur road down the eastern side of the airport. The nearby Perlan attraction offers an elevated, albeit distant, view of the airport.

Spotting Hotel

Icelandair Hotel Reykjavik Natura
Nauthólsvegur, Reykjavik | +354 444 4500 | www.icelandairhotels. com A part of the old airport terminal, the Icelandair hotel is a good place for spotters visiting the city as one side of the hotel faces the airport's main runway and both of the main ramps. It's a good place to keep track of aircraft transiting the airport. Photography is possible of the aircraft sitting on the ramp outside, or on the runway beyond, if you have a higher floor room.

INDIA

Delhi Indira Gandhi International

DEL | VIDP

India's largest and busiest airport, and home to most of the nation's airlines. Delhi has three active runways. The original Terminal 1 is to the north, whilst terminals 2 and 3 are in a central area. A further three terminals are in the planning stages, along with a fourth runway.

To the east of the central area you'll find busy cargo facilities and maintenance areas for Air India and a number of stored Indian Air Force aircraft. To the north, alongside the shorter runway, is the military base, and a small Air Force Museum.

The tall concrete walls around Delhi Airport makes exploring the perimeter difficult, and the city's heat and pollution can make any photographs you do take look hazy.

Your safest bet for spotting here is to obtain a room at the Radisson Blu hotel, but be aware that this is where spotters were arrested after their equipment aroused suspicion to a cleaner.

Another good location is along the southern perimeter where the UER II road meets the intersection with the Old Delhi Gurgaon Road. By the side of the road you'll often see people gathered to watch aircraft, along with food stalls and lots of rubbish. Here you can see aircraft using runway 11/29, and photography is possible.

Spotting Hotel
Radisson Blu Plaza Delhi
Near Mahipalpur Extension, Nh 8, New Delhi, 110037 | +91 11 2677 9191 | www.radissonblue.com Situated at the eastern side of

the airport near the main motorway linking it to the city. This is a large and very comfortable and western hotel. Depending on your room you should be able to see aircraft arriving on runways 27, 28 and 29, and some departures. The terminals are a little far away, and higher rooms are better for seeing over the surrounding trees.

This is the hotel where a maid reported spotters for suspicious behaviour, leading to their arrest. So caution should be taken over your activities and leaving equipment such as binoculars, cameras and SBS units on display.

Goa Dabolim Airport

GOI | VOGO

This is one of India's only tourist airports, with many resorts nearby. As well as the usual domestic and low cost traffic, it sees many seasonal charters from Europe and Russia. You can also visit the nearby Naval Aviation Museum.

The airport has one runway, and is also a military base so extra care must be taken. Despite what you may be told, photography is permitted within passenger terminals in India, and also on board aircraft if you have a ticket.

Locals also often congregate near Dabolim Railway Station which is close to the western end of runway 26.

Naval Aviation Museum

Vasco da Gama, Goa | www.goatourism.gov.in A small museum in Goa, with a complete Indian Navy Lockheed Constellation aircraft on display amongst others. Open daily (except Monday) from 10am to 5pm.

Mumbai Chhatrapati Shivaji International

BOM | VABB

India's second largest and busiest airport, and one of the world's busiest for movements, having broken the 24-hour record twice.

Mumbai has two runways, which cross in the middle. To the north is the brand-new Terminal 2, whilst the older Terminal 1 is to the west. Air India performs maintenance on its fleet at locations around the airport site, and there's a busy general aviation and corporate hub on the southern side of the airport.

The best spotting location at Mumbai is an area of raised ground alongside the threshold of runway 27. It affords incredible photographs of aircraft on the runway and taxiway, and locals often gather here. However, officials will usually interrogate or move on spotters if they pass by. You may need local assistance to reach the location, which is behind houses off Magan Nathuram Road as it passes the eastern side of the airport. The area is very dirty and smelly.

Another location is off the Western Express Highway at the 09 end of the runway. It is acceptable to park up at the side of the service road alongside the highway and watch (or even risk photographing) aircraft movements.

Spotting Hotels

Orchid Hotel
Adjacent to Domestic, 70-C, Nehru Rd, Vile Parle East, Mumbai, 400099 | +91 22 2616 4000 A well-known hotel for spotters at Mumbai. It is found near Terminal 1 and the runway 14 threshold. Its roof terrace has a pool and good views over this part of the airport. Security, however, is now very tight and anyone using cameras or binoculars are usually spoken to immediately. Rooms on the top floor can have great views, with 702-707 reportedly good. Anyone with access to the executive floor can use the

INDIA

special lounge all day, which itself has good views. Spotting is allowed, but again no cameras.

Hotel Taj
Chhatrapati Shivaji Airport (Domestic Terminal), Off Western Express Highway, Santacruz (East), Mumbai, Maharashtra 400099 | +91 22 6211 5211 | www.tajhotels.com Quite a luxury hotel, and different from the well-established Orchid as a spotting location. The Taj is situated behind the domestic terminal, so rooms overlook the parking stands and runway beyond. Great for photography and service.

INDONESIA

Denpasar Bali Ngurah Rai International

DPS | WADD

Denpasar Ngurah Rai International is the third busiest airport in Indonesia, and a busy tourist resort – particularly among Asians an Australians. The airport sees a good mix of exotic domestic aircraft and large international carriers on a daily basis, and is a hub for Garuda, Indonesia AirAsia, and Wings Air. Unfortunately, due to terrorist activity the airport became much more security conscious and increasingly more difficult to spot at; the best spotting location has now disappointingly been fenced off.

The airport spans a narrow strip of land between the ocean and an inlet to the east. It has a single runway, 09/27, which extends into the sea on reclaimed land.

Much of the northern side of the runway is taken up by the airliner parking stands and passenger terminal, while the south side has a smaller ramp for executive aircraft. On the departures level of the terminal, a narrow corridor can be found which has large windows overlooking the apron and runway. Photography is not ideal due to the glass, but it is the only worthwhile spot inside the building.

Kutra Beach was once an amazing position for photographing aircraft on the runway and taxiways close up. However, fences have now been erected on the breakwater which prevents you getting close and blocks any decent photography. Nevertheless, you can still see aircraft movements from this beach and read registrations.

The resort village of Jimbaran on the south side of the airport has a number of streets which lead to crash gates fronting the runway. It is easy to photograph aircraft through holes in the fence here, however security will often move spotters on from these locations. Jimbaran's beach also has opportunities to watch movements, but is not good for photography.

Spotting Hotel

H Sovereign Bali
Jl. Raya Tuban No.2, Tuban, Kuta, Kabupaten Badung, Bali 80361, Indonesia | +62 361 3015555 | www.hsovereignhotels.com Just north of the airport at its eastern end. Fairly basic but comfortable. Rooms in the range 5021-5026 should all offer good views of aircraft movements on the runway, with slight obstructions by trees. The rooftop area also has good views.

Jakarta Halim Perdanakusuma

HLP | WIHH

Formerly the city's main airport until Soekarno Hatta opened in 1985, Halim is now a military base and is once again growing as a commercial airport, with domestic flights from Batik Air, Citilink, Pelita Air, Susi Air, TransNusa and Wings Air. Cargo operators are also common here.

Halim is also home to a maintenance base on its south side which often has aircraft in long-term storage. Although not as easy as it used to be, recent reports state it is still possible to arrange airside photography access at Halim. There are not many spotting locations outside the airport, and with the military presence it is not wise to act suspicious. Halim is located within the city, around 20 minutes' drive from the main airport.

Jakarta Soekarno-Hatta International

CGK | WIII

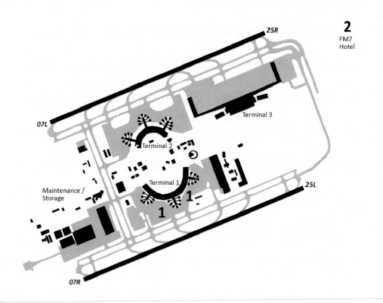

Jakarta's main airport is the busiest in the country and has three terminals, with the two main ones having viewing galleries. It is the home base of Garuda Indonesia, Batik Air, Indonesia AirAsia and Lion Air.

The airport layout sees a pair of parallel runways, with the original Terminal 1 facing the southern runway, Terminal 2 facing the northern runway, and the brand-new Terminal 3 also facing this direction. The latter handles most of Garuda's flights, and it is anticipated that Terminal 4 will also be built in the future.

Jakarta was somewhere enthusiasts flocked to see older classic jet and prop types, but these days are now gone save for some aircraft languishing in long term storage near the maintenance areas on the western portion of the airport.

There are a couple of good spotting hotels here, including one inside Terminal 2. You can travel freely between the three terminals using the monorail.

Spotting Locations

1. Terminal 1
This terminal has a number of so-called waving galleries along its length. Each is free to enter and offers a slightly different view to others. They offer good opportunities to photograph domestic aircraft, and some galleries look over the maintenance and storage areas. However, at the time of writing all but one of these galleries were closed and it is uncertain whether they will reopen in the future.

2. Spotting Hotels
(see later)

Spotting Hotels

Jakarta Airport Hotel
Terminal 2E, Soekarno-Hatta International Airport, Jakarta 19110 | +62 21 559 0008 | www.jakartaairporthotel.com This hotel is situated upstairs in Terminal 2 and all rooms look out over the gates and northern runway. The corridor leading to the rooms has windows looking towards the domestic side of the airport and maintenance areas. Perfectly nice place to stay, but can be expensive and is often fully booked.

FM7 Resort Hotel
Jl. Raya Perancis No. 67, Benda, Kec. Tgr, Banten 15125 | +62 21 559 11777 | www.fm7hotel.com The FM7 Resort Hotel is situated close to the end of Runway 25R, and one of the main benefits is the proximity of aircraft approaching this runway, which can be photographed quite easily. Although the hotel is only two stories high, rooms on the top floor can be found that have good views and are not too obstructed by the surrounding trees. Some rooms also have views across to runway 25L, but flicgh trackers

are necessary to identify them as they disappear behind the buildings. A rooftop bar area also has views – this is open from 5am-1am, with an additional roof area open at the manager's discretion.

Surabaya Juanda International

SUB | WARR

One of Indonesia's busiest airports, located in central Java, around 500 miles east of Jakarta. It is a busy domestic hub and sees international service from some Asian carriers.

The airport has one runway and two terminals – one either side of the runway. Ultimately two more runways and a replacement terminal will be built as part of future plans. To the east of Terminal 2, directly opposite Terminal 1, is a military base which often has transport aircraft present.

In the south-west corner of the airfield is a compound full of stored and retired airliners and the Merpati Training Centre. The aircraft cannot easily be seen, and it helps if you're in a departing or arriving aircraft to catch a view of all of them.

A waving gallery is located in Terminal 1 for views across the parked aircraft and runway. Photography is possible, and the military area can be seen opposite.

Spotting Hotel
Ibis Budget Hotel
Terminal 1, Jl. Ir. Juanda, Kec. Sidoarjo, 61253 | +62 31 8688115 | www.ibis.com Set within Terminal 1 at Surabaya. Its rooms are above the terminal, and any facing the airport has a ramp and runway view, so you can spot and usually photograph as you wish. The hotel is basic, but comfortable.

IRELAND

Dublin Airport

DUB | EIDW

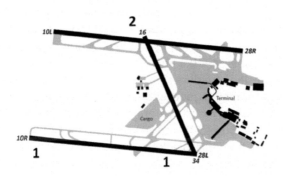

Dublin has become one of the fastest growing European airports thanks to the growth in Aer Lingus and the airport's US pre-clearance facility which makes transatlantic services much easier. The airline links these services with connecting regional flights from across the UK and Europe.

The airport has two runways. A new parallel runway 10L/28R to the north is due to open soon. The cross runway, 16/34, is only used when the wind condition dictates, and at other times can be used as a taxiway.

Many terminal developments have taken place over the past decade to improve the passenger experience. There are now four piers, with commuter aircraft parking on remote stands.

Biz jets park on an apron at the northern side of the airport, which is difficult to see from the terminal or even aircraft windows. The cargo apron is opposite the passenger terminal, to the north of the main runway. Look out for a retired Ryanair Boeing 737-200 (EI-CJD) in the same area.

Sadly no official spotting facilities remain at Dublin, but a number of locations around the perimeter are popular.

Spotting Locations

1. Runway 10/28
Following the road away from the terminal, turn on to Old Airport Road, which follows the perimeter. You'll soon be alongside the main runway, and depending on the direction in use you can find raised spots at either end of the runway which give you an elevated position for photography. Many spotters congregate here. Photography is good, and most traffic will pass you eventually. Follow the road around for spots on the northern side of the runway. Buses #16 and #41 heading for Dublin will drop you ½ a mile from this location (Dardistown Cemetery). A car is recommended.

2. Runway 16
Following the perimeter road around will lead you past the fire station and to the threshold of Runway 16. Parking along the side of the road, you can take good photographs here. This runway is not used as much.

The road here has already been rerouted as construction begins on the new runway. Once complete, there will likely be similar views of aircraft using the new strip from around this location.

Spotting Hotel
Radisson Blu Dublin Airport
Dublin Airport | +353 1 844 6000 | www.radissonblu.com Rooms facing the airport have a view of arrivals on runway 28 and 34, and distant views of departures. You can see parts of the international pier, but no other gate areas. Too distant for photography.

Shannon Airport

SNN | EINN

Shannon still sees its fair share of traffic crossing the Atlantic, including Aer Lingus and the technical stop for British Airways' London City-New York A318 service, plus seasonal links with Air Canada, American Airlines, Delta and United. Otherwise, traffic consists of summer charters, and European schedules by Aer Lingus and Ryanair. Cargo traffic is fairly busy with carriers such as ASL Airlines, Turkish Airlines Cargo and UPS Airlines.

The passenger terminal occupies the southern side of the airport. Maintenance and storage areas are on the eastern and northern peripheries of the airport, with a main 06/24 runway. There is a complex patter of disused runways now used as taxiways.

Often you'll see exotic aircraft at Shannon undergoing maintenance or painting, or in storage. There's also an old Iberia Boeing 727 (EC-CFA) used by the fire service, visible to the east of the terminal.

There is a public viewing area next to the Lufthansa Technik hangar on the northern perimeter of the airport, close to the runway 24 threshold. The majority of aircraft use this direction for landing, so you will see most movements. The fence is a little high for photographs unless you have a step ladder. From the terminal head along the N19. At the second roundabout, turn left for Newmarket-on-Fergus, then second exit (Ballycally) at the next roundabout. Turn left when the hangar comes into view, then immediately left again.

ISRAEL

Tel Aviv Ben Gurion International

TLV | LLBG

Ben Gurion is the largest airport in Israel, serving Tel Aviv as well as the capital Jerusalem 28 miles away. The airport has three runways in a triangle pattern, with the passenger terminals on the southern side.

El Al is based here, as well as Arkia, Israir and Sun d'Or. Other airlines from across Asia, Europe, the Middle East and North America fly in daily.

Security can often be a concern in Israel. Using radio scanners is not permitted, and security officers will often come to speak to you if they see you with cameras and binoculars. However, they are often happy to let you proceed if you explain what you are doing. Spotting is not uncommon in Israel, but avoid the military parts of the airport.

There is an official viewing terrace near Terminal 3. Head up the driveway to the terminal (where there are also some views), go past the terminal turn right into Tamar Street. Before the gate turn left into Ya'af Street and look for the elevated metal viewing terrace. This is a good spot for watching runway movements and taking photographs.

ITALY

Bergamo Orio al Serio International

BGY | LIME

Acting mostly as a third airport for Milan, this airport is located some 28 miles north east, and just south of the city of Bergamo itself. This airport grew in prominence during the low cost boom of the 2000s and today is a base for Ryanair. Many seasonal leisure flights also use the airport, and it is a busy cargo hub for DHL.

The terminal is on the south side of the main runway, whilst to the north is a military base and parking areas and hangars for executive aircraft, and a smaller general aviation runway. Among the trees and hangars you may see some derelict Fokker F27s.

You can spot from the top of the car park to the left of the terminal building, with views across the runway and some of the stands.

There is a viewing area with parking alongside the road at the eastern end of the airport, underneath the approach to runway 28. To reach it follow Via Orio Al Serio east from the terminal, past the cargo terminal. It turns into Via Matteotti. You may need to find somewhere to park before the road turns towards the runway end as the park has no spaces.

Bologna Guglielmo Marconi Airport

BLQ | LIPE

Bologna has grown in prominence over the past few years. It now boasts long-haul links to North America and the Middle East, as well as a busy mix of scheduled and low-cost carriers from all over

Europe. Ryanair has a base here and during the summer Italian carriers add plenty of additional seasonal flights. The airport has one runway, 12/30, and a single passenger terminal. A cargo facility handles flights from DHL.

South from the terminal is a riverside walk with views of the end of runway 30 and its approach. You can take good pictures of aircraft on the ground and in the air. Follow signs from the airport to Lippo, and when you see the runway and the road bends to the left, you can park by the side of the road and walk up the hill to find a good spot.

Spotters should avoid the area north-west of the terminal near the FlyOn conference centre due to its use by the army.

Catania Fontanarossa Airport

CTA | LICC

Catania is the busiest airport on the island of Sicily; its location close to Mt Etna can make for some stunning backdrops to your photographs. The airport is busiest during the summer months, with a lot of low cost and charter flights from across Europe. Throughout the year there is a steady stream of domestic routes to other parts of Italy.

The airport has a single runway and the terminal is on the north side. To the east is the sea and beaches. There is a separate heliport further south from the airport which should be avoided as it is also a military installation.

To the east of the airport is the long beach which is a great place to relax and to watch arrivals over the sea. Viale Presidente Kennedy runs behind the beach past the end of the runway and is also a good spot to watch from. You may get Etna in the background from this area.

If 08 is in use, the industrial area just off the motorway has some space alongside the roads and fields off Strada Comunale Passo Cavaliere.

Milan Linate

LIN | LIML

The older and much smaller airport of Milan. Linate is situated closer to the city than the larger Malpensa Airport, however it has always been limited by space and facilities. It recently underwent upgrades to its terminal and facilities. On the western side of the runway is a ramp for executive and government aircraft, as well as a smaller general aviation runway often used for parking.

Linate is served by many scheduled airlines from across Europe, plus Italian domestic routes.

From the terminal, head in the direction of Milan and then take a left towards Linate village. This side of the airport is used by the military and government, and you will eventually pass a number of spots where views across the airfield can be had along Via Baraca and Via Milano, which encircles the southern end of the main runway. Most aircraft can be read off from here with a good pair of binoculars. Various opportunities for photography can be had around this area.

One of the most popular spots around the perimeter is the cemetery. After passing the end of runway 36, turn left on to Via Walter Tobagi and pass through the industrial estate. Eventually, turn left at the T-junction on to Via IV Novembre and follow to the end. The car park next to the cemetery fronts the perimeter fence. Aircraft using the runway and taxiway are at extremely close quarters here. The terminal cannot be seen, however.

Milan Malpensa

MXP | LIMC

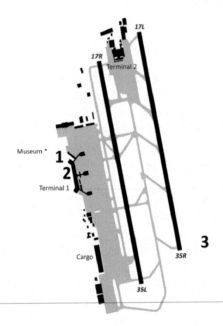

Malpensa is a large, modern and busy airport. It has two main terminals (the older Terminal 2 is to the north). To the south of Terminal 1 is a busy cargo terminal, whilst to the north are maintenance facilities used by Alitalia.

Alitalia has a strong presence at Malpensa, as do easyJet, Neos and Ryanair. Cargo services are dominated by FedEx Express and Cargolux, but you'll see most of the world's major freight airlines here.

As with all Italian airports, the police and security presence is obvious, and spotters do not always have their approval. However, a number of spots around the airport are frequented by spotters and offer the chance to log and photograph aircraft.

Just behind Terminal 1 is the Volandia aviation museum (see later).

Spotting Locations

1. Terminal 1 Car Park P1
Car park P1 offer views over the ramp around the cargo area and parts of the gates from ground level. You can take photographs of some aircraft.

2. Terminal 1 Windows
Behind the check-in area in Terminal 1 are large windows with views out over the apron and part of the gates and runways. Photography is possible, but through glass.

3. Runway 35R
From Terminal 1, drive south along the SS336 motorway and exit for Malpensa Cargo City. At the roundabout take the first exit, then turn left for Castano P. At the next roundabout take the second exit, crossing the motorway onto Via Molinelli/SP14. Follow this road past the ends of the runways then turn left onto Via Case Sparse. Eventually you will reach a small car park and play area on the left, with parking. Spotters regularly congregate here and this spot is great for photographs, especially if you use the picnic benches or climbing frame! Movements on both runways can easily be read off.

MUSEUM

Volandia Museum

via per Tornavento, 15 Casenuove, 21019 Somma Lombardo | +39 0331 230 007 | www.volandia.it A popular museum of flight and park near Malpensa. Lots of historic aircraft, both civil and military, relating to Italy's history. Also covers space and balloons. Generally open 10am to 7pm, but days vary depending on the month.

Rome Ciampino – G. B. Pastine International

CIA | LIRA

Rome's smaller (original) airport, situated closer to the city, is Ciampino. It is a busy military, cargo and business aviation airport, and is a hub for Ryanair and Wizz Air. Other low-cost carriers have now mostly reverted back to Fiumicino.

The Italian Government's transport aircraft are also based here, along with the yellow fire-fighting CL-215s. Cargo operations see daily flights by UPS and DHL.

Because of the military and government presence, spotting must be done very discretely. Police and security are known to regularly move on anyone using cameras and binoculars here.

It is possible to log some aircraft from the car park outside the terminal by taking fleeting looks along the main apron.

The Hotel Palacavicchi and the High Altitude Parking area are good places to watch arrivals from the north.

Rome Leonardo da Vinci – Fiumicino Airport

FCO | LIRF

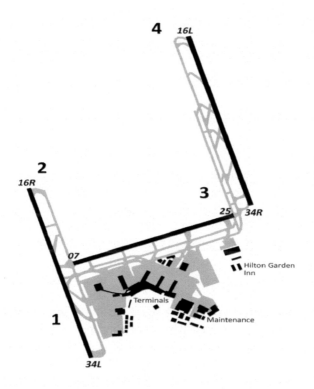

Rome Fiumicino is the largest and busiest airport in the capital, and indeed in all of Italy. It is the major hub for Alitalia and also on the route networks of most European, North American, Middle Eastern, African and Asian airlines. Many low-cost and leisure carriers can usually be found here, and heavy maintenance works are carried out on the national carrier's fleet here.

The airport has four runways (although one is primarily a taxiway) and three terminals occupying the central area. The few freight movements are usually handled to the south-west of the passenger terminals, and at a dedicated terminal east of the maintenance area.

For the enthusiast, a good road system hugs the perimeter of most of the airport giving views of most movements. Additionally, some locations in and around the terminal buildings offer glimpses of aircraft on the ground and opportunities for photography. As always, be aware that security personnel rarely look favourably on this pastime in Italy.

Spotting Locations

1. Runway 16R/34L Road
Running the length of this runway is the Viale Coccia di Morto road which has many points along both sides where you can pull in and view aircraft. Photography is not really possible unless an aircraft has just lifted off. Be careful of traffic and beware of police patrols. To reach this road, leave the terminal area in the direction of Fiumicino. You will soon pass the end of 34R and turn parallel to its length.

2. Runway 16R
Following the perimeter road from location 2, at the 16R end of the runway the road will bear right around a waterway. Around here are a number of places to pull in and watch aircraft passing overhead on short finals to the runway. Excellent for photography.

3. Between Runways
Following the perimeter road from the previous two locations, when you reach a T-junction, turn right. A number of spots here give views of aircraft on Runway 06L/24R. Continuing along the path will give you views of aircraft using Runway 25, and also across to the maintenance ramps. Beware this road leads to private properties and is patrolled.

4. Runway 16L
From the previous spot retrace your path (or turn left at the T-junction) and continue along the road. At the next crossroads,

turn right over the bridge and follow the road round past the end of runway 16L which is mostly used for arrivals. You can choose which side depending on the sun for the best photographs.

Spotting Hotel

Hilton Garden Inn Rome Airport
Via Vittorio Bragadin 2, 00054 Fiumicino, Italy | +39 06 6525 9000 | www.hilton.com Ask for an odd-numbered room on the 5th or 6th floors and you will have views of nearly all movements at the airport. Views are too distant for photography and SBS or flight tracking may be needed for registrations.

Turin Airport

TRN | LIMF

A busy airport in northwest Italy. Turin is a base for Blue Air and, unlike many of Italy's airports, is busier in the winter than summer thanks to skiing charters from all over Europe.

Other carriers you'll see regularly include Alitalia, Air Moldova, Blue Panorama, British Airways, Brussels Airlines, easyJet, Iberia Regional, KLM, Lufthansa, Royal Air Maroc, Ryanair, Volotea, Vueling and Wizz Air.

The top floor of the car parking garage outside the terminal is the easiest place to spot from. You can take pictures of aircraft on the runway and some gates with a zoom lens.

Another good spot for photographs of aircraft on the runway is along the fence north of the terminal. Drive north from the terminal and at the roundabout take the first exit followed by the second exit at the next roundabout. After the fire station the small road (Str. Vecchia di Malanghero) turns to follow the fence.

There is a Douglas DC-3 mounted on poles alongside the SP-2 road south of the airport terminal.

Venice Marco Polo Airport

VCE | LIPZ

The main airport for Venice, situated just north of the city on the mainland and fronting the bay. The airport has two parallel runways, with a terminal on the north side. Cargo facilities are to the south of the terminal, and a maintenance area is further to the north. You will often see Sukhoi Superjet aircraft being worked on here by Leonardo.

The main carriers at Venice are Alitalia, easyJet and Volotea, and most flights are by leisure carriers or domestic routes within Italy. Seasonal long-haul flights operate to the USA and Canada. Cargo airlines include DHL, FedEx, UPS and Volga-Dnepr Airlines.

Spotting opportunities are limited, but it is possible to see movements from the departures level outside the terminal and the café alongside it. Once airside the views are good.

JAMAICA

Montego Bay Sangster International

MBJ | MKJS

A popular tourist airport serving nearby resorts on the island. Montego Bay sees around 4.5 million passengers per year mainly through airlines from Canada, the USA, Europe and around the Caribbean.

The airport has a single runway. At the southern end is an area known as Dead End Beach with some resorts and bars nearby. Aircraft arriving on runway 07 pass very close by and can be photographed.

JAPAN

Chubu Centrair International

NGO | RJGG

Chubu Centrair is one of Japan's newest airports built, like several others in Japan, on an artificial island close to the coast near Nagoya. It was opened in February 2005 to replace the older airport at Nagoya; its name is a play on its location, serving the heavily populated central region of Japan. It is around 180 miles from Tokyo.

Because of its newness, Centrair is a very modern airport with amenities to attract discerning travellers.

It has a single, large terminal with one central pier, and two piers stretching in either direction away from the central building. In front is the airport's only runway, 18/36, and to the north is one of Japan's largest cargo terminals.

The Coast Guard also base aircraft at this airport, with facilities at the northern end of the site.

Enthusiasts will want to visit the brand new Flight of Dreams centre at the airport, which features one of the prototype Boeing 787 Dreamliner aircraft, ZA001, donated by the manufacturer.

By far the easiest and best location for spotting at Chubu, the official Observation Deck runs along the top of the central pier atop the terminal with good views of the gates and runway. This is a large, popular deck which is open from 7am-9pm, free of charge. It has tall wire fencing running along its length, but it is still possible to poke a camera through to take photographs.

If the weather isn't good enough to be outside, you can shelter in the domestic gate area of the terminal where large windows offer

JAPAN

154

plenty of views of the aircraft and runway beyond. You can't see the international gates from here, but aircraft will be visible when using the runway.

Spotting Hotel

Centrair Hotel
1 Chrome-1 Centrair, Tokoname | +81 569 38 1111 | www. centrairhotel.jp The closest hotel to the airport terminal. It is a tall hotel, and upper rooms facing the airport have views of movements on the runway and domestic side of the terminal.

Fukuoka Airport

FUK | RJFF

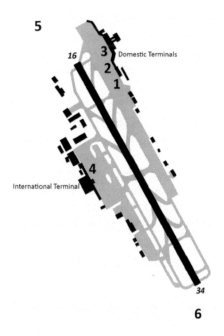

Fukuoka Airport handles a mix of domestic and intra-Asian flights from a variety of airlines. It is the fourth busiest airport in Japan.

There are three domestic passenger terminals - 1, 2 and 3 - on the northern side of the single runway, and an International Terminal on the opposite side. A Coast Guard station is situated alongside the International Terminal. As with most Japanese airports, enthusiasts are catered for by observation decks on all terminals.

Spotting Locations

1. Domestic Terminal 1 Observation Deck
All three domestic terminals have their own observation deck. The one at Terminal 1 is outdoor and accessed from floor 2F in the departures area. It is free of charge and open from 7am to 8pm. This is a good all-round location for aircraft using the runway and domestic terminals. Large fences front the deck, which can hinder photography but is usually acceptable.

2. Domestic Terminal 1 Observation Room
Accessed via a spiral staircase from floor 3F, Terminal 1's alternative observation area is indoors and fronted by glass windows. This can sometimes hinder photography, but the views are great and it's a nice warm place to spot in harsh weather. Free of charge, and open 7am to 8pm.

3. Domestic Terminal 2 Observation Deck
You can access this rooftop deck from floor 3F near the games room. A slightly more spacious area to spot, which has glass windows instead of fences. The glass is usually clean enough to take photographs through. Views are of the southern end of the domestic terminal and the runway. You can see across to the International Terminal too. Free of charge, and open from 7am to 9.30pm.

4. International Terminal Observation Decks
There are two observation decks atop the International Terminal and accessed from either end of the building. These have views over the international gates, runway, and across to the domestic terminals. The decks are surrounded by glass, so photographs are not always perfect. Free of charge and open from 7am to 8pm.

5. Runway 16
There are a few points around the perimeter fence close to the end of Runway 16. From these you can take good unobstructed views of aircraft landing on this runway, and you'll often find other spotters here. You can see some movements on the ground through the fence. You can reach these points by walking alongside the fence from Terminal 2 for around 15 minutes.

6. Runway 34
Two spots near the end of this runway are great for photographs of aircraft landing and lining up for departure. The first is a mound next to a small road (where you can park). Take bus 43 from the domestic terminal and get off at Tsukiguma. This is good on the morning.

The second spot is a footbridge on the other side of the runway which is good on the afternoon for photography. The gas station nearby is useful for supplies.

Kagoshima Airport

KOJ | RJFK

Located at the southern tip of Japan on Kyushu. Kagoshima is a busy domestic hub with international links to China, Hong Kong and South Korea. There is a viewing area on top of the terminal building which is great for photography on an afternoon. You will see all movements from here.

Nagoya Komaki Airfield

NKM | RJNA

Nagoya's original airport is in the north of the city, and home to Fuji Dream Airways and a military air base, but little else of note. It has a single runway. The passenger terminal has an observation deck which is fine for watching movements, and logging aircraft at the military part of the airfield. You can also take photographs here.

The Aichi Museum (https://aichi-mof.com/) south of the terminal has a number of aircraft exhibits, as well as its own viewing terrace.

Okinawa Naha

OKA | ROAH

A single runway airport which is a joint military base. Okinawa is Japan's seventh-busiest and serves mainly domestic flights, with a mix of international services to the likes of China, Hong Kong and Taiwan. The terminals and cargo complex are in the north-east corner of the airport. To the south is the expansive JASDF base, whilst on the western side is a Coast Guard station. It makes for an interesting mix of movements.

There are two observation decks on top of the Domestic Terminal from which all movements can be seen, including anything operating from the military side. There is a fee to enter.

Osaka Itami

ITM | RJOO

The original airport for Osaka, Itami is now relegated to domestic operations, with international services flown out of Kansai International to the south of the city.

Itami is surrounded on all sides by the city, and it is one of the busiest in Japan for aircraft movements. A perfect place to catch up on the domestic airline fleets, here you will primarily see the country's two main operators - Japan Airlines and All Nippon Airways (and their feeder carriers) operating throughout the country with various aircraft types from commuter turboprops to widebodies.

There are two parallel runways at the airport. The terminal building, which is split into two section, plus the parking apron, are on the northern side.

The airport's observation deck is located on top of the terminal building and overlooks the runways and many of the gates. Photography is good from here, although air bridges can get in the way of closer shots. The observation deck is open from 8am-10pm and is free of charge. You can access it on the 3rd floor.

An alternative is Itami Sky Park, which is situated on the opposite side of the airport. This garden-like structure has various levels allowing photography above the fence of aircraft on the main 14R/32L runway. The Sky Park extends for quite a distance along the airport perimeter and is an excellent spot in good weather. It's free to use, with nearby convenience stores for supplies. You can take bus #25 from the terminal every 30 minutes (alight after passing the tunnel under the runway).

Osaka Kansai International

KIX | RJBB

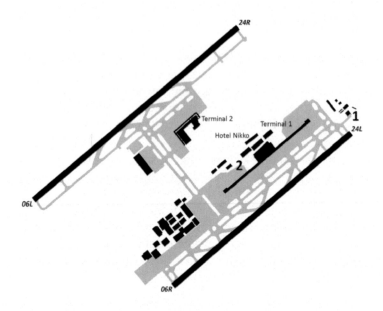

Kansai Airport is the main international gateway to Osaka, located on a man-made island in Osaka Bay with two runways and terminals. It is anticipated that a third runway will also be built.

Kansai is also a major cargo centre – one of the busiest freight airports in the world. Freighters of all the world's major cargo airlines are a daily sight, using facilities to the south-west of the passenger terminals.

All major Japanese and Asian airlines fly to Kansai, as well as a number of low-cost carriers and airlines from Europe, North America and the Middle East.

Spotting Locations

1. Sky View Observation Hall
The official spotting location at Kansai is an elevated platform at the eastern end of the airport, close to the threshold of runway 24L. It has excellent views over this runway and the terminal gates, so you won't miss any aircraft or registrations. Photography is also good, with the classic view of aircraft passing over the road bridge possible. The Observation Hall is free and open 8am-10pm (10pm at weekends). You can reach it via the bus from the terminal (Nankai bus stop), signposted to the Observation Hall.

2. Outside Terminal 1
At departures level of Terminal 1, you can walk outside in either direction and come to positions where views of the apron, taxiways and parked aircraft are possible.

Spotting Hotel

Hotel Nikko Kansai Airport
Kansai Airport, Osaka 549-0001 | +81 455 1111 | www.nikkokix.com This hotel is linked to the terminal and railway station. Rooms on the top floor facing the airport have views of the taxiway, runways and part of the terminal.

Sapporo New Chitose

CTS | RJCC

The largest airport on the northern island of Hokkaido. New Chitose is a joint civil-military airport, which is home to a JASDAF squadron as well as the government transport aircraft on the western side of the airport (with its own parallel runways).

The civilian airport operates from the eastern side of the site, with two parallel runways and a semi-circular domestic terminal building. The small international terminal is behind, on the western side.

The airport sees a good mix of international and domestic scheduled services, and in particular is good for the smaller regional aircraft of the various Japanese airlines.

There is an outdoor observation area on the fourth floor of the domestic terminal, open 9am to 5pm in the summer, but closed in winter. Indoors, another observation hall is available year-round.

Sendai Airport

SDJ | RJSS

Sendai has a main east-west runway, with a shorter strip crossing to the south and used mostly by general aviation traffic.

The passenger terminal is at the eastern end of the airport. Despite its modern design, it still finds space for a small observation deck overlooking the gates and main runway, known as the "Smile Terrace". It is open from 6.45am to 8pm daily.

At the western end of the main runway you'll find Sendaikukorinku Park where locals and enthusiasts gather to watch aircraft at close quarters. It's great for photography of aircraft on the runway and taxiway. There is a large car park, or it takes an hour to walk from the terminal.

Tokyo Haneda International

HND | RJTT

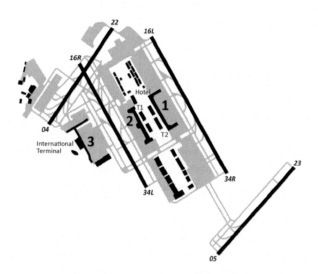

Haneda is one of the best airports for spotting in Japan. It provides observation decks on all terminals, including the newer International Terminal, giving you plenty of options to observe the vast number of aircraft passing through the airport.

Many more international flights now fly from Haneda, having transferred from Narita. Combined with the large number of domestic and intra-Asian flights, it makes Haneda a very busy airport indeed – so much so that it can be difficult to cover everything given the different aspects faced by each viewing deck. Spotters must move about to catch as much as possible, using the position of the sun to determine the best place to be for photographs.

The layout of Haneda is quite complicated. Two pairs of parallel runways run in two different directions, with the most recent built on reclaimed land in the bay. The domestic terminals sit centrally, between the 16/34 runways, whilst the ANA and JAL maintenance hangars are to their south.

Over on the south-west side of the airport is the International Terminal, whilst in the north-west corner are areas used by executive aircraft and the Coast Guard.

Spotting Locations

1. Terminal 2 Observation Deck
On the opposite side to the Terminal 1 deck, this one overlooks runway 16L/34R. It is also open from 6.30am to 10pm daily, and free of charge. This deck covers ANA and its associates, plus Air Do and Solaseed. It is better for photography from mid-morning onwards, but fewer movements are seen overall.

2. Terminal 1 Observation Deck
Terminal 1's observation deck overlooks that terminal and the new International Terminal across runway 16R/34L. You will see JAL and its associate airlines here. It is free to enter, and open from 6.30am to 10pm daily. The deck is accessed from the centre of the building via lift or escalator. Although there are tall fences around the deck, enlarged holes are provided for sticking camera lenses through. Photography is best in the morning.

3. International Terminal Observation Deck
This newer terminal also has a free deck on top, which is open the same times and is free of charge. It looks over the international gates, runway 16R/34L and across to Terminal 1. Light is best from mid-morning, but again you'll have to grapple with the high fence and limited holes to stick a lens through. You'll see most movements from here.

Spotting Hotel

Haneda Excel Hotel Tokyo
3-4-2 Hanedakuko Ota, 144-0041 Tokyo | +81 3 5756 6000 | www.tokyuhotelsjapan.com/en/ Linked to Terminal 2, this hotel offers

some of the best views at the airport if you get the right room. Ask for a higher floor room facing the airport. It is quite expensive to stay at this hotel, but the location is superb. The observation decks at the terminals are only a short walk away.

Tokyo Narita International

NRT | RJAA

Narita is Japan's second busiest airport, situated some 60 miles north of Tokyo. Primarily an international gateway, much of this traffic has now transferred back to Haneda. Narita is, however, trying to attract new routes and developing the site, with a third runway expected to be built, and the shorter runway 16L/34R finally to be extended.

There are three passenger terminals in the central area and a large cargo terminal to the north. To the south, Japan Airlines handle maintenance of their fleet.

Spotting Locations

1. Terminal 1 Observation Deck
The largest of the official spotting locations at Narita. It is located atop Terminal 1 and is free to enter. It has views over the gates, taxiways and the main runway, and photography is good on a morning (through holes in the fence). You will see most international and cargo flights from this deck. It is accessed from level 4F inside the terminal, and open from 7am to 9pm. There is no WiFi at this deck.

2. Terminal 2 Observation Decks
Terminal 2 has two observation decks - one either side of the pier. They are both free to enter, and open from 7am to 9pm, with WiFi. The southern deck has better views of the taxiways, but the northern one has views of some gates that are not visible to the other. You will see the low-cost carriers better from Terminal 2. Photography is possible through enlarged holes in the fence, and light is best in the afternoon.

3. Museum of Aeronautical Sciences/Runway 34L
Whilst the Aviation Museum is worth a visit in its own right, it also features an observation deck which is good for views of aircraft approaching runway 34L and on the taxiways linking it. It makes for good photographs. If you don't have a car, take bus from Terminal 1 stop No. 30.

From the museum you can walk around the southern end of Runway 34L to Hikoki-no Oka Park where photography on an afternoon is perfect if aircraft are landing in this direction.

4. Sakura no Yama Park
Situated near the end of runway 16R and ideal if aircraft are landing on this runway. Good for photographs, although the

perimeter fence can sometimes get in the way. You also have good views over the western side of the airport. Many people come here, although you'll need a car (follow Route 44 southeast from the airport). It is a 15-minute walk from the Marroad Hotel.

Spotting Hotel

Marroad International Hotel
763-1 Komaino, Narita-shi, Chiba 286-0121 | +81 476 30 2222 | www.marroad.jp/narita/ Situated close to the threshold of runway 16R. If you ask for a room facing the airport, you will have views of this runway, the cargo apron and part of Terminal 1. Photographs are possible, and most movements can be logged. The hotel's top-floor restaurant also has good views. Reasonably priced, with a free shuttle to the airport.

Museum of Aeronautical Sciences

111-3 Higashisanrizuka, Narita 288-0112 | +81 479 78 0557 | www.aeromuseum.or.jp Located close to the end of runway 34L at Tokyo Narita Airport, with its own observation deck. This museum has a nice little collection of civil aircraft and helicopters. The largest preserved type is a NAMC YS-11 airliner and a Boeing 747 nose section. The museum is open 10am-5pm Tuesday-Sunday (daily in January, May and August), with a 500 yen entrance fee.

Shuttle buses depart from Terminal 1 (first floor, stop No. 30) and Terminal 2 (third floor, stop No. 2) for the museum. The trip takes 15 minutes and costs 200 yen. There are only four buses per day. Alternatively, a taxi ride from the airport costs about 1600 yen.

KUWAIT

Kuwait International

KWI | OKBK

Kuwait International is a joint civil-military base with strict security. It is home to Kuwait Airways and Jazeera Airways, and served by many international carriers – particularly from around the Middle East and Asia.

Two new terminals were opened in recent years, taking the total to four. They are all in the central area, with the military base and maintenance areas to the north. A third parallel runway, and the brand new Terminal 2 are under construction and due to open in 2022.

There are no spotting areas. Try the Safir Hotel among the terminal complex as it has views over some of the parking gates, maintenance area and runway.

LATVIA

Riga International

RIX | EVRA

This main gateway to Latvia and home to airlines like airBaltic, SmartLynx and Wizz Air who provide much of the operations. Other airlines like Ryanair, Norwegian, Aeroflot, Finnair and Lufthansa are also regular visitors.

The airport has a modern passenger terminal with two piers and remote parking ramps to the north and south. FBOs offer hangars and parking space for biz jets, while freighters are a common sight. It's worth keeping an eye out for stored airliners which are often parked and stored to the north of the terminal, and also on the west side of the runway among the trees.

Behind the terminal and within walking reach is the Riga Aviation Museum (www.airmuseum.lv).

The official spotting location at Riga is on the west side of the runway from where all movements can be seen. Photography is good, but through the fence. To reach the spot head away from the airport on the P133 road and join the A10 motorway north. Then turn onto the A5 motorway south and exit towards Skulte. Turn left and follow the road to the end where you'll see the spotting area.

LEBANON

Beirut Rafic Hariri International

BEY | OLBA

The main airport in Lebanon is on the coast just south of Beirut city. It has three runways in an unusual pattern, with a terminal in the central section to the north. Stretching north on either side area maintenance hangars and cargo areas.

Beirut is the home to Middle East Airlines but sees a lot of scheduled traffic from across Europe and the Middle East, as well as cargo airlines.

Naturally security is sensitive in this region and spotters should take care when brandishing cameras and binoculars. There are no dedicated spotting locations, but local spotters use Choueifat Public Park to the south of the airport alongside runway 03/21 which has views over the airport and is good for photography. This is near a shopping mall which has parking and distant views of aircraft taking off.

LITHUANIA

Vilnius Airport

VNO | EYVI

The main airport in the country is located a couple of miles south of the city. It has one active runway, 01/19, and is a base for airBaltic, Ryanair and Wizz Air. The passenger terminal is fairly modern, but quite small. As a result, remote parking gates are used at busy times.

A new 24 hour outdoor spotting area has opened alongside the perimeter fence with opportunities for viewing and photography of aircraft on the runway and parallel taxiway. From the terminal, drive (2 minutes) or walk (15 minutes) south along Rodūnios kl. You'll eventually see the fence line. The viewing area is in Salininkai Gardens, and there is parking available.

LUXEMBOURG

Luxembourg Findel Airport

LUX | ELLX

This is the country's only airport of significance and is located at Findel to the east of the city. Passenger traffic is fairly minimal, with based Luxair providing most of the movements, alongside some other scheduled and low-cost traffic. easyJet and Ryanair have both recently upped their presence here.

The airport is, however, a significant cargo hub, which is home to Cargolux's fleet of Boeing 747s. Many other cargo aircraft use the airport, too, with China Airlines Cargo and Qatar Airways Cargo using it as a base. The cargo facilities and ramp are at the eastern side of the airport, alongside the threshold of runway 24.

For spotting, head away from the terminal on the E44 motorway and leave at Exit 10 for the cargo center. Leave the roundabout at the second exit and look for the rough area on your right where you can park and watch movements on the runway through the fence. You may need a ladder.

As an alternative, head west from the terminal on the A1 for 3km. Turn left at the lights towards the staff car park and park outside as you are not allowed to drive in. You can then walk to a position that suits you near the fence to watch movements on runway 06.

Spotting Hotel

Ibis Budget Luxembourg Airport
Route de Treves, Rue Lou Hemmer, 2632 Findel | +352 43 88 01 | www.ibis.com Make sure you book the Ibis Budget and not the other Ibis at the airport. Rooms on the side facing the airport have good apron views and can see movements on the runway in the distant. Photography good through glass with a decent lens.

MACAU

Macau International

MFM | VMMC

Macau International has a single runway 16/34 built on reclaimed land in the sea. Most arrivals are from the south. The single, small terminal and parking apron are underneath the Tam Hill Garden which overlooks the airport and is a good place to watch movements (though too far for photography).

Movements are dominated by based Air Macau and its narrow body Airbus fleets. Other carriers from across the Far East and China all visit, but there are few long-haul links or cargo services. Because of its reputation as a gambling centre, Macau Airport also sees plenty of executive movements. It is not, however, a particularly busy airport compared to many others in China.

MALAYSIA

Kuala Lumpur International

KUL | WMKK

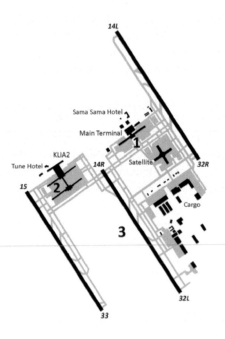

A large hub airport known to most as KLIA. It is one of Asia's busiest airports, and was opened in 1998, replacing the cramped Subang Airport close to the centre of the city.

It is the home base of Malaysia Airlines, AirAsia and AirAsia X and on the route network of many cargo airlines, as well as carriers from around the world.

The airport is split into two sections – KLIA1, which is the original complex, and KLIA2, which opened for low-cost operators in May

2014. Both main terminal buildings have official viewing facilities. KLIA1 has a satellite building, which doesn't have any spotting areas, although it is possible to view from certain gates. You can travel between the two areas using a train, which costs less than £1/$1.

KLIA has three runways and a large cargo complex. Arrivals and departures are predominantly in the 32/33 direction, with most of the low-cost airlines using runway 15/33 next to KLIA2. As well as the locations below, you can drive the perimeter roads to explore the best locations – but beware security may move you on.

Spotting Locations

1. KLIA 1 Terminal Viewing Gallery
Upstairs in the main terminal building, close to the food court, is an official viewing area. Situated indoors, this large room overlooks the airfield, including all gates at the main building, and some of those on the satellite terminal. The cargo area and KLIA2 are not really visible from this location, and the runways are a little distant, but most movements will be visible at some point. Photography can sometimes prove awkward because you're shooting through glass, but in general is quite good.

2. KLIA 2 Terminal Viewing Gallery
The viewing areas in KLIA2 can be found on level 3 departures. Follow the signs for the smoking area and food courts. You will come across the outside viewing area next to McDonald's. It is split into two sides, with each overlooking around nine different gates. The central parking area is not visible from the viewing area, but aircraft can be seen taxiing in and out from the left section. You can also see aircraft on the new runway 15/33 from here.

3. Mound
A raised mound overlooking the airport and runway 14R/32L is a good spot for photography away from the terminals. You'll need a 300mm lens for aircraft of B737/A320 size. To reach the location, follow road 27 from the KLIA2 terminal around the perimeter and turn towards security post 6. Follow the road parallel to the airport

fence, take the first left and then first right to reach the mound. You can drive up to reach the view.

Spotting Hotels

Sama Sama Hotel
Jalan CTA 4 B, 64000 KLIA – Sepang, Selangor Darul Ehsan | +603 8787 3333 | www.samasamahotels.com
Located alongside KLIA 1, making it close enough to walk to the viewing area. Rooms on the top floors and facing the airport allow most movements to be seen, although they can be a little distant for photography or reading off.

Tune Hotel
Lot Pt 13, Jalan KLIA 2/2 6400 KLIA, Selangor Darul Ehsan | www.tunehotels.com A new hotel built alongside the KLIA 2 low-cost terminal and connected via a covered walkway. Some rooms on the sixth floor face the nearest runway and associated taxiway. No gates can be seen at either KLIA1 or 2. Rooms get free WiFi.

Kuala Lumpur Sultan Abdul Aziz Shah (Subang)

SZB | WMSA

The original Kuala Lumpur Subang airport is still an operational airport, albeit a shadow of its former self. The airport has a single runway, with facilities on either side. The main terminal was demolished when KLIA opened, but its former Terminal 3 is now operating as a terminal for passenger flights, with operators such as Citilink, Firefly and Malindo Air providing domestic links. The airport is also home to a busy cargo terminal and maintenance base. Eurocopter Malaysia are also based here, as are some private jet operators.

The airport is around a 30-minute drive from KLIA, or can be reached from Sentral Station via bus. Some aircraft can be seen by

MALAYSIA

driving or walking around the fence, but security may move you on. A café inside the terminal overlooks one of the parking ramps.

Penang International

PEN | WMKP

Situated on the southern tip of Penang Island off Malaysia's western coast, Penang International is Malaysia's third busiest airport in terms of passengers with links around the country and Asia. All Malaysian carriers have a presence here, and interesting other airlines include Cathay Dragon, China Airlines Citilink, China Southern, Lion Air, Lucky Air, Qatar Airways, Scoot and Thai Smile.

Cargo is also a major part of Penang's operation, with a dedicated cargo terminal on the opposite side of the runway to the passenger terminal.

Most arrivals and departures use runway 04. If you have a car, an industrial and commercial area on the north east side of the airport has some good views of aircraft departures and those taxiing (through the fence). From the terminal follow signs for George Town and Tokong Ular on route 6. Then turn left on Jalan Mayang Pasir. Turn right on P8, then right onto route 6 again. After you cross the river, turn left immediately and follow the road round until you see the runway.

MALDIVES

Malé Velana International

MLE | VRMM

The main gateway for the Maldives. The single runway airport occupies an entire island to the east of the city, and is naturally quite cramped. However, recently a new runway has been built to replace the original, and a new seaplane terminal opened which is busy with passengers flying off to resorts around the country.

Given its location, Malé Airport has a good mix of scheduled services from Africa, the Middle East and the Indian subcontinent. It also handles seasonal flights from Europe.

The main seaplane operator is Trans Maldivian Airways, which has a fleet of DHC-6 Twin Otter float planes.

The airport doesn't have any useful spotting locations, but you can see most movements from the roads around the airport and the seaplane base.

MALTA

Malta International

MLA | LMML

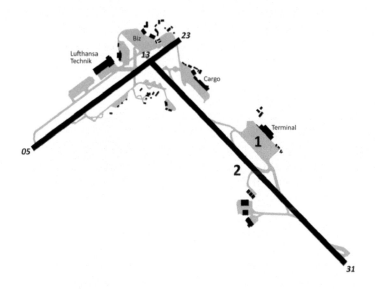

Located at Luqa near the capital Valletta, Malta's main airport is home to Air Malta and a hub for various low cost airlines including Ryanair. During the summer months it is busy with holiday flights from across Europe. At other times you will see regular flights from Italy and North African countries.

The airport has two runways. Lufthansa Technik has a sizeable maintenance hangar on the north-western side of the airport, which sees a number of interesting aircraft come and go. There is also a cargo apron and terminal just north of the present passenger terminal. Flight training and corporate aircraft use an apron at the northern corner of the airport.

Thankfully, Malta is safe for the spotter, with a few decent locations and a friendly local spotting community.

Spotting Locations

1. Terminal Viewing Terrace
On the third floor of the terminal is an official viewing area, situated near a restaurant. It is free to use, and offers good views across the parking apron and main 13/31 runway. Photography is through clear glass. It is accessed via elevator next to the security check.

2. Spotters Platform
From the terminal it is possible to drive or walk to the spotters' platform on the opposite side of the main runway. Simply head through the tunnel under the airport, then turn left at the roundabout on the other side. You'll soon find the raised platform on your left which is the place where many classic photographs of aircraft at Malta are taken from. Parking is available.

MEXICO

Cancún International

CUN | MMUN

The second busiest airport in Mexico, and most likely to be visited if taking a holiday to the country from Europe. It has two parallel runways and four passenger terminals running alongside the southern runway; a ramp for biz jets is to the south east.

Cancún has an interesting mix of operators, with mainline scheduled operators from the USA, Canada and South America common, along with Mexican low-cost airlines and a good mix of scheduled and charter carriers from Europe.

It is difficult to spot at the airport, however a number of resorts are within view of arrivals and departures. Terminal 3 is the best for spotting through the windows, with all aircraft at this terminal visible, along with some at Terminal 2.

The Moon Palace resort is a good option for spotting as arrivals pass overhead on their approach to landing at Cancun.

Mexico City International

MEX | MMMX

This airport handles around 50 million passengers per year and is a major Latin America hub. It is the home base of Aeromexico, Aeromar, Interjet, Magnicharters and Volaris, as well as the government and Police transport fleets.

The airport has two parallel runways, with arrivals mostly from the south. Terminal 1 is on the north side of the runways, whilst Terminal 2 and the military ramp is on the south side.

A lot of retired and stored aircraft can be found at Mexico City, including older Boeing and Douglas types worth trying to see on your visit.

Views are possible around the airport, such as from the footbridge near Terminal 1. But be careful in some of the neighbouring areas as they are not always completely safe and the police are known to look for bribes. If you can get a good room at the Camino Real or Hilton hotels, which are connected to Terminal 1, it is the best bet for spotting.

Spotting Hotels

Camino Real Hotel
Peñón de los Baño, Venustiano Carranza, Mexico City | +52 55 3003 0033 | www.caminoreal.com The best spotting hotel at Mexico City. Rooms on the 7th and 8th floors facing the airport are ideal, with movements on taxiways and runways visible, as well as some of the distant maintenance ramps. It's not amazing for photography.

Hilton Mexico City Airport
International Mexico City Airport, 15620 Ciudad de México | +52 55 5133 0500 | www.hilton.com Located above the terminal building. There are views from some of the rooms, as well as the public areas in this hotel (such as the bar and restaurant), of aircraft parked at the gates in front, and the runways beyond.

Tijuana

TIJ | MMTJ

This airport is built right up to the US border and easily reached from San Diego. You can even consider spotting from the US side, with movements visible and some of the aircraft on the ground.

Tijuana doesn't really have any good spotting locations landside, apart from the multi-storey car park. Police and security are likely to move you on.

Movements include Mexican low-cost and domestic carriers and some international flights. On the ground are some stored and derelict airliners, including a Boeing 747SP.

MONTENEGRO

Tivat Airport

TIV | LYTV

Tivat has a single runway, with a small terminal and parking apron at the northern end. Flights are mostly seasonal with holiday carriers from Russia in particular, plus Europe and the Middle East.

If you follow the road past the terminal heading south, you'll soon reach an open area with good views through the fence onto the apron where biz jets and light aircraft park

From the terminal drive north and turn left soon after, towards Kalardovo. This road (named Aerodromska) passes the end of runway 14 with great views from both sides and an area of open ground to park on. You can see the main parking ramp here and get great shots of aircraft approaching the runway from the north (a rarity) or departing from the south.

MOROCCO

Marrakech Menara

RAK | GMMX

Popular with low cost carriers such as easyJet and Ryanair, and also a hub for Royal Air Maroc. Marrakech Menara is a joint civil-military base, with the passenger terminals to the south of the runway.

The airport is quite close to the city, so movements can often be seen from its various attractions and hotel rooftops. Spotting is possible from Avenue Guernassa which links the airport to the city – particularly if arrivals are from the east.

Inside the terminal the windows are good for seeing most of the aircraft at the gates, but not the more remote executive stands.

NEPAL

Kathmandu Tribhuvan International

KTM | VNKT

Kathmandu is the main international airport for Nepal. Regional flights and and helicopter services link this airport with places like Lukla and Taplejung.

This airport is overcrowded and unable to expand, leaving the single runway and terminal overworked a lot of the time. You can expect to see a lot of local airlines, plus carriers like Air Arabia, Air India, China Eastern, China Southern, Etihad, FlyDubai, Korean Air, Malaysia Airlines, Qatar Airways, Thai and Turkish Airlines among many others.

The best places for spotting are around the southern end of the airport where you can watch and photograph arrivals onto runway 02 (used for landing most of the time). You'll need to take a taxi to get there, and do some walking to find the best spot.

Lukla Tenzing-Hillary Airport

LUA | VNLK

Lukla is one of the most hair-raising airports in the world, with a short runway perched on the side of a mountain and a sheer drop at one end. Daily flights (weather permitting) arrive from Kathmandu from a variety of local airlines.

All movements can be seen from behind the runway 24 threshold and alongside the terminal by following the walkway. You can also walk to various points alongside the runway.

NETHERLANDS

Amsterdam Schiphol

AMS | EHAM

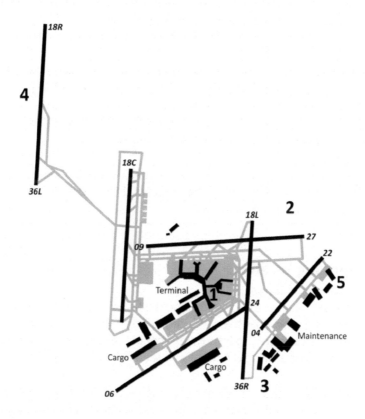

Schiphol is one of the world's largest and busiest airports and can be a joy for the spotter thanks to the various viewing locations, and the number and variety of movements.

Naturally KLM and its Cityhopper partner make up most of the movements, alongside Delta Air Lines, easyJet, Transavia and TUI fly Netherlands. However, the mix is good with many long-haul airlines visiting every day. The airport is famous for having a single terminal concept, with various piers and concourses.

Cargo is also an important aspect of Schiphol, and you'll see a cargo terminal to the south of the terminal, and another on the eastern perimeter alongside runway 06/24.

Along the eastern side of the site is Schiphol-Oost. This is the site of the large maintenance base for KLM, as well as the original control tower and the apron used by biz jets and general aviation traffic.

Many aircraft use the newer 'Polderbaan' runway 18R/36L which is a good distance away from the airport and requires long taxi times. Thankfully there are some viewing locations there. Enthusiasts are well catered for at the airport, with facilities both atop the terminal and around its perimeter.

Schiphol is now pretty full and it is expected that in the near future Lelystad Airport will take some of the strain by handling low-cost and leisure airlines.

Spotting Locations

1. Panorama Terrace
This official terrace is located along the top of the central terminal area. Although it has been reduced in size, it still has good elevated views across piers C to E and a number of the runways. Aircraft that are not seen arriving can usually be seen taxiing at some point.

Entrance to the terrace is free. You can reach it from the ground floor by taking the stairs, escalator or elevator at Café Rembrandt. On the next floor (in Departure Hall 1) you take the stairs or escalator at desk row 1 to the second floor, where a footbridge leads you to the Panorama Terrace Opening times: from last Sunday in October 9am to 5pm; from last Sunday in March 7am to 9pm.

2. McDonalds

One of the official viewing areas is located alongside a McDonalds restaurant on the northern side of Runway 09/27. Most of the airport's movements can be seen here, as well as the maintenance and business jet ramps. Photography is not perfect here due to the south-facing aspect, however some aircraft are at close quarters on the runway. There are seats to use. You can drive to the spot, or reach it from the terminal on bus #300 or #342. Head north under the motorway from McDonalds and you'll see a retired Boeing 747-400 outside the Corendon Village Hotel.

3. Runway 36R

When landings are on this runway, this spot offers great photographs. From the terminal head south on the A4 then take the N201 followed by the N232. When you see the gas station, turn left and park along Breguetlaan. Alternatively you could take bus #187 from the airport to Oude Meer/Fokker Logistics Park. Look out for the preserved Fokker F27 on the lake.

4. Runway 18R/36L Polderbaan

Two official viewing locations have been sited alongside the new sixth runway, which have become favourites among spotters. You will need a car or cycle to get there, but there is a car park to use. You will have good views of traffic arriving or departing on this runway. To get there head away from the airport on the A4, then turn north on the N201 towards Hoofddorp/Aalsmeer. Follow it until you reach a crossroads with a gas station on the left; turn right along IJweg and keep going until you reach the spotters car park. There are paths in either direction along the runway for you to find the best position.

5. Schiphol Oost

Continuing past location 2 on bus #300 or #342 leads to the Schiphol Oost area. You won't see many movements on the airport from here, but it allows you to log the biz jets and aircraft receiving maintenance around the hangars. Simply reverse the journey by bus to return, or continue walking south to reach position

Spotting Hotels

CitizenM Hotel

Jan plezierweg 2, 1118 BB Amsterdam Schiphol | +31 20 811 7080 | www.citizenm.com A modern, affordable hotel which is part of a popular chain. All rooms have double beds and are very compact. Check-in is via a computer in the lobby, however staff can then make changes if you request them, such as a room overlooking the airport. Rooms on the 4th and 5th floor should be fine, and look out over the low-cost H pier, plus the runways and taxiways beyond. You shouldn't miss much if you use SBS or flight tracking website. Photography is possible of aircraft around the H pier only.

Sheraton Amsterdam Airport

Schiphol Boulevard 101, Amsterdam Schiphol | +31 20 316 4300 | www.marriott.com Good for spotting most movements if you ask for a high room facing the airport. You will see aircraft parked at a number of the piers, along with taxiways and some of the runways. The hotel is a little too distant for photography. Can be expensive.

Eindhoven Airport

EIN | EHEH

The second busiest airport in the Netherlands. Eindhoven is a mixed civil/military facility which handles most of the Royal Netherlands Air Force fleet, including their transport and tanker aircraft. Ryanair, Transavia and TUI fly Netherlands have bases here and provide most of the passenger flights, alongside other low-cost and leisure carriers.

The airport has a single runway. The military base occupies facilities on both sides, while the passenger terminal and apron is in the north-east corner.

The aptly named Spottersweg road runs past the end of runway 21 and has an official parking lot for spotters to use, which offers great views of aircraft landing from the north. You may wish to walk a little further south for photography. To reach it drive or walk north from the terminal along Luchthavenweg and turn left onto Spottersweg after the ASL building.

Inside the terminal there is a viewing area located upstairs near the restaurant which is behind glass. Its views are limited, but you'll see anything that uses the runway.

Lelystad Airport

LEY | EHLE

Lelystad is at present the main general aviation airport in the Netherlands, and quite a busy one. It will in the future become more of a commercial airport with its new passenger terminal and plans to transfer in low-cost and leisure airlines from Schiphol.

At present you can walk along the line of hangars from the airport entrance road, and it's often possible to arrange airside access in advance. This will probably change in the future.

Another reason to visit Lelystad is for the excellent Aviodrome museum.

MUSEUM

National Aviation Theme Park Aviodrome

Pelikaanweg 50, 8218 PG Lelystadt Airport | +31 900 284 6376 | www.aviodrome.nl This museum has many restored historic aircraft, with particular emphasis on Dutch aviation. Most notable are the last flying DC-2 in the world, the first Fokker F27 Friendship built, flying Antonov AN-2 and Catalina, Lockheed Constellation, Fokker 100 and a former KLM Boeing 747-206B (SUD). Pleasure flights are often available in the flying aircraft. It is a great family day out and perfect for the enthusiast. Open daily except Tuesday, from 10am to 5pm.

Maastricht Aachen Airport

MST | EHBK

This airport close to the German border and city of Aachen is fairly quiet for passenger flights, which are mainly made up of Ryanair and Corendon Airlines aircraft, with more flights in the summer. The airport is fairly busy as a cargo hub, however, with worldwide links from airlines like Emirates SkyCargo, Silk Way, Sky Gates Airlines, and Turkish Airlines Cargo. There are also often airliners in storage at Maastricht.

Spotting is possible from the viewing area next to the passenger terminal.

Rotterdam The Hague Airport

RTM | EHRD

Rotterdam is a fairly busy regional airport serving the city and nearby The Hague. It is an easy 45 minute drive from Amsterdam, but there's nothing of major interest that you won't see at the Schiphol Airport.

Transavia operates a base here, with other low-cost and leisure airlines regular. There's quite a number of based general aviation aircraft which park around the hangars off to the right when looking from the terminal.

There's a viewing area inside the terminal which offers views over the main ramp and runway through glass.

A short walk past the car parks along Fairoaksbaan should reveal any aircraft parked behind the hangars.

Finally, for approach shots on runway 06 walk from the terminal towards the Best Western Plus hotel and follow Vliegveldweg until you see the approach lights.

NEW ZEALAND

Auckland Ardmore

AMZ | NZAR

This former WWII USAF bomber base is now a general aviation airfield around 15 miles east of Auckland International. It has three runways and is the busiest airport in New Zealand by number of movements. Air Auckland and Sunair fly some local services from here. There is a warbird restoration company in residence with a number of aircraft. Spotting is best done by car, driving around the many hangars all around the airfield; some are friendly and allow access to spotters.

NZ Warbirds Association

Harvard Lane, Ardmore Airport, Papakura | www.nzwarbirds. org.nz A renowned organisation which restores, displays and flies vintage warbird aircraft. As well as seeing the aircraft at the museum, you can take flights in the DC-3, Spitfire, Kittyhawk P40, Mustang P51 and Harvard AT6!

Auckland International

AKL | NZAA

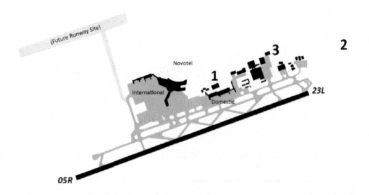

The busiest airport in New Zealand for passenger flights, and the principal gateway to the country. Auckland is also the main base of national carrier Air New Zealand and its worldwide network. The has a single runway, 05/23. However, work was started on a second, parallel runway, to the north of the site. This has been put on hold, but will likely continue in the future as the airport continues with its expansion plans.

There are two terminals at Auckland - the International Terminal to the west, and the smaller Domestic Terminal to the east. It is in the airport's master plan to combine these into one building in the future.

Further east is an area of freight aprons and maintenance hangars. For the enthusiast, a number of viewing locations are provided, and a good mix of airliners pass through every day.

As well as local carriers, Auckland also handles many airlines from Asia and North America, including many widebody aircraft. It's also a good place to see the Air Chathams fleet regularly.

Spotting Locations

1. Domestic Terminal Parking
The top level of the car park behind the domestic terminal is good for viewing movements on the runway. Photography is possible with a zoom lens.

2. Puhinui Road Viewing Area
Two viewing areas are available alongside Puhinui Road as it runs east away from the airport. There are car parking spaces on either side of the road. The elevated position makes it a great spot for watching and photographing arrivals on runway 23. You can also photograph aircraft lining up for departure on 23 if you have a long lens.

3. Laurence Stevens Drive
This road runs east from the roundabout outside the Domestic Terminal and leads you past the cargo and maintenance aprons. Delving into the various gaps between buildings will yield many of the aircraft parked out of view of the terminal areas. Photography is possible through the fence.

Spotting Hotel

Novotel Auckland Airport
Ray Emery drive, Auckland 2022 | +64 9 257 7200 | www.novotel. com A decent hotel linked to the International Terminal at Auckland. It is quite tall, so a room on one of the top floors will allow you to see over the terminal building and to the runway beyond. Only one side of the hotel has views of aircraft, and there are no views of the domestic or cargo aprons.

Christchurch

CHC | NZCH

This is the second busiest airport in New Zealand, and the main airport on the South Island. Airlines include domestic New

Zealand carriers, plus international carriers like China Southern, Emirates, Fiji Airways, Qantas and Singapore Airlines.

Spotting at Christchurch is easy if you have a car. From the terminal, it is possible to drive a lap of the perimeter and stop at various places where you can photograph and watch aircraft through the fence. Harewood Road has a spot which is best for morning shots, whilst Jessons Road and Pound Road are best on an afternoon. The flying club on the opposite side of the runway to the terminal also has a terrace which has good views.

Wellington International

WLG | NWZN

At the southern tip of the North Island, Wellington is known for its windy weather and is a busy hub for inter-island flights by Air New Zealand, its partners and Jetstar Airways. Other carriers of note include Air Chathams, Fiji Airways, Virgin Australia and Air Post. Its short runway currently limits operations, but a plan to extend it could open the airport to more international flights.

Like Christchurch, if you have a car you can easily tour the perimeter to find spots that suit you; walking a circuit takes about an hour. One favourite is a car park and lookout between Moa Point Road and Lyall Bay on the south western corner (near the tunnel). From here you can find a spot alongside the runway to watch and photograph the action, or walk north to log aircraft parked at the general aviation area.

At the north east corner, there is a small car park off Calabar Road which looks down on the threshold of runway 16.

NORTH KOREA

Pyongyang

FNJ | ZKPY

The main airport in North Korea, serving the capital. It is the base for Air Koryo and its fleet of old and young Russian airliners. Enthusiasts have had access in recent years through a number of organised tours, which has allowed ramp access to the small airport. However, spotting outside of these organised tours should not be attempted.

International flights into Pyongyang are by Air China and Air Koryo. The new passenger terminal has views from the gate areas.

NORWAY

Bergen Flesland Airport

BGO | ENBR

Norway's second busiest airport. Bergen is a base for Widerøe and many operators who service the North Sea oil fields and remote communities along the coast.

The airport's passenger terminal has gates around a circular pier, with a newer extension to the south which has more gates. Commuter aircraft park at gates to the north.

A separate helicopter terminal is to the north of the passenger terminal. There is a single runway.

It is possible to spot and take photographs from the top floor of the main car park behind the terminal of aircraft on the taxiways and some stands, with the runway visible beyond.

On the west side of the airport, and better in the afternoon for photography, is a hill which overlooks the runway and terminal gates beyond. To reach the hill by car, drive south from the terminal and turn right at the roundabout onto Fleslandsvegen. Drive past the horse riding school and take the third left along a gravel road. You'll see some boulders at the entrance to stop you parking. Follow the road up the hill until you find the good view.

Bodø Airport

BOO | ENBO

A joint civil-military airport in northern Norway. It is busiest with domestic flights from Norewgian, SAS and Widerøe (who are based here), and in the summer wakes up to a number of seasonal charters to the Mediterranean. The military base occupies land on the south side of the runway.

One of the best spotting locations is from the Norwegian Aviation Museum to the east of the airport, which has an elevated 'control tower' looking over the runway and across to the military base.

You can also walk or drive to the west from the terminal along Langstranda to reach the maintenance base of Widerøe and get some views across to the runway.

MUSEUM

Norwegian Aviation Museum

Olav V gate, 8004 Bodø | +47 75 50 78 50 | www. luftfartsmuseum.no Despite Bodø's remote location, this is a good quality aviation museum with a number of historic displays. Around 40 aircraft on display including a Spitfire, Fokker F-28, Junkers Ju-52, U-2 spy plane and DHC-6 Twin Otter. Open daily 10am to 4pm (11am to 5pm Saturday and Sunday).

Oslo Gardermoen

OSL | ENGM

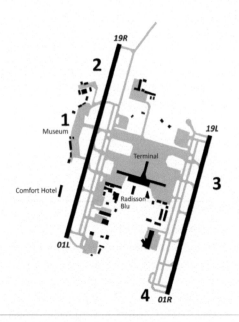

Gardermoen has been Oslo's main airport since October 1998 when Fornebu Airport was closed. It had already been operating as a military air base and civil airport since the 1940s.

The airport is large and modern, with two parallel runways and all terminal, maintenance and cargo areas in between. It is the busiest in Norway, and the second busiest in Scandinavia.

Gardermoen is a busy hub for Norwegian, Scandinavian Airlines and Widerøe, and is served by most European airlines, plus many from further afield.

The Norwegian Air Force maintain their base at the airport, with Lockheed Hercules aircraft stationed and their own operating area on the northern and western sides of the field. It's also worth visiting the SAS Museum (www.sasmuseet.net).

There are a number of places to watch aircraft at Oslo, although the distance between the runways can make it difficult to monitor all movements.

Spotting Locations

1. SAS Museum Terrace

Alongside the SAS Museum on the western side of the airport is a specially-built spotting terrace. This is open 24 hours, free of charge and gives views over Runway 01L/19R and the freighter ramp in front. You can also see aircraft around the terminal area, but from a distance. You can drive here (address Gardermovegen 1, 2030 Nannestad), or take bus 420 from stand 48 outside the arrivals hall to 'SAS-museet'.

2. Spotting Mound

A short distance north of the SAS Museum along the Gardermovegen road and past the GA terminal is a mound in the forest which gives you elevated views of aircraft using Runway 01L/19R. To reach it, go over the roundabout and then turn right into the woods just after (not suitable in snow/mud). It is perfect for landing shots, and you can see across the airfield. It is too distant from the terminal to see much there, however.

3. Eastern Mound

Alongside Runway 01R/19L is another mound which gives you elevated views of the runway, and across to the International Pier and SAS Hangar. You'll need a car to reach this location, and it's best to avoid when there is snow on the ground. Follow the E16 motorway east from the airport, and turn onto the 174 to Jessheim. Take the next exit onto Fv460 where you see McDonalds and some hotels. At the second roundabout turn right onto Vibergvegen. Turn left onto Blikkvegen and follow for 2 miles. You'll see a dirt track ahead, where you can drive down and park, and climb up for a view of the airport.

4. Runway 01R

Drive or walk past the P3 parking lot along Henrik Ibsens veg. Just before it ends at a turning circle, you turn along the rough road to your left. Eventually it opens up into an area where you can park and walk up a hill with some benches on top. It has great views of aircraft lining up or landing on runway 01R.

Spotting Hotels

Radisson Blu Airport Hotel Oslo
Hotelvegen, P.O. Box 163, N - 2061 Gardermoen | +47 63 93 30 00 | www.radissonhotels.com Quite expensive, but ideally located. Has many rooms higher up that have views of movements on runways 01L/19R. Hotel can usually accommodate your request.

Comfort Hotel RunWay
Hans Gaarders veg 27, Gardermoen 2060 | +47 63 94 88 88 | www.nordicchoicehotels.com Situated next to the perimeter fence overlooking Runway 01L/19R. To get there from the airport you either take the dedicated S44 hotel shuttle bus at 70NOK or the cheaper normal service bus 855 which involves a short 2 minute walk from the stop to the hotel. Rooms facing the runway allow you to read off all movements, but tress can get in the way of photographs and views across to the terminal.

Stavanger Sola Airport

SVG | ENZV

The third busiest airport in Norway. Stavanger has two runways at right angles to each other with the passenger terminal occupying the position in between.

The airport is a hub for Norwegian, SAS and Widerøe, and is a busy base for helicopter traffic linking to the various oil platforms in the North Sea. The summer is busier with holiday charter flights. There is a historic aircraft museum next to the airport (see later).

Spotting is possible from the top level of the car park next to the terminal, from where all movements can be seen across the airport, but photography is not ideal.

If aircraft are using runway 11, you can park alongside the road which passes its threshold and even use the beach to take photographs. From the terminal take the second exit at the first and second roundabouts, and follow Nordsjøvegen as it skirts around the end of the runway.

The Scandic Hotel (www.scandichotels.com) at the terminal also has good views from many rooms.

MUSEUM

Flyhistorik Museum

Flyplassveien 129, 4055 Sola | www.flymuseum-sola.no An interesting collection of aircraft, both civil and military, is preserved at this museum just to the north of Stavanger Airport. Aircraft include a Fokker F-27, Convair 440 and DH114 Heron. Open 12pm to 4pm on Sundays and school holidays only.

OMAN

Muscat International

MCT | OOMS

Muscat Airport is the principal gateway to Oman. It is home to Oman Air and sees flights from across the Middle East, Asia and Europe. The country is a growing tourist destination, and it's not far from the popular United Arab Emirates.

From the drop-off zone outside departures, you can walk left and right in front of the terminal for views of some gates. Once inside the building, before check-in, most of these gates (eastern side of piers A and B) can be seen too. Go down one level to Arrivals then walk to the very ends of the terminal building for the best, but limited, views.

However, you must be careful spotting landside, as you would anywhere in this part of the world. Even airside, try to keep a low profile when using binoculars and cameras.

Once through immigration and security, the departure gates are on three piers, A (north), B (south) and C (west) with C straight ahead, B is left and A right. There are decent views from the windows in each.

PANAMA

Panama City Albrook International

PAC | MPMG

The smaller, 'downtown' airport of Panama City, is situated a couple of miles to the west. It is a small facility with a single runway and terminal. The principal operator is Air Panama with its variety of regional and jet aircraft, which come and go throughout the day. You'll also see some executive movements here.

From inside the terminal you have views over the gates and part of the airfield. Outside you also have some views of the areas around the terminal. However, if you have a car you can drive to the opposite side of the airfield where there are plenty of views across the field through the fence. You'll be able to work along and read off aircraft around the various aprons and hangars.

Panama City Tocumen International

PTY | MPTO

Tocumen is the principal international gateway to Panama. It is a short distance to the east of the city and has two staggered parallel runways, with a central terminal area. It is the busiest and largest airport in Central America, handling traffic from a range of carriers, with Copa Airlines being the principal operator.

If you have a car it is possible to drive alongside the northern of the two runways. There is a car park near the threshold of runway 03L (north of the terminal) where locals watch the aircraft.

Cargo operations are quiet extensive, and flights use a separate parking area to the north of the airport which is a little more difficult to see due to a road check a long way before reaching it. There is an area of stored airliners here.

Airside spotting is great if you are flying out of Tocumen, with plenty of windows at gates and looking towards the runways.

PERU

Cusco Alejandro Velasco Astete International

CUZ | SPZO

The majority of tourists in Peru head to Cusco, which is an attraction in its own right, and the starting off point for trips to Machu Picchu. The city's high elevation and position amongst the Andes makes it an interesting place to fly in to. Its airport underwent modernisation in the mid-2000s, with a new pier and jet bridges on the terminal.

International services have been operated in the past, but presently all flights are domestic with airlines such as Amazonas, Avianca, LATAM Peru, Star Peru and Viva Air Peru. There are usually some smaller local operators present, too. Capacity constraints mean that there are large parts of the day with no movements.

Spotting from the gate area is easy and you can monitor movements. Otherwise a car or taxi is necessary to reach and spotting positions around the perimeter, which are quite numerous thanks to the city streets encroaching on the airport. Some good views can be had from the rough road at the end of runway 28.

Lima Jorge Chávez

LIM | SPJC

Lima is the main international gateway into Peru. It is from here that most tourists connect on to destinations such as Cusco.

The airport has a single runway and a single, large passenger terminal which is split into international and domestic sections. Since the airport is operated jointly with the military, there are areas to the south of the terminal where air force and police aircraft park up. A new runway and passenger terminal will by the mid-2020s.

The airport is a hub for Avianca Peru, LATAM Peru, Sky Airline, Star Peru and Viva Air Peru. Many international airlines also visit.

To the north of the terminal is the military apron, as well as maintenance hangars. There is a large area behind the military base where various airliners were stored awaiting scrapping. These are only visible from departing aircraft.

Lima does not present too many spotting opportunities. Loitering is not advised due to the strong military presence. If you are flying out of the airport, give yourself extra time and you will be able to log the comings and goings from the large windows in the departure gates. All gates look out to the runway, with the international section looking towards the cargo and military part of the airport, and the domestic section towards the military and maintenance areas.

If you have a car or hire a taxi, there is a good spot along the Gambetta Highway (100) north west of the airport. Head south from the terminal along Av. Elmer Faucett then turn right along Av. Morales Duarez. Turn north onto the Gambetta Highway and continue through the tunnel. Shortly after there is a place to park on the right which has good photographic opportunities of aircraft approaching runway 15.

PHILIPPINES

Clark International

CRK | RPLC

This civil airport serves Angeles City to the north of Manila. Construction work is underway to develop its terminal facilities as a viable alternative to the capital's airport. At present it has airline flights from the likes of Asiana, Cathay Dragon, Cebu Pacific, Emirates, Jetstar, Philippine Airlines, Qatar Airways and Scoot. It is also a busy cargo hub, with a UPS Airlines base.

A storage area on the northern side of the site is home to various decaying airliners and commuter aircraft. You can see them from the taxi rank outside the current terminal.

Exploring the smaller roads south of the terminal you'll have fleeting views to the cargo and military ramp, and also find the Air Force Park with a number of preserved military types on display.

Mactan-Cebu International

CEB | RPVM

Situated on an island opposite the city of Cebu and linked by road bridges and ferries, this is the Philippines' second-busiest airport.

Cebu has a single, long runway. The two passenger terminals and the small Mactan Air Base are located on the northern side. A second, parallel runway will be built in the coming years.

Movements include a mix of low-cost airlines and domestic flights, along with links to other Asian and Middle Eastern countries. With some cargo flights and the military transport movements, it's an interesting airport to visit.

General Aviation Road runs along the southern boundary of the airport. As the name suggests, it passes the general aviation area where many light aircraft are located. You can find various spots looking through the fence for runway shots and spotting. A wooden shelter near the 04 end is often used (tip the owner). Another good spot is the fire station, further up the road.

Manila Ninoy Aquino

MNL | RPLL

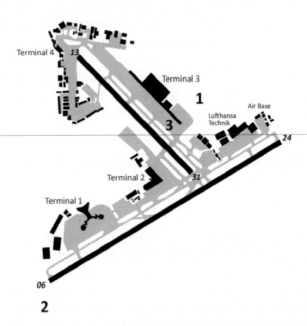

The principal airport in the Philippines and home to its indigenous airlines. Ninoy Aquino is a few miles south of the city centre and has two runways which cross close to their centre – 06/24 and 13/31. The majority of movements use the former.

The airport has four terminals – the newer Terminal 3 is on the north-east side of runway 13/31, while all others, including the older Terminal 4 domestic facility are on the south-west side.

Further to the east is a Lufthansa Technik maintenance base which often has a number of heavy airliners present.

Around the northern side of the airport is a host of smaller hangars and companies engaging in flight training, maintenance, operations and cargo. It is this area which was always of interest to enthusiasts as many smaller types operate from here, and for years a collection of rusting old airliners was stored. Some are still present, but not on the scale of the past.

Manila is not as busy as other Asian hubs like Hong Kong or Tokyo's airports, but can still get crowded and offers a good variety of airliners and in particular the domestic traffic not seen elsewhere. There are good views from the departure areas of the terminals.

Spotting Locations

1. Holiday Inn Express
Perhaps the easiest and least conspicuous area. See later section.

2. Runway 06 Arrivals
If you have a car or walk 25 minutes, this is a great spot for arrivals on runway 06, which is the primary direction of traffic. You can't see the rest of the airport, apart from aircraft lining up for departure. Photography is great here. To reach this location from Terminal 1, walk along the Paranaque – Sucat Road, then turn south along Multinational Ave (where you see the brown metal footbridge crossing the road. Walk past the end of the runway and find a good spot – often there are local spotters here.

3. Terminal 3
Inside this terminal there is a new walkway signposted 'Airport Runway' on the 4th floor, near the food court. There are no seats, but you can use the windows for a quick view of anything outside.

Spotting Hotel

Holiday Inn Express Manila Airport
Newport Boulevard, Pasay 1309 Metro Manila | +63 2 908 8600 | www.ihg.com Formerly the Remington Hotel. This hotel is excellent if you get a good room overlooking the airport. Generally, rooms on the fifth floor upwards in the range xx009-xx0017 and xx0068-xx0073 will be perfect. Photography is possible from the rooms of aircraft on the nearby taxiway and runway. It is also next to the Air Force Museum.

MUSEUM

Philippine Air Force Museum

Nr Andrews Ave, Pasay City, Manila | +63 2832 3498 | www.paf.mil.ph/UNITS/pafmuseum/pafmuseum.html Located near Terminal 3, on the Villamor Air Base side of the airport. This museum has around 20 aircraft on display, including both fighters and transport types. Open 8am-12pm Monday to Saturday. Admission PHP20 per person.

POLAND

Gdańsk Lech Wałęsa Airport

GDN | EPGD

Situated on the northern coast of Poland, Gdansk is the third busiest airport in the country. It is a base for LOT, Ryanair and Wizz Air and sees mostly flights from nearby Scandinavia, Germany and Finland.

Walk or drive east from the terminal along the service road (not the 472 road) parallel to the railway line. Eventually it turns right. Follow to the end where you'll see a spotting area beside the fence, with space for parking. You have views onto the taxiway and eastern end of the runway, but are facing into the sun most of the day. There are also two spotting platforms along the main road running along the southern boundary of the airport.

Kraków John Paul II International

KRK | EPKK

Krakow is Poland's second busiest airport, though still quite a small facility which is shared with a military base. The terminal and main apron are at the eastern end of runway 07/25, with the military base occupying much of the southern side. There are often transport aircraft based.

Low cost airlines like easyJet, Jet2, Norwegian, Ryanair and Wizz Air are the busiest here, alongside national carrier LOT Polish Airlines.

On the opposite side of the E77 motorway under the approach to runway 25 is a path where you can get great approach shots and see some of the main apron. It's easiest to reach if you have a car.

Warsaw Chopin Airport

WAW | EPWA

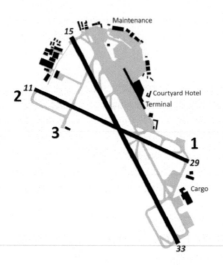

The largest and busiest airport in Poland is Warsaw (until the new airport is built). In addition to a number of low-cost airlines, national carrier LOT is the busiest operators here, flying to many European and worldwide destinations. Local charter carriers such as Enter Air and Travel Service also have a strong presence, and you will see the Polish Government's various Russian aircraft here to the north of the terminal, along with the LOT maintenance area.

Long-haul airliners arrive from places like China and the Middle East, but few from North America or the rest of Asia will be seen.

Warsaw has a single terminal split into North and South areas. There are two runways which cross in the middle, and a cargo area to the south-east which handles most European cargo airlines.

POLAND

There are various opportunities for logging aircraft at the airport. If you are travelling through there are plenty of views once airside.

Spotting Locations

1. Runway 29

Easy to walk to from the terminal (or drive; there is parking available), this spot is alongside the end of runway 29 and between the two cargo areas. You have views through the fence of aircraft taxying past or arriving on the runway. From the airport, head east on Wiktora Narkiewicza (don't join the main motorway). Turn south on Wirazowa and after a short distance turn right where you see the blue fence. Follow the road to where you can park by the side of the road and look through the fence. The 'Terminal Cargo' bus also runs past here.

2. Spotter Hill

There is a patch of raised ground next to the end of runway 11 which is great for approach shots. You are above the fence line. To reach this location from the terminal, drive north along 634 (signposted 'Centrum'), then turn left at the lights towards Krakow/Wroclaw on road 706. At the junction, turn left again for Krakow/Wroclaw. Look out for a large retail complex on your right, with a Burger King restaurant alongside the road. At this point you need to reverse your course, so turn into the retail park and then exit back onto the main road back towards the airport, but turn immediately right along a track next to the perimeter fence. You'll come to the hill on your right, with rough ground for parking.

3. Fire Station Viewing Platform

A better spot on the western side of the airport is behind the fire station. There is a raised platform with steps to the top which lifts you above the fence line for great shots of aircraft on runway 11/29. There are also holes cut in the fence at ground level for cameras, and look out for some retired aircraft at the fire station in front of you.

To reach it, park at position 2 and walk south past the airport car park. Just after, a track leads across the fields parallel to the car park directly to the platform.

Spotting Hotel

Courtyard Warsaw Airport
Żwirki i Wigury 1, 00-906 Warszawa | +48 22 650 01 00 | www.marriott.com A large, modern hotel outside the passenger terminal. The terminal buildings largely obstruct any views, but if you secure a top-floor room facing south you can see across to the runways and some of the gates at the southern end of the terminal.

Warsaw Modlin Airport

WMI | EPMO

This airport opened at a former air force base in 2012; it is 25 miles north of the city and used primarily by Ryanair and its new Ryanair Sun subsidiary.

The terminal is brand new and modern, sited to the south of the single runway, with a large parking apron stretching in front. You may see some general aviation and executive traffic. Walk either side of the terminal for a view through the fence.

PORTUGAL

Faro Airport

FAO | LPFR

Serving the popular Algarve region on Portugal's south coast, Faro is a holiday airport served primarily by European charter and low-cost operators.

Faro has a single terminal building, upgraded recently, and a single runway 10/28. There are no official viewing locations, but photographers will love the opportunities alongside the runway, especially given the year-round sun is always behind you. Naturally Faro is busier in the summer months.

Spotting Locations

1. Runway 28
To the east of the terminal, among the car parks and car rental areas, you'll see a small road running alongside a fence. This leads to a water treatment plant, and then turns into a dirt road which leads to the end of runway 28, with parking available. You'll be facing south, but can see and photograph aircraft landing on this runway. If you walk a little further, over the footpath bridge, you'll come to a spot where you can photograph aircraft lining up on the runway.

2. Runway 10 and Perimeter Track
A track runs along the length of the runway on the southern side, and you can find a spot to suit your needs. One of the better locations is at the end of Runway 10. From the roundabout at the airport entrance, drive behind the gas station along Estrada Praia de Faro, which loops past the end of the runway. Shortly afterwards turn left onto a small road which leads to the

perimeter fence. You can park along here and walk to find the best spot for you. A stepladder may be needed for photographs.

Lisbon Airport

LIS | LPPT

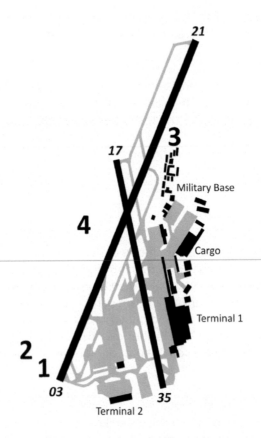

Although one of Europe's quieter capital city airports, a trip to Lisbon can still yield a number of exotic aircraft, and the opportunity to spot in the sun is never to be missed.

Lisbon is served by most European airlines, plus a number of long haul carriers from North and South America, and Africa (such as TAAG Angola). It is a hub for easyJet, TAP Air Portugal, Ryanair and Azores Airlines. The airport is also a military base.

There are two runways and two terminals here. Terminal 1 is the larger facility, on the east side, while Terminal 2 is the newer, smaller facility to the south used by low-cost carriers. Some remote parking spots for airliners can be found between the runways, whilst cargo, military, executive and aircraft undergoing maintenance use aprons to the north of the terminal.

Runway 03/21 is the primary strip used by most flights, with runway 17/35 used occasionally.

Spotting Locations

1. Runway 03
From the main E1 road running along the southern boundary of the airport, take exit 4 and at the large roundabout take the first exit onto Av. Santos e Castro. Almost immediately take the exit on your right, and park on the rough ground between the road and the fence. Here you have a view of aircraft lining up and landing on runway 03. You may need a stepladder to see over the fence.

2. Runway Overlook
A great spotting location at Lisbon is the runway overlook which lifts you above the fence and street furniture for a great view over runway 03/21 and the airport beyond. You'll need a good lens for photography. Following directions for location 1, take the second exit off the roundabout along Eixo Central. Up the hill on your right is the viewing location, with limited parking spaces for cars. You can reach this location by public transport by taking bus 798 from Campo Grande Metro Station.

3. Northern Taxiway
A spot nearer the northern end of the airport and main runway has views of the taxiway and aircraft on the runway. Follow the

PORTUGAL

road to the AT1 (Aerodromo Transito Nr 1), which is the air force base and VIP area. Spotting is rarely a problem, but it's difficult to fit your camera through the gaps in the fence.

4. Runway Overlook 2
A second overlook is further north of position 2. Continue up Eixo Central, over the next roundabout. Turn right at the end onto Av. Nuno Krus Abecassis, then left on R. Vasco da Gama Fernandes. At the end turn right onto Av. Santos e Castro and follow it until you see the rough parking area and view on your right.

Madeira Airport (Funchal)

FNC | LPMA

The main airport serving the island of Madeira is at Santa Cruz, east of Funchal. Chances are you will have seen some stunning photographs and videos of aircraft operations here. The airport is built on the side of a hill overlooking the sea, and with much of the runway built on stilts. The approach to the airport from the south involves a turn shortly before landing, similar to that at the old Kai Tak airport in Hong Kong. With swirling winds from the sea, it can often be a hair-raising event for pilots and passengers.

The airport terminal is on the south, served by daily links to the Azores and Portuguese mainland, as well as the Canary Islands. It is also served by many low-cost and leisure airlines from northern Europe – particularly in the summer months.

Spotting Locations
1. Airport Terminal
An observation deck atop the terminal is great for watching and photographing aircraft at close quarters. It has both landside and airside sections.

2. Viewing Hill

For the famous views often seen from this airport, the hill overlooking the airport off Rua Santa Catarina is a great vantage point. You can either walk from the terminal or, if driving, take exit 21 from the VR1 and use the signs leading to Aqua de Pena. Park in the parking area on your right, and then walk up the footpath heading up the hill. Further up the road is a small snack bar with views over the threshold, too.

Porto Airport

OPO | LPPR

Porto is now a major airport in its own right, with a growing number of scheduled services across Europe, Africa and the Americas. It is a hub for TAP Air Portugal, easyJet and Ryanair, and has a busy DHL cargo terminal on the west side.

The airport has one runway, 17/35. There are few spotting locations, but passengers have good views once in the departure lounge.

From the airport access road, you can drive along R. de Pedras Rubras, veering left onto R. de Tras. This becomes R. do Monte and then R. das Bicas. Eventually you'll come to a turn in the road with a small area to park and a view onto the runway through the fence. Photographers will need a ladder. All movements can be seen.

There are also views from the west side of the airport if you continue from the first location under the runway tunnel.

QATAR

Doha Hamad International

DOH | OTHH

Doha's flagship new airport opened in April 2014 to much fanfare, replacing the original airport only a few miles away. It is dominated by Qatar Airways any many other airlines flying into this Middle East country.

There is a panoramic window in the check-in hall overlooking some stands and part of one of the parallel runways. Once airside, windows at most gates give an opportunity to log aircraft and restaurants in the 'Eat Street' area overlook some of the C gates and taxiways.

Sadly there are no easy spotting locations around the airport. As with most countries in this region, spotting is not understood and often you will be challenged by the authorities if they see you using binoculars and cameras openly.

RÉUNION

Sainte-Denis Roland Garros

RUN | FMEE

The island's only airport has two runways hugging the shoreline to the east of Sainte-Denis. It receives widebody aircraft from Air France, Air Austral, Air Mauritius and Corsair International. There is a small marina and pier at the end of runway 30 which gives spectacular views of aircraft arriving only a few metres above your head. The access road to the marina from the roundabout has parking alongside the road which is perfect for watching movements on this runway.

ROMANIA

Bucharest Henri Coandă International

OTP | LROP

Bucharest's Henri Coandă International was formerly known as Otopeni Airport. It has recently become the only airport in the city served by passenger airlines (Baneasa Airport no longer has scheduled flights).

This airport has two parallel runways. The passenger terminal sits between them at the western end, while a cargo and commuter ramp is also between them, and further east is a FBO ramp. The south side is occupied by an active air force base.

Officially, spotting is not allowed without a permit. You can risk it by visiting the area north of the terminal for views of traffic on runway 08L, or by driving through the tunnel to the central area where you will see the executive apron, cargo aircraft and two stored BAC 1-11s, plus the northern runway.

RUSSIA

Moscow Domodedovo

DME | UUDD

Domodedovo is the second busiest airport in Russia and one of three major airports serving Moscow. Airlines that do have hubs here include S7 Airlines, NordStar, Ural Airlines, Red Wings and Yamal Airlines. Sadly, few Russian aircraft types operate here today, and many of the long-term stored airlines have been removed.

The airport has a single large terminal, with the new Terminal 2 being slowly opened and added to. There are two runways, and areas of remote parking opposite the terminal for stored airliners, and around the western side for cargo and commuter aircraft.

There are no official spotting locations and it is unwise to openly use cameras and binoculars in Russia. The best views inside the terminal are now post-security, but good if you are flying through the airport.

Along the northern perimeter there is a good spot underneath the approach to runway 14L. To reach it walk or drive north from the terminal along the A-105 and turn right after half a mile, following the road until you reach the perimeter wall. Turn left and find somewhere to park up.

Spotting Hotel

Domodedovo AirHotel
стр. 6, Domodedovo, Moskovskaya oblast', Russia, 142015 | +7 495 795 38 68 | www.airhotel.ru An affordable hotel behind the passenger terminal. Higher rooms facing the airport have good

views of both runways and the terminal aprons, but not good for photography. Room 928 is reportedly the best.

Moscow Sheremetyevo International

SVO | UUEE

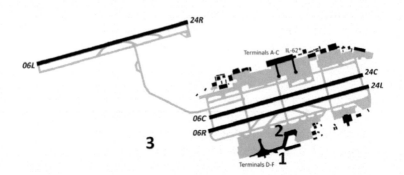

The busiest airport in Moscow, situated to the north of the city. This is the home of Aeroflot and the government transport aircraft fleet.

After years as a very old fashioned airport with traditional Soviet-era architecture, Sheremetyevo is now in a phase of expansion and upgrade to bring it in line with the expectations of international travellers and airlines with modern aircraft. It has managed to attract a number of airlines from Domodedovo as a result.

The airport has six terminals, A-F, split over the north and south sides of the southerly parallel runways (a newer runway is to the north). Those on the north are A, B and C, with B the largest and C currently being reconstructed. To the south are D, E and F (which will be the next to be reconstructed). Much of the ramp space in the northern area is used for longer term parking and Aeroflot aircraft undergoing maintenance.

Look out for a preserved Ilyushin Il-62 on the 'north side of the airport.'

Spotting Locations

1. Radisson Blu Hotel
(see later)

2. Terminal F Restaurant
Until it is reconstructed, Terminal F's Ocean Restaurant on the fourth floor is one of the best places for watching aircraft movements at the airport. You can see aircraft on the nearby gates, runways, and northern stands in the distance, and take photographs through glass. You will need to buy food or drink, but it is not expensive.

3. Runway 06C/R Approach
West of the airport along the main Sheremetyevskoye shosse road which leads to the M-11 motorway there are a couple of spots where you can watch and photograph arrivals on runways 07L/R. The first is near the approach lights, where you can park and stand in the field. There are bus stops along the road which link it with the airport.

Spotting Hotel

Radisson Blu Moscow Sheremetyevo
Mezhdunarodnoye Shosse 1a, Sheremetyevo Airport, Khimki, Moskva, 141400 | +7 495 280 34 20 | www.radissonblu.com A new hotel at Sheremetyevo which has stunning views over parts of the aircraft parking ramps and runways beyond. The hotel is also linked directly to the terminals. Rooms on the 7th-10th floors facing the airport have good views of the action. The Altitude restaurant on the 11th floor also has great views.

Moscow Vnukovo International

VKO | UUWW

Vnukovo is the third main airport for Moscow and the third busiest in Russia. Airlines operating here are mainly low-cost and seasonal, and it is the main base for Pobeda and UTair. It is, however, a good airport for seeing plenty of Russian domestic airlines and aircraft that don't usually venture out of the country.

Terminal A is the only terminal in use today, with other facilities closing in 2017. It is located on the eastern side of the airport, while on the western side there are maintenance hangars and aprons usually with large numbers of old Russian types parked up. They are hard to see.

Look out for a Tupolev Tu-104 mounted on poles near the airport entrance.

The M3 runs along the southern perimeter of the airport. There are some good places to stand along it, close to the gas station and the end of runway 01. You can either stay close to the approach lights, or cross over and stand nearer the gas station. Buses run here from the "Yugo-Zapadnaya" Metro station, but not the airport itself. A taxi is a more direct option.

Moscow Zhukovsky

ZIA | UUBW

Moscow's fourth airport. Many enthusiasts know this as the site of the MAKS Airshow held every other year.

A new passenger terminal opened in 2016 and there are plans to build more, increasing the airport's capacity and growing passenger numbers. Today it is served by various domestic carriers, with Ural Airlines the most prevalent.

Along the northern side of the field are hundreds of retired airliners and other aircraft from the Soviet era, but they are largely out of view unless you have airside access or can find views through tracks in the neighbouring forests.

Otherwise the best you can hope for are distant views from the terminal area, or through the window of a departing area, or by visiting the MAKS show.

St Petersburg Pulkovo

LED | ULLI

The busiest Russian airport outside of Moscow, Pulkovo is a hub for Rossiya and S7 Airlines, and sees a lots of domestic flights along with European and some long-haul links.

The airport has a complex layout, with two parallel runways. Terminal 1 is situated between the runways, whilst terminal Pulkovo 1 is alongside the northern of these runways. Further north, close to a disused runway, is terminal Pulkovo 2, which is now used for government and executive flights. These types of aircraft can usually be found parked on the apron outside it.

Spotting is possible from the car park outside the departures level of Terminal 1, or from the windows inside. Excellent photographs can be taken of aircraft on the taxiway or runway if you have a good lens. The Park Inn hotel is also good for spotting.

Vladivostok International

VVO | UHWW

Vladivostok is the closest major Russian airport to the hubs of the Far East. It is only a short distance across the sea from Japan, and close to the land borders with China and North Korea. It handles flights from all across the Far East, as well as links to Moscow and other Russian hubs, plus local communities within the region.

The airport has a pair of main parallel runways and a modern terminal area to the east. In the south of the site is the older domestic terminal, plus a military and general aviation area with two smaller runways. An express train links the newer international terminal with the city.

Just outside the international terminal you'll see a preserved Yakovlev Yak-40. From here you can see some aircraft parked at the gates. There are also views from the departure lounge.

There are a number of retired airliners and transport aircraft around the airport, particularly around the military area, but these are difficult (likely impossible) to see from the ground.

SERBIA

Belgrade Nikola Tesla Airport

BEG | LYBE

The home base of Air Serbia, and a focus city for Wizz Air. Belgrade is also served by most European and Middle Eastern carriers. The on-site aviation museum behind the terminal is also worth a visit (see later).

The airport has just one runway, with the aircraft parking aprons forming an L-shape, with the southern part used for maintenance and storage. A number of retired airliners were hidden away behind a hangar in this area and may still be present for a while yet. They're visible by walking along the main road from the terminal.

A small park behind the car park near the terminal is the best place to look through the fence and see movements on some of the remote stands and the runway beyond.

MUSEUM

Museum of Aviation Belgrade

Сурчин, Београд | www.muzejvazduhoplovstva.org.rs This museum has over 200 aircraft in its collection, on display both inside and outside, close to the airport terminal. The collection is based around Yugoslavian and Serbian aviation history. The largest aircraft is Sud Aviation Caravelle YU-AHB, although a Boeing 727 is also due to join.

SINGAPORE

Singapore Changi

SIN | WSSS

Singapore's Changi Airport is one of the world's largest aviation hubs, and a major transit point for travellers heading between Europe and Asia. It is home to Singapore Airlines and its cargo division, plus its Scoot and Silk Way low-cost offshoots. The airport is never quiet and offers a really interesting mix for the enthusiast, with many smaller regional Asian carriers coming and going regularly among the big international traffic.

The airport layout is based around two parallel runways, with all of the terminals located in the central area between. After undergoing plenty of transformation recently, there are now four terminals in use, with another under construction alongside the new Jewel multi-use interconnecting structure which will add retail, entertainment and dining options for both passengers and visitors. The amenities and quality of the facilities here have ensured Changi is consistently voted the best in the world by passengers.

On the western side of the airport is a small site used by the Singapore Air Force, largely hidden by trees. You can often see its Fokker 50 and KC-130 aircraft arriving and departing, however.

In addition to being one of the busiest airports in the world for passengers, Changi is also a busy cargo hub, using a large complex of facilities to the north of the terminals, as well as Singapore Airlines' engineering hangars.

Thankfully there are a number of good spotting opportunities at the airport and enthusiasts can often be seen using them.

Spotting Locations

1. Terminal 1 Viewing Mall
Nicely air-conditioned, you can enjoy some good views of movements from this indoor area inside Terminal 1. It has views of the central apron and more distant views of aircraft on the runways. Singapore Airlines aircraft don't usually park here. Photography is acceptable, but through glass, and better on the afternoon. To reach the area, go up the escalators from the check-in hall.

2. Terminal 2 Viewing Mall
Smaller than the Terminal 1 Mall, this is another indoor room which looks out over parking stands used by Singapore Airlines and some other airlines, plus runway 02C/20C. You can reach this

area by heading up the escalators to the floor above departures, following the signs. Again, photography is possible through glass.

3. Terminal 3 Viewing Mall

This indoor area looks out over runway 02L/20R, which is usually the arrivals runway. Photography is not good here, but you can still log movements with ease. Reach the area from the check-in area via escalators, following the signs.

4. Changi Beach Park

If aircraft are arriving on runway 20R, head to the beach area north of the airport for great approach shots. You can move further down depending on the position of the sun. You can park at the ferry terminal, and there are bus stops here (take the 34 or 53 bus from the airport to Tampines Ave, then 9 bus to the ferry terminal).

Spotting Hotels

Crowne Plaza

75 Airport Boulevard #01-01, Singapore 819664 | +65 6823 5354 | www.crowneplaza.com The best hotel for spotting at Singapore Changi, but can be expensive. Views from the even numbered rooms are excellent if you get one on floors 7, 8 or 9 facing the airport (ask for a runway view). You will have views of some Terminal 3 gates and runway 02L/20R. Corridors can also be used for views of the central terminal area.

Changi Village Hotel

1 Netheravon Road, Singapore 508502 | +65 6379 7111 | www.villagehotelchangi.com.sg If you ask for a room facing the sea, you will be able to read off arriving aircraft landing on runway 20R and see aircraft using 20L, or 02L/R. You'll need flight tracking websites for night-time movements.

SINT MAARTEN

Princess Juliana International

SXM | TNCM

This airport is a major draw for aviation enthusiasts because of its location and the position of Maho Beach which borders the approach end of the airport's runway. This is the only place that is worth trying to spot, as it really is the best. Many people congregate when large aircraft are due to witness arrivals and departures at close quarters, and the neighbouring bar usually posts a list of the day's planned arrivals on a chalkboard every morning.

The airport was devastated by two hurricanes in recent years and has been rebuilding its infrastructure, terminal, as well as traffic levels. St. Maarten handles inter-island commuter aircraft throughout the day. Medium haul traffic from the US and Canada arrives a few times per day, as do long-haul aircraft from Europe – usually Air France and KLM.

Spotting Hotel

Sonesta Maho Beach Hotel
1 Rhine Drive, Sint Maarten | +1 721 545 3100 | www.sonesta.com/mahobeach The natural choice for spotters. Situated alongside the beach, if you take a room facing the airport the aircraft will be at the same level (or lower) as your balcony, making it a great position for photography.

SLOVENIA

Ljubljana Jože Pučnik Airport

LJU | LJLJ

Ljubljana is not a particularly busy airport, but the main gateway to the country. It also handles passengers from southern Austria and eastern Italy as part of its catchment area. It gets busier in the summer months with low cost and leisure traffic. There is a preserved Inex Adria Douglas DC-6 (YU-AFF) behind the terminal building, near the car park and police station.

The airport has a single runway. The small terminal is on the eastern side, with cargo apron to its north, plus general aviation, corporate ramp and military base to the south.

The terminal has a viewing area (signposted 'Terasa' from outside the entrance to the building) overlooking the apron. It is good for photographs for much of the day, but you are shooting through glass.

SOUTH AFRICA

Cape Town International

CPT | FACT

Less busy than Johannesburg, but still a major gateway to South Africa. It is served by airlines from across Africa, Europe, the Middle East and Asia. South African Express and Mango operate a hub operation at the airport.

The passenger terminal and other aprons stretch along the western side of the main 01/19 runway. The smaller 16/34 is used by general aviation traffic. In the domestic side of the terminal there is an observation deck with good views across the parking stands, taxiway and runway. The upper floors of the P1 parking garage also have good views.

Another favourite spot is south from the terminal past the car hire parking, onto Tower Road. It is at the end of the road and gives you good views of aircraft on the runway through the fence. This facility used to fly jet aircraft until one of its Lightnings crashed at an air show.

Johannesburg O R Tambo International

JNB | FAOR

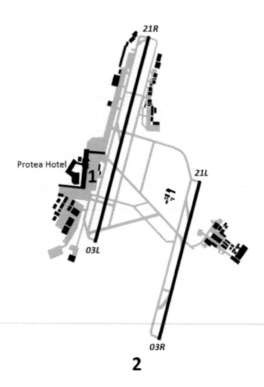

The main gateway to South Africa. O R Tambo is a large airport with two parallel runways and six terminals (albeit in a compact complex). The airport has a complicated layout of ramps, hangars, maintenance areas and storage areas.

As well as being a hub for South African Airways, Airlink, Comair, Mango and Kulula, many interesting African airlines us the airport. Spotting is fairly easy, but as always in South Africa be careful when outside and use a car if possible.

Spotting Locations

1. International Terminal Viewing Area
On the third level of the terminal. The large window has a commanding view over the parking apron and gates, with the runway beyond. Photography is through glass, but this spot is generally good from midday onwards. It is free to use, and has the benefit of food and drink nearby.

2. Hi-Flyerz Aviation Bar
Located to the south of the airport and under the approach path to runway 03R. This is a bar and restaurant with the cockpit of a Boeing 747 (formerly ZS-SAL) as part of the bar. It is great for morning photography and spotting all day, with air traffic control transmissions streamed on speakers. Viewpoint road, Bartlett, Boksburg, +27 11 897 0106, www.hiflyerz.com

Spotting Hotel

Protea Hotel by Marriott O R Tambo
Gladiator St, Kempton Park, 1619 | +27 11 977 2600 | www.proteahotels.com The hotel of choice for spotters at Johannesburg. It is located opposite the passenger terminal and high rooms facing the airport look out over part of the parking apron and aircraft which day stop. You can also see runway 21R in the distance. Photography is possible of some movements with a long lens.

Johannesburg Rand

QRA | FAGM

Originally the main airport for the city, today Rand is a busy general aviation airport to the east of Johannesburg which has an interesting aviation museum. Skyclass Aviation are also based at the airport, offering charters on board their Douglas DC-3 and DC-4 aircraft (www.flyskyclass.com). It is possible to spot from the café in the old terminal, and ramp access may be possible on occasion.

MUSEUM

South African Airways Museum Society

Rand Airport, Transvaal Aviation Club Building, Germiston 1419 | +27 76 879 5044 | www.saamuseum.co.za Uncovering the history of aviation in South Africa. A static display of aircraft includes two Boeing 747s of South African Airways, 737-200, 707 section, Douglas DC-3, DC-4 and C-54, amongst others. Open Wednesday to Sunday, plus public holidays, from 9am-3pm.

Lanseria

HLA | FALA

A secondary airport for Johannesburg, to the north west of the city. It mainly handles FlySafair, Kulula and Mango regional flights, but is also a busy biz jet base. The airport has a single runway and terminal, but a number of hangars and parking areas can be found on both sides of the runway, which include some stored airliners on the south side.

A café in the terminal acts as an observation area for many spotters since it has great views across to the runway.

SOUTH KOREA

Jeju International

CJU | RKPC

The air route between Seoul and the island of Jeju is the busiest in the world, with a great number of flights every day operated by a number of airlines.

All South Korean domestic airlines fly through here many times per day, but traffic is also made up of many international carriers, including Air China, Asiana, China Eastern, China Southern, and Cathay Dragon, Korean Air and Shenzhen Airlines. It's possible to watch the aircraft coming and going from the seashore near Jeju City, as well as from a few spots on the road running alongside the main runway.

Seoul Gimpo

GMP | RKSS

Gimpo is Seoul's original airport, and today is busy mostly as a domestic facility for the capital. Movements are dominated by Asiana Airlines and Korean Air, along with other domestic carriers such as Air Busan, Eastar Jet, Jeju Air and T'way Airlines. Over a hundred flights a day link Gimpo with Jeju Island – the world's busiest air route. Many aircraft operate here which will not be seen at Incheon or outside the country, so it is worth the visit. Some international flights are allowed, particularly to China, Japan and Taiwan through Air China, All Nippon Airways, China Airlines, China Eastern, China Southern and Shanghai Airlines. Domestic aircraft tend to repeat after a few hours.

The airport has two parallel runways and two terminals at right angles to each other. A Korean Air maintenance and cargo base are to the south-east. General aviation and helicopters use facilities on the south-western side of the runways.

An viewing terrace can be found on the domestic terminal. Head upstairs to food court and follow signs for the Observatory.

An observation deck with both indoor and outdoor areas can also be found on the sixth floor of the Korea Airport Corporation building between the domestic and international terminals (the entrance is alongside a supermarket). It is good for logging all movements on the parallel runways and aprons, and is also fairly good for photography. It is open from 9am to 5pm, and closed Mondays.

Seoul Incheon

ICN | RKSI

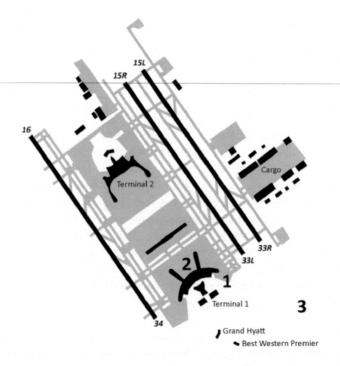

Seoul Incheon was opened in March 2001 after it became apparent that Gimpo airport was bursting at the seams and unable to expand. Incheon is a modern airport and has recently opened its new Terminal 2 and a third parallel runway. Passenger traffic is busy, with a heavy presence of both Korean Air and Asiana Airlines. Elsewhere, the airport has six cargo terminals on the northern side of the airport, which proves to be a very busy operation.

Security in South Korea is very tight and aircraft spotters are not officially tolerated. Therefore, beware that you are likely to be moved on or told to stop spotting by security personnel. Using binoculars, poles and cameras can add suspicion, so be very discrete. Nevertheless, if you are departing from Incheon you can easily walk past most gates logging aircraft parked there.

The airport's website helpfully gives arrival information for all aircraft, including cargo flights.

Spotting Locations

1. Outside Domestic Terminal
Just outside the domestic part of Terminal 1 there is a smoking area which offers some views over the domestic gates and aircraft approaching runways 33L/R. You can also see aircraft departing in the opposite direction. It is possible to take photographs discretely from here.

2. Panorama Restaurant
Up on the 4th floor of the international part of Terminal 1 is the Panorama Restaurant which has views out over the gates around the terminal, and across to the satellite concourse. You must buy food and drink if you wish to stay here, and it can be quite expensive.

3. Haneul Garden Park
A park directly under the approach to the northern runways is a short drive/taxi ride or a 30 minute walk from Terminal 1 (a shuttle

bus also passes). It has benches and is popular with locals. You can easily take photographs of aircraft when landing from the south, but much of the airport is out of sight.

Spotting Hotels

Grand Hyatt Incheon Hotel
208 Yeongjonghaeannam-ro, 321 Beon-gil, Unseo-dong, Jung-gu, Incheon 400-719 | +82 32 745 1234 | incheon.grand.hyatt.com Located close to the end of runway 33, rooms facing the airport have views of this. Aircraft are quite far, so need a good pair of binoculars to read off. The hotel is fairly expensive. There is a free shuttle bus to the terminal.

Best Western Premier Hotel Incheon Airport
48-27 Gonghang-ro 424beon-gil, Jung-gu, Incheon | +82 32 743 1000 | www.airportshotel.co.kr/en Located in a similar position to the Hyatt, it is a little more reasonable but offers views of runway 33L and some views of the terminals from some rooms on floors 9 and 10. In-room TVs have a channel listing arrivals and departures, including cargo and GA movements.

SPAIN

Alicante Elche Airport

ALC | LEAL

Alicante is a popular holiday destination near the tourist resorts along the Costa Blanca; it has one of Spain's busiest airports. The airport is a hub for Ryanair, Norwegian, Vueling and Air Nostrum.

The main terminal opened in 2011, closing the existing terminals 1 and 2 until new uses can be found for the buildings. Alicante only has one runway.

Although no official viewing areas are provided, if you have the use of a car the best spot to get a good overview of all movements and opportunities of photographing aircraft on the runway is along the southern perimeter. To reach this spot from the terminal, head along the local road towards Elche, then turn left at the next roundabout onto CV849. Eventually you'll see a gravel track on the left running alongside the perimeter fence. You can park here and use the mound to get elevated views.

Barcelona El Prat

BCN | LEBL

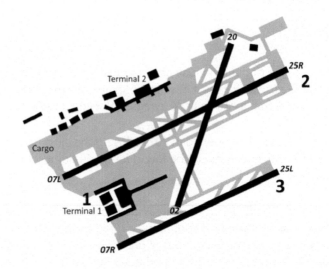

Barcelona's El Prat airport has developed significantly despite the dominance of Madrid, with an extensive network of domestic, intra-European, and long-haul flights by many airlines. The main Spanish carriers all have a strong presence here, as do Europe's low-cost airlines. In addition to this, Barcelona is served by a number of airlines from North and South America, Asia and the Middle East; Russian airlines are particularly prevalent compared to other airports in Spain.

The airport has two terminals. Terminal 1 is used by most major carriers, including Iberia and all of its partners. Terminal 2 on the northern side of the airport is used mainly low-cost carriers.

Of the three runways, the parallel 07/25 runways are used most of the time.

Bus route PR3 is really useful for getting around the airport. It runs from the El Pray metro station (one stop from the airport) and travels past spotting locations 2 and 3 in the summer months.

Spotting Locations

1. Terminal 1 Balcony
At departures level outside terminal 1 there is a balcony which overlooks the runway 07L threshold and nearby taxiways and aprons. A good location if you don't have a car.

2. Spotting Tower
An official spotting location provided for viewing aircraft, with benches and an elevated tower which raises you above the fence. It is situated next to the threshold of runway 25R and plenty of people congregate here to watch aircraft pass at close quarters as they approach. The location is off Platja de El Prat, with parking available at the nearby cemetery. Bus route PR3 will take you to the spot if you exit at Tanatori.

3. Runway 25L
Follow the road from the Spotting Tower location until you reach the end of Runway 25L. Again, there are places to park. Aircraft approaching the runway are very close to you and fine for photographs. A ladder is needed for good shots over the fence.

Ibiza Airport

IBZ | LEIB

The majority of Ibiza's passengers arrive during the summer months when this small island becomes a significant holiday destination. Many leisure and low-cost airlines from across Europe can be seen – particularly those from the UK and Germany. Otherwise the airport is relatively quiet, with regional airliners linking to the mainland.

The small airport has a single runway and terminal. The main parking apron is large enough to handle executive jets and any visiting cargo aircraft, with a small extension at the eastern end for light aircraft.

Walking or driving to the east of the terminal will lead to opportunities of views over the runway and apron down tracks leading from the main road. The best of these is Cami Aeropuerto. Aircraft will also pass overhead the beaches to the east of the airport.

Lanzarote Arrecife Airport

ACE | GCRR

One of the main airports in the Canary Islands. Lanzarote handles mainly holiday traffic, mixed with inter-island commuters and links to the mainland with Iberia, Vueling etc. Ryanair operates a base here.

The single runway hugs the shoreline, with the terminal and main parking apron at the northern end. A small military base occupies a site further south of the terminal, with its own apron.

Most spotters use the beach and road at the end of runway 03 since the majority of aircraft approach from this direction and good photographs are possible. To get there from the airport, head west on the LZ-2 motorway, then turn south on the LZ-40 for Puerto del Carmen and Matagorda. Once you reach the beach there is a car park and you can walk to a position that suits you.

Spotting Hotels
Hotel Beatriz Playa
Puerto del Carmen, Las Palmas | +34 928 51 21 66 | www. beatrizhoteles.com A perfectly positioned hotel alongside the end of runway 03. Rooms facing Arrecife face the end of the runway,

where aircraft on the ground and on approach can be seen and photographed. Rooms 3028-3050 are reportedly the best. It's a short walk to the end of the runway from the hotel.

Las Palmas Gran Canaria

LPA | GCLP

This holiday airport has two parallel runways and a single terminal, which was renovated and extended in 2014. It is a base for Binter Canarias, CanaryFly, Norwegian, Ryanair and Vueling, and most of Europe's low-cost and holiday airlines pass through year-round given the climate of the islands. A new runway opened recently, parallel to the existing strip.

A large Spanish Air Force base exists on the eastern part of the airport site, offering some interesting movements on occasion.

The small town of Las Puntillas to the south of the airport terminal is a good place to watch aircraft movements. You have a view of the 03L/R thresholds and taxiways. To reach it, head south on the GC-1 motorway and leave at exit 18. Turn left at the roundabout and drive under the motorway, taking the second exit at the next roundabout onto Calle Kant. Take the first left, then right onto Calle Estevanez and drive to the end.

A small airfield and aeroclub around 15 miles south of Las Palmas Airport has a preserved Douglas DC-7 airliner.

Madrid Barajas Adolfo Suárez

MAD | LEMD

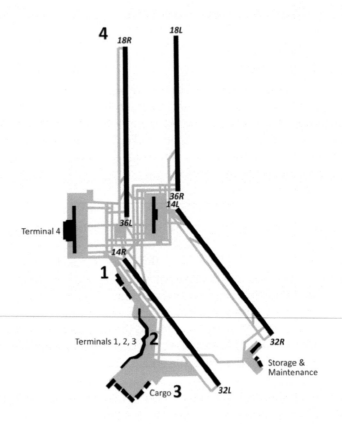

Madrid has always held a strong position as a hub airport for national carrier Iberia and its partners, and also as the European connection point for Latin America. It is the recent opening of bases here by easyJet, Norwegian and Ryanair that has improved access to the airport, especially to the city break and domestic market.

The quality of movements at Madrid has drawn enthusiasts for many years, with a number of spotting locations giving handy

250

access. Although the influx of low-cost carriers may not interest many, they provide affordable access for quick breaks.

The airport has a complex layout, especially since expansion took place to the north, leaving a lot of the original site as one large area of parking aprons to the south. There are three passenger terminals to the south, with Terminal 4 in the north. Next to Terminal 1 is an area used for biz jets, light aircraft and cargo airliners.

There are usually a number of stored and retired aircraft on the storage and maintenance areas on the east side of the airfield, and keep an eye out for a preserved DC-9 outside Terminals 1 and 2.

Spotting Locations

1. Metro Station Mound
The most popular spotting location at the centre of the airfield. Take the Metro to Barajas, the small town adjacent to the airport. Once there, walk along Av. De Logroño and turn left along Ctra. Cementerio Nuevo. Walk across the white pedestrian bridge and along to the raised area which allows you to log almost every movement, even aircraft using the distant new runway and Terminal 4. Photography is only really possible for aircraft passing on the taxiways nearer to you. It is possible to drive here if you follow signs for Barajas and then head towards the road tunnel under the airport. The mound is alongside this tunnel, with various places to park nearby.

2. Terminal 2
Inside Terminal 2, head up to the second floor using the stairs in the middle section and find the café. Windows along the passageway have views over the terminal gates, runway 32L arrivals, and you can se aircraft parked on the cargo aprons. Photography is through glass.

3. Cargo Area
Alongside the DHL buildings you can see aircraft on the cargo and southern aprons and taxiways. To reach the spot from Terminal

1, follow signs for Centro de Carga Aerea and continue along Av. Central. After the majority of the cargo buildings have passed, turn left at the roundabout onto Calle November. The fence is in front of you. You can follow the road along for a closer view on runway 32L.

4. Northern End
This locations is a long distance from the airport terminals, but great for photographing arrivals from the north on runways 36L/R. To get there, drive north on the M-12 and exit the large roundabout for Alcobendas at the BP gas station. At the third roundabout take the first exit, passing underneath the E-5 motorway, and leading to a sewage works. You can park here or risk driving further along a dirt track under the R-2 motorway. Once on the other side you can walk under the approach to whichever runway you prefer.

Spotting Hotel

Hotel B&B Madrid Airport
Calle de Lola Flores, 2, 28022 Madrid | +34 917 48 16 57 | www. hotel-bb.com An affordable hotel to the south of the airport, on the road to Torrejon Air Base. Rooms offer views of aircraft arriving on runway 32L, or (more distant) departures in the opposite direction. You can also see arrivals into Torrejon.

Malaga Airport

AGP | LEMG
A busy holiday gateway which opened a large new terminal in 2010 and a second runway in 2012. The older 1970s and 1990s terminals still exist and link to the new one, with many views across the different aprons and runways once you are in the departures area. Traffic mainly consists of low-cost carriers, with Ryanair and Vueling basing aircraft here. In the summer months the airport is generally busier, with more holiday flights from

northern Europe, and seasonal long-haul services from Air Transat, Delta Air Lines, Kuwait Airways, Qatar Airways and Saudia.

On the south side of the airport alongside runway 13/31 is a small military base which sometimes has transport and firefighting aircraft present. You can see across from gates in the Terminal 2 piers.

An apron for executive aircraft is largely hidden from view of the terminals, but can be found by driving or walking south. Here you'll also find a small museum which also has a viewing balcony and some aircraft exhibits, including a DC-3, DC-9 cockpit, Convair 440 and Beech 18.

The best spotting location is alongside runway 13/31 where a rough parking area and mounds exist near the village of Churriana. Photographs can be taken through the fence, or of aircraft taking off. To reach it continue south from the airport along MA-21 and follow signs for Churriana. Turn right at the third roundabout and keep driving, bearing right onto Calle Rigoberta Menchu which leads to the fence.

An alternative location where spotters congregate is alongside the new road close to the end of runway 13. Continue past the terminals on the main central N-340 road towards the P3 parking. You will be directed onto a side road which passes through a tunnel. At the roundabout turn left onto the dirt road. This spot is great if aircraft are using this runway as you'll be able to photograph arrivals and aircraft taxying for take-off, although the sun will be in front of you at certain times of the day.

Menorca Airport

MAH | LEMH

The quietest of the three Balearic Islands. Principally a holiday destination, with low-cost and charter airlines busiest in summer.

Menorca also has commuter links to the mainland with Air Europa, Iberia and Vueling.

From the terminal, head north to the roundabout with a pyramid on and turn left towards San Climente. Then turn right after down a small road signposted Poblat Talaiotic da Torello. Along here you can find a spot facing the approach to runway 19 when approaches are from the north.

When approaches are from the south, a road runs past the threshold on its way to Binisfuller. This road joins the main San Climente to Es Canutels road. Various places to watch and photograph aircraft can be found along here.

Palma de Mallorca Airport

PMI | LEPA

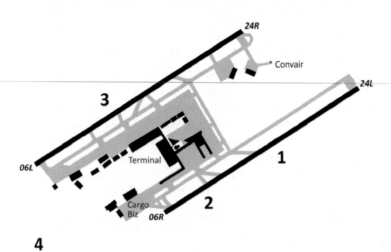

Palma Airport, on the Balearic island of Mallorca, is at the heart of one of the most popular holiday destinations in Europe. Millions flock here year-round from all over northern Europe. The airport is currently the third busiest in Spain. Most common airlines here are Air Europa, easyJet, Jet2, Ryanair, TUI and Vueling.

The airport has a pair of parallel runways. The terminal area is in the centre, with different modules (concourses) on three sides. Cargo and executive aircraft parking areas stretch to the west on both sides.

A small military base is in the north-east corner of the airfield. Languishing here is former Spantax Convair 990 EC-BZO which you may be able to see from an arriving or departing aircraft window.

Spotting Locations

1. Runway 24L Mound
Ideal for morning to mid-afternoon photography. This mound is situated alongside the runway 06R/24L at roughly the midway point. To reach it drive along the Ma-19A road to Manacor, pass the industrial estate and rental car offices, then turn down the dirt road at the first roundabout (you may have to double back to turn along the road).

2. Industrial Estate
Retracing your steps from location 1 back towards the Son Oms industrial estate you can find a couple of buildings with rooftop parking areas on Carrer Son Oms 4. When runwy 06R is in use, these offer a perfect position for photography high above the fence.

3. Runway 06L/24R
A dirt road runs along much of the length of the northern runway 06L/24R, with a dirt mound at one point that is good for photography later in the day. Drive north from the airport an exit at the large retail park with a Carrefour supermarket. From the car park follow signs for Mercapalma, then for Sa Tapia. This will lead you to the fence.

4. Beach
When arrivals are coming from the sea, as they often do, the nearby beach next to Can Pastilla is fine for logging and some photography of arrivals.

Spotting Hotel

Hotel Alua Soul Palma

Calle Maestro Ekitai Ahn 40, 07610 Cala Estancia, Mallorca | +34 971 46 67 11 | www.aluahotels.com Probably the most popular hotel at Palma with spotters, located in Ca'n Pastilla (formerly the Marina Luz). Its rooms have views of aircraft on one of the runways, and it is a short distance from the airport. Ask for a top-floor room facing the Bay of Palma for the best views. This is an adult-only hotel.

Seville Airport

SVQ | LEZL

Seville is an interesting airport in south-west Spain. Scheduled airlines link it with the rest of Spain and further into Europe, with Iberia, Ryanair and Vueling the busiest carriers.

The passenger terminal and L-shaped apron are on the north side of the main 09/27 runway, as well as a cargo apron served by ASL Airlines Belgium, DHL and UPS Airlines.

Also located here is an Airbus facility which produces the A400M Atlas transport aircraft for air forces around the world. The manufacturing site is on the east and south-east sides of the airport, often with aircraft in various states of construction parked outside.

Finally, a small military base can also be found on the south side of the airport.

The elevated roadway on either side of the terminal is good for catching aircraft on the main apron, but not for photography.

If you want to see the Airbus aircraft and aircraft on approach to the runway from the east, drive along Barrida del Avion from the terminal, signposted Via Servicios Aeropuerto. When this comes to a roundabout, take the first exit (signposted Airbus Military) and turn off the road onto rough ground when the airport comes into view. From here you can walk to some paths alongside the river and find a good vantage point.

Tenerife North

TFN | GCXO

The original airport serving the island of Tenerife, and infamously the site of the worst air disaster when two Boeing 747s collided on the runway in March 1977. Today it is served by a handful of inter-island and European scheduled airlines like Air Europa, Binter Canarias, CanaryFly, Iberia, Norwegian, Royal Air Maroc, Ryanair and Vueling.

A derelict Vickers Viscount is located near the control tower. Follow the road past it for a couple of miles and turn right onto the TF-265 (signposted La Esperanza). Continue by turning right up a side road to the TF-24 On the south-east side of the airport the TF-24 road, and then take a sharp left where you see a restaurant up on the hill. Here you can park and have great views over the runway threshold.

Tenerife South Airport

TFS | GCTS

Built to serve the tourist resorts on the south of the island and to relive the often fog-bound Los Rodeos airport. Tenerife South is the busier of the island's airports and used by many of the charter and low-cost airlines from Europe, and a fair number of scheduled flights from the mainland.

In the summer months it can be quite busy. The winter months are still fairly busy given the year-round warm climate, and the prevalence of low-cost flights. The airport has a single runway and terminal.

As its name suggests, the airport is at the southern end of the island, close to the main resorts of Los Cristianos and Playa de la Americas.

To spot arrivals onto runway 07, head west from the terminal on the motorway and take exit 62 following signs for the TF-65 towards Los Abrigos. Once in the village, take the first left onto Calle la Gaviota and at the end you can turn up the rough track on your left which leads to the end of runway 08 (the track does improve). This is a good spot for photography of aircraft both landing and lining up on this runway, and you can continue along the southern perimeter to find a better spot. You will need supplies as you can be exposed to the sun here.

Continue from Los Abrigos along the main road to El Medano. Before you reach it, after passing through the small village of La Tejita turn left up a dirt road immediately after the last hotel. Follow this to the fence line and turn left. You'll come to a purpose-built spotting tower with steps and seats on top. This is at the mid-point of the runway and elevates you above the fence for better photographs. You could walk or drive to this spot from location 1 also.

Teruel Airport

TEV | LETL

A relatively new airport built to take advantage of alternative income streams such as airliner maintenance and storage. Teruel is situated around 100 miles south of Zaragoza and 95 miles inland from Valencia off the A-23 and N-234 roads. It has a single runway and associated aprons, with a large number of parking areas arranged for the long-term storage of aircraft. Viewing the stored aircraft can be difficult, but is possible with perseverance and a car! Security will likely question you if you loiter too long.

Valencia

VLC | LEVC

Valencia is a fairly busy and interesting airport which isn't as heavily influenced by holiday traffic and instead handles more scheduled carriers and low cost airlines such as Ryanair, Transavia, Vueling and Wizz Air. Iberia links the city to many Spanish destinations through its Air Nostrum subsidiary, which is based here.

The airport has a single runway and terminal, with cargo carriers such as UPS Airlines using a ramp to the north west of the terminal. Air Nostrum has a maintenance base on the south side of the airfield, and there are often stored airliners in this area, as well as executive and light aircraft.

Inside the terminal you can view the main apron from the upstairs area through large glass windows. Most movements can be seen from here.

SWEDEN

Gothenburg Landvetter

GOT | ESGG

Sweden's second-busiest airport and an important passenger and cargo hub in the west of Sweden. Most of the passenger flights are domestic and European, however there are some longer routes by Iran Air, Qatar Airways and holiday airlines.

ASL, Amapola Flyg and DHL Aviation are the main cargo operators. There is a separate cargo building and apron to the north of the passenger terminal. Further south is an apron used for parking commuter airliners.

It's not easy to spot at Gothenburg and enthusiasts have been moved on regularly. Under the approach for runway 21 there is a hut built to shelter spotters. To reach it you need to walk quite a distance. Head north past the Schenker Logistics building and turn left to follow alongside the airport fence until you reach the hut. Good for photos, but south-facing.

The top floor of the multi-storey car park outside the terminal has good views of the southern end of the runway and some of the parking stands, but is quite distant for photographs.

Malmö Airport

MMX | ESMS

Malmö in the south of Sweden is the home base of cargo carrier West Air Sweden, and a hub for other cargo carriers like Amapola Flyg, ASL and UPS Airlines. The cargo aprons and hangars are to the south of the passenger terminal. Passenger services are provided by AIS Airlines, BRA Braathens Regional, Norwegian, Ryanair, Scandinavian Airlines and Wizz Air, with additional charters in the summer.

There is a small viewing area outside the terminal. Turn left as you leave the building and you'll see it near the parking garage. There are also views through the fence if you turn right.

Stockholm Arlanda

ARN | ESSA

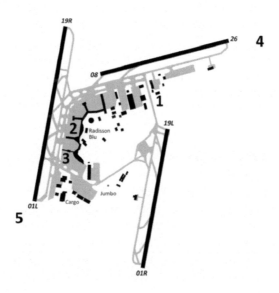

Stockholm's main airport at Arlanda is some 26 miles north of the city. The airport is one of the hubs of Scandinavian Airlines, as well as Norwegian, Thomas Cook Scandinavia and TUI fly Nordic.

Arlanda has four terminals. Terminals 3 and 4 are used for domestic flights, whilst 2 and 5 are used for international flights. All terminals are joined together, and the central Sky City is a connector building with places to eat, shop and relax; it has large windows looking out over the runways.

There are also a number of cargo facilities south of the terminals, and maintenance hangars to the east where sometimes you'll see airliners in temporary storage.

There are three runways at Arlanda. Enthusiasts are catered for near the newer runway 01L/19R with a covered building known as the Spotters Hut. Views are also possible elsewhere around the airport.

The vast majority of movements at Arlanda are operated by Norwegian and SAS, including some by the long-haul fleet. Most European carriers frequent the airport, and a number of long-haul airlines provide links with North America, Africa, Asia and the Middle East. If you explore a little you can find no fewer than four retired 1960s Caravelle airliners around the airport.

A former Pan Am Boeing 747-200 is used as a hostel on the airport grounds (see www.jumbostay.se). A novel place to stay when visiting Arlanda!

Spotting Locations

1. Spotters Hut
A popular official location provided for the viewing of aircraft is a hut at the northern end of Runway 01R/19L. It also has views over parts of runway 08/26, and the de-icing area. You can't see any of the terminal stands. Aircraft can be seen at close quarters when landing on runway 19L and taxying past. You can drive to the spot, which has a car park alongside, or take bus line 579 from Terminal 5.

2. Sky City
Sky City is located between terminals 4 and 5. It has large windows around the food court area which look out on to the aprons and Runway 01L/19R. The glass can make photography difficult, but logging aircraft is not a problem. A mezzanine area has comfy seats to enjoy the view from.

3. Terminal 3

Terminal 3 is simply a pier with a couple of gates from which most domestic commuter aircraft depart. Before going through security, there are windows on either side of the pier from which you can see most movements around terminals 2, 3 and 4. You can also see across to the cargo ramp and business ramp.

4. Runway 26

Driving away from the airport, instead of taking the motorway to Stockholm, turn left on the 273 and head past the Spotters Hut entrance. Immediately after the small lake, turn left and follow the road until you can see the runway approach lights. Turn right onto a gravel road and park up. This is a perfect spot for photographs if aircraft are using runway 26.

5. Runway 01L

Drive south from the terminals on the 273 and leave at the first exit, signposted E4 Sunsvall/Uppsala. Turn right for Cargo and at the next roundabout take the first exit, then pull off to the left at the second exit where there is a rough road and an area to park. The runway lights for runway 01L are in front of you and perfectly positioned for photographs.

Spotting Hotels

Comfort Hotel Arlanda Airport
Tornvägen 2, 190 45 Stockholm-Arlanda | +46 8 444 18 00 | www. nordicchoicehotels.com A brand new hotel outside Sky City in the central terminal complex at Arlanda. The hotel has rooms facing the airport and runways, with some of the gates visible, from the upper floors. Photography is possible with a 300mm+ lens.

Radisson Blu Sky City Hotel
Stockholm Arlanda Airport, SE-190 45 | +46 8 506 740 00 | www. radissonblu.com Located above the terminals and linked into the Sky City area. Rooms higher up and at each end of the building offer great views over the movements – particularly of Runway 01L/19R. Photography is not really possible, however. The hotel can be expensive.

Stockholm Bromma

BMA | ESSB

Stockholm's original airport. It was replaced by Arlanda in the 1960s when it couldn't expand. Despite this, Bromma is still a busy commuter airport with flights all over Sweden and to some neighbouring countries. BRA Braathens Regional Airlines has a hub here, with Brussels Airlines, Finnair, Sun-Air of Scandinavia and Widerøe operating international routes.

You can also expect to see a lot of executive movements here, plus air taxi, general aviation and pleasure flights in a based DC-3.

A hill behind the terminal is a great vantage spot for photographing aircraft on the runway and watching all movements. You can see many of the parking areas from here. It's easiest reached from the P2 car park.

SWITZERLAND

Geneva Airport

GVA | LSGG

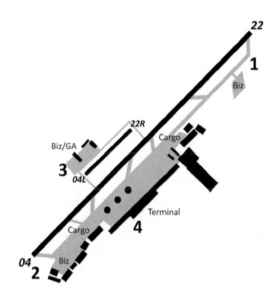

Geneva's airport is located in Cointrin just the north of the city centre on the border with France. It still uses a system of remote satellites with their own aircraft gates, linked by underground passage to the main terminal. Since 1956, an exchange of territory has been agreed with France, whereby the terminal allows passengers destined for France to exit via different channels and ultimately onto the road heading straight to the nearby border. For departing passengers, a separate area of the terminal has been set aside for those travelling to France. Naturally Air France is the dominant user of this area.

Geneva is very much an international city, with organisations based here including the European headquarters of the United Nations. There are also many conferences held in Geneva annually, with the European Business Aviation Convention (EBACE) the most notable for spotters. As a result Geneva handles more business jet movements than most other European airports, with dedicated parking aprons and based FBOs like TAG Aviation.

Additionally, during the colder winter months Geneva plays host to an influx of leisure passengers destined for the nearby ski resorts in the Alps.

Aside from the based easyJet and Swiss aircraft, Geneva sees links from all over Europe, the Middle East, Africa and North America. DHL has a cargo facility, and look out for a retired Boeing 737-200 used by the fire service on the apron north of the terminal.

Spotting Locations

1. Runway 22
When aircraft are arriving over the lake, follow the road from the terminal towards Lausanne. Exit at Gd-Saconnex and follow signs for France. Take the first right after passing over the highway. Turn onto the road Chemin Des Clys and find somewhere to park. Bus route 28 from the terminal passes nearby this spot in the direction of Jardin Botanique. Get off at Tunnel Routier stop and walk the rest. This is good for photography in the morning. You will also walk past the remote biz jet ramp where aircraft often stay longer, or are stored.

2. Runway 04
At the Runway 05 end, leave the terminal and head for Meyrin. Turn right at the lights for Meyrin, and then turn right at the Tag Aviation signpost. After a U-turn, you will pass some buildings before the road turns left. Park in the car park on the right and then walk back in the direction you came from, and down a pedestrian path which leads to a fence near the runway threshold. Bus 28 to Hopital La Tour leaves the terminal in this direction. Alight at Blandonnet and walk towards Tag Aviation and the pedestrian path.

3. General Aviation and Aero Bistro

On the northern side of the airfield is the general aviation area, which also sees more executive jets parking. Along Route H. C. Forestier you'll find the Aero Bistro next to the Aero Club, which has refreshments and views of the runway. A short walk further leads you to the biz jet parking ramp.

4. Le Chef Restaurant

For great views while you enjoy some food or drink, go to Le Chef upstairs in the terminal (before security). It has good windows overlooking the parking gates.

Zürich Airport

ZRH | LSZH

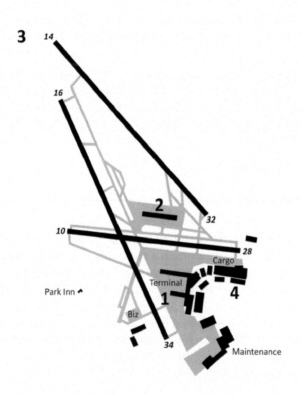

SWITZERLAND

Zurich is a popular choice in Europe for aviation enthusiasts as it provides some excellent facilities for enthusiasts. The airport is the busiest in Switzerland and is the main operating base for national carrier Swiss International Air Lines and its partners. Other airlines from across Europe, North America and Asia make up the numbers with daily flights, and an interesting mix of executive jets regularly occupy the ramps.

The airport has three runways. 14, 28 and 34 are the most common for arrivals. The terminal has two piers in the main area, with a satellite pier further north. Swiss's maintenance facilities are to the south, whilst biz jets use parking aprons on the east and west sides of the field.

Each January the World Economic Forum is held close to Zurich in the town of Davos. This brings in leaders from around the world and their private jets and government transports, both big and small. Enthusiasts flock to the airport for this feast of rare types and registrations, despite the usual cold weather!

The official viewing locations at Zurich are amongst the best in Europe. There are, however, some useful unofficial spots around the airport which can produce stunning photographs. Whilst movements are not as numerous as other European hubs Zurich is still worth a visit.

Spotting Locations

1. Pier B Terrace
The observation deck on top of Pier B is the original and best spot for watching and logging aircraft movements at Zurich. Aircraft pass by and park very close to this location and you will see movements on runway 16/34 and part of 10/28. You will need to wait for runway 14 arrivals to taxi closer to the terminal. The BUCHairSHOP is located here, along with a restaurant and refreshments. This terrace is signposted within the terminal, and opens daily from 8am-8pm (summer) and 9am-6pm (winter). There is a CHF5 entrance fee.

A behind-the-scenes bus tour is available from the Pier B Terrace and takes in the Airside Centre, Piers A and B, Runway 28, nature reserve, cargo and maintenance areas, and the emergency services, and includes some time close to runways 16 and 28. The tour lasts over an hour and tickets can be bought from the terrace or through the website www.zurich-airport.com, but be advised that they can book up early so get them as soon as possible.

2. Pier E Terrace

To get close to the action on the satellite Pier E, there is an observation deck on top. Buses run from the Pier B terrace every 30 minutes from midday. You'll be closer to aircraft using runways 16 and 28.

3. Runway 14 Viewing Area

Another official viewing location can be found close to the end of runway 14 and is great for photographic arrivals. It is located on Bülachstrasse. To reach it, leave the airport north on Autobahn 51 and leave at exit 6. Cross two roundabouts and turn right onto Oberglattenstrasse. Eventually you'll see the spotting area and car park on your left. You can't see much else on the airport from here, but it's great for arrival shots. Bus 510 will take you as far as Oberglatt, from where it's a 15 minute walk.

An alternative spot exists on the other side of the runway 14 threshold, at the end of the small Im Hell road. It also has a car park.

4. Car Park 6

The top level of Car Park 6 gives good views over runways 14 and 28 and the executive jet aprons, which is useful during the World Economic Forum. You can see many movements from here, although some will be out of sight. The car park is covered.

Spotting Hotel
Park Inn Zurich Airport

Flughofstrasse 75, 8153 Rümlang | +41 44 828 8686 | www.
parkinn.com If you request a room overlooking the airport, you
won't be disappointed. Most of the action is visible from here,
although photography is a little limited due to the distance and
glass. This hotel can be fairly expensive.

Radisson Blu Zurich Airport
Flughafen, 8058 Züich | +41 44 800 40 40 | www.radissonblu.
com Not all of the rooms here have views, but ask for a high level
facing the airport and you should be able to see movements.
Room 409 is reportedly good for all round views. The hotel is next
to the terminal buildings, so is central for visiting the viewing
areas.

TAIWAN

Kaohsiung International

KHH | RCKH

A busy airport in the south of Taiwan. All of Taiwan's domestic airlines have a heavy presence here.

Kaohsiung has a single runway and two terminals – domestic and international – both in the southwestern corner of the airport.

The best place to watch the action is in the covered walkway between the domestic and international terminals, were seating and large windows have views over many of the gates and ramp areas. This area is actually signposted the View Deck, so is easy to find (on the departures level).

Nearby is the Republic of China Air Force Museum.

Taichung

RMQ | RCMQ

A busy gateway on the west coast of Taiwan, which replaced the old downtown airport. The current facility is shared with the military, so caution should be exercised.

The airport sees cross-straits flights to China by Air China, China Airlines, China Eastern, Mandarin Airlines, Tianjin Airlines and Uni Air, with others including EVA Air, HK Express, Tigerair Taiwan, T'way and Vietjet.

There are good views of the ramp within the terminal. Those with a car could use the car park of the Chingchuankang Golf Course near the threshold of runway 18 if aircraft are arriving from that direction, for good approach shots.

Taipei Songshan

TSA | RCSS

Taipei's original airport, close to downtown, transitioned into a mostly domestic facility from 1979 when Taoyuan Airport opened. This grew into a significant operation before the decline of domestic air travel in Taiwan.

Today the airport is still a hub for domestic flights, with both Far Eastern Air Transport and Uni Air based here. However, it also now sees a good number of international flights across the Taiwan Strait to China, and north to Japan.

The airport shares its single east-west runway with Songshan Air Base. The facilities are located immediately east of the passenger terminals, and mostly sees transport operations such as those to move the President and his government. Look out for a preserved Douglas DC-3 just outside the base.

The Observation Deck is accessed upstairs between the domestic and international terminals and signposted clearly. This viewing area has great views over the terminal gates and runway. Photography is through tinted glass unfortunately. There are toilet and refreshment facilities next to the deck. Free to enter.

Near the threshold of runway 10 there is a multi-storey car park (walk along Minzu East Road). The top levels have good views and is perfect for photography.

Air Force One Coffee is a café and restaurant on the north side of the airport, close to the runway. It has an elevated, outdoor viewing area which is good for photography (albeit backlit a lot of the time) and spotting aircraft parked at the terminal and air base. Spotters are welcome, just remember to buy food and drinks.

Taipei Taoyuan

TPE | RCTP

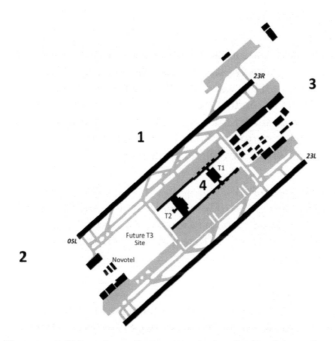

Taoyuan is Taiwan's modern mega-hub, which is located 25 miles west of the city and the original Songshan airport. It is served by airlines from all over the world, with a heavy focus on traffic from the Far East. Almost 45 million passengers used the airport in 2017, with 246,000 aircraft movements.

The airport has a pair of parallel runways, the northerly of which was opened in 2015. In between you'll find the airport's two passenger terminals, with gates facing both runways. A third terminal is expected to open in 2020 which will greatly expand the airport's passenger capacity.

Taoyuan is also one of the world's busiest cargo hubs, with areas to the north and south of the terminals used by freighters. There are also maintenance bases and hangars for based and visiting airlines.

Spotting Locations

1 Miracle Café

On the north side of the airfield you'll find the "Miracle" Café, named due to it narrowly escaping damage when an Airbus A300 crashed alongside. It has views over the northern side of the airfield, and from its rooftop you can take acceptable photographs from afternoon till sunset. The cafe is situated on highway 15 road running along the northern perimeter, with parking outside the EMC car garage which uses the same building.

2 Runway 05L Sports Park

You'll need to drive to this location, which is close to highway 15 and next to the approach path to runway 05L. You have good photographic opportunities. There is a car park at the sports field which you can use.

3 Runway 23 approach

At the north eastern end of the airport there are locations which are good for runway 23L and R arrivals depending on the time of day. It's best to drive there, where you'll find the bridge over the river (Hangxiang Road), next to the DoDoHome Parking. Continue on and there's an old road you can also use. Find somewhere safe to park, and move on if asked.

4 Terminal Viewing Decks

Recently opened, these two viewing decks are situated on the north and south sides of Terminal 2 and offer an elevated position for spotting and photographing movements (through the fence).

Spotting Hotel

Hotel Novotel Taipei Taoyuan Airport

1-1 Terminal South Road, Taoyuan County, Dayuan Township, 337 Taipei | +886 3398 0888 | www.novotel.com The closest hotel to the airport, and situated between the two runways alongside the roads which lead to the terminals. Even numbered rooms on floors 7, 8 and 9 face towards the runway 05L/R thresholds, and as such you can get views of many (but not all) movements depending on the direction in use.

THAILAND

Bangkok Don Mueang

DMK | VTBD

Originally Bangkok's main airport, Don Mueang closed when Suvarnabhumi opened in 2006, but has since grown again as a hub for low cost and domestic flights as a result of overcrowding at the new airport. The country's low-cost airlines are based here, and many other similar carriers fly in.

It now has two terminals – Terminal 1 for international flights, and Terminal 2 for domestic. There is a pair of parallel runways. Incredibly, there is a golf course wedged in between the two runways!

A number of airliners can be found stored to the south of the terminals, and there is a military aviation museum to the east of the airfield (see later). Military movements, including the Royal Thai transport aircraft, add to the interest of visiting this airport. They operate from the base on the eastern side of the airport.

The best place to spot is at the two viewing terraces inside the terminal, split into north and south sections; each section is better depending on the direction of runway use, and you'll need to visit both to see different parts of the airport and distant military aprons. Photography is though glass.

A number of stored aircraft are present at this airport. If you take bus 59 to the stop next to the Bangkok Airways hangar and then walk back to the terminal you will see many of these aircraft.

You can also see the storage area from the multi-storey car park at Jae Leng Plaza.

MUSEUM

Royal Thai Air Force Museum

171 Paholyothin Road, Don Mueang Airport | +66 2 534 1853
Located on the opposite side of the airport to the passenger
terminals. A small museum dedicated to the history of the
Royal Thai Air Force. Aircraft exhibits are mainly military but
of historical interest. Open daily (except holidays) from 9am
to 4pm with free entry.

Travel Between Bangkok Airports

A free shuttle bus links the two airports, operating from early
morning till late at night. At Don Mueang the bus is on the ground
floor at Terminal 1. At Suvarnabhumi the bus is level 2 between
gates 2 and 3.

Bangkok Suvarnabhumi

BKK | VTBS

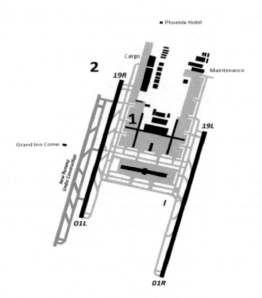

Suvarnabhumi Airport is home to Thai Airways and many other airlines from the country. It is one of Asia's busiest airports, and the diversity of airlines both local and from around the world makes it a real draw for enthusiasts – especially with good spotting locations and hotels to use.

The airport has a large terminal between the parallel runways, which spreads out in various directions, and a new satellite terminal for domestic flights; another parallel runway is planned.

Other areas of note at Suvarnabhumi include the maintenance base for Thai Airways, and a large freight facility, both north of the main terminal and visible from aircraft when arriving or departing.

Spotting Locations

1. Observation Area

Inside the terminal is an area set aside for watching aircraft, which is signposted. The views are good over the western side of the airport, and photography is possible with a long lens. Having nearby eateries and coffee shop also makes this a comfortable place to watch aircraft. You will not see the whole apron, but most movements will be visible at some point.

2. Western Perimeter

King Kaeo Road runs along the western side airfield, following alongside runway 1L/19R and the planned third runway site. It is possible to walk towards the airport from this road at various locations and take photos of arrivals or log what is visible parked at the passenger and cargo terminals. A long lens is needed. You will probably need to direct a taxi drive to reach the location.

3. Spotting Hotels

See later.

Spotting Hotels

Phoenix Hotel
88 Ladkrabang 7, Ladkrabang Road, Bangkok 10520 | +66 2 737 1446 | www.phoenixhotelbangkok.com The best-known hotel for spotting at Suvarnabhumi airport. Management understand the needs of spotters and will grant access to the rooftop area and balcony facing final approach to runway 19R. The hotel is only 2 miles from the terminal and very affordable. Ask staff and they can provide you with a list of the day's arrivals.

Grand Inn Come Hotel
99 Moo 6 Kingkaew Road, Rachathewa, Bangkok 10540 | +66 2 738 8191 | www.grandinncome-hotel.com A basic but pleasant hotel situated alongside the airport perimeter to the west. Top floor rooms overlook runway 19R/01L, with 541 reported as having great views. Most movements can be seen and tied up with SBS or flight tracker websites. Photography is possible if you have a long lens and can cope with the heat haze.

Chiang Mai International

CNX | VTCC

The busiest airport in northern Thailand, with a significant presence by Bangkok Airways and Thai AirAsia. Most flights are domestic, but international services are also operated by Asiana, Cathay Dragon, China Eastern, EVA Air, Hainan Airlines, Korean Air, Qatar Airways, Scoot, Sichuan Airlines and Spring Airlines among others. Flights to China are among the most common.

A Royal Thai Air Force Douglas DC-3 is based at the airport, usually parked near the end of runway 18.

The airport has a single north-south runway, with a passenger terminal on the eastern side. A footbridge crossing the main road running past the southern end of the airport is a great place to watch movements, and photograph arrivals on runway 36.

Khon Kaen

KKC | VTUK

A small regional airport with links to Bangkok from the country's domestic and low cost carriers. There is a small terminal and just one runway, 03/21. Views are possible of the runway and apron from the car park next to the terminal.

Koh Samui

USM | VTSM

A fairly busy airport serving the island of the same in the Gulf of Thailand. It has a single runway which aircraft must backtrack on due to the lack of parallel taxiway. Traffic is made up mainly leisure and low cost carriers flying to destinations in Thailand, Singapore, China and Malaysia.

There is a great spot just to the south of the terminal where you can park for free and get good views over the runway and terminal apron.

Phuket

HKT | VTSP

Phuket is one of Thailand's busiest airports thanks to the island's thriving holiday resorts. Traffic comes from Europe, the Middle East, Australia and the Far East, as well as from across Thailand. It is a mix of scheduled, low-cost and charters, with many wide body aircraft visiting. The busiest season is between November and March.

The airport spans a narrow point at the northern part of the island, with a single runway 09/27, and three terminals crowded round a parking apron at the western end. Nai Yang Beach and the Andaman Sea forms the western boundary. A smoker's terrace airside in the international terminal has good views.

Nai Yang Beach is one of the most popular places to spot from. Photographers love the proximity to aircraft landing and the stunning location. It is only good if aircraft are landing on runway 09, however. To reach the beach, the nearest parking is along Soi Mai Khao 6, to the north of the airport. You'll then need to walk around half a mile along the path (or hire a scooter taxi).

Spotting Hotels

Centara Grand West Sands Resort
Soi Mai Khao 4, Mai Khao, Thalang, Phuket 83110 | +66 76 372 000 | www.centarahotelsresorts.com A family resort hotel located close to Phuket Airport with great amenities and nearby beach. Some rooms have balconies and views of the airport apron and runway approach. Jonathan Payne, the Executive Assistant Manager, is keen to accommodate the needs of spotters. Call ahead to make a request for a room with the best views.

The Sixteenth – Naiyang Beach Resort
19/16, Mu1, Saku, Thalang, Phuket 83110 | +66 76 530 187 8 | www.the16naiyanghotel.com A new hotel a few minutes from the airport (with a free shuttle). Rooms are clean and air conditioned, and the hotel has a rooftop pool bar area which looks over the airport, with most parking stands visible. Single rooms face west towards the parking area, whilst twin rooms face east.

TURKEY

Antalya

AYT | LTAI

Antalya is a busy and very popular holiday airport in Turkey. It has featured on the radar of enthusiasts in recent years for its combination of good weather and interesting tourist flights from across Europe and, in particular, Middle East, Russia and the CIS.

The airport has three parallel runways, with three small terminals; one in the centre, and the other two at the north side of the airport.

Many spotters choose to base themselves at the Lara Hotel which is good for monitoring all movements and even taking photographs.

Just outside Terminal 2 is an area used by buses at the departures level. You have a view across to the eastern runway and taxiways from here, and photography is good in the late afternoon and evening. Some spotters also choose to watch aircraft arrivals on the airport approach road, near the IC Hotel, and also from an area of waste ground on the eastern perimeter, off Havaalan-Lara Yolu road.

Spotting Hotel
Lara Hotel
Güzeloba Mh., Antalya | +90 242 349 2930 | www.larakaprisotel.com Away from the tourist resort hotels, the Lara is still a comfortable and affordable place to stay on the cliffs to the south of the airport. All rooms face the sea, with balconies, and aircraft approaching can be seen on either side, depending on the runway in use. Additionally, the pool area is also a good place to

watch aircraft, but you may need to use an SBS to tie up some – especially if departing over the hotel towards the sea.

Dalaman Airport

DLM | LTBS

Dalaman is a busy tourist gateway to the coast of south-western Turkey. It is at its busiest from March to October, and at other times only has a handful of domestic and leisure flights.

The roads between and around the two terminals have views of some parts of the main apron. Some aircraft park remote, which makes them more visible.

If aircraft are arriving from the north, the point where the airport road meets the road from the beech is a good spot to watch aircraft. There are not many places to park, but people often congregate here.

If arrivals are from the south, follow the road down to the beach where aircraft will pass low overhead and you shouldn't have much difficulty spotting and photographing.

Istanbul Airport

IST | LTFM

Turkey's flagship new airport to serve the capital Istanbul. It was built to replace Ataturk Airport, and to operate alongside Sabiha Gokcen. Ultimately this new airport has plans to be among the biggest and busiest in the world, working with the ambitious Turkish Airlines to create an East-West transfer point linking more worldwide cities than any other.

The airport initially opened with two runways and a main passenger terminal capable of handling 90 million passenger per year. However, over the coming decade a further two runways and expanded terminal will be constructed to help realise its full potential.

The airport is situated 35km north of the city, on the European side. It is currently on the road network, but will soon be linked to Istanbul's Metro network for easy access.

No official spotting locations exist. There are some views from the multi-storey car park, and if aircraft are approaching from the north, the beach at Arnavutköy is less than two miles out.

Inside the airport, there are good views around gates B13 and D17.

Istanbul Sabiha Gökçen

SAW | LTFJ

The secondary airport for Istanbul. Traditionally a low-cost hub, this airport is the home base of Pegasus Airlines, and is also a hub for AnadoluJet. It handles over 30 million passenger per year, making it quite busy. The new second runway and terminal expansions will see it grow further.

The passenger terminal is in the north-east corner of the airport, while to the south are maintenance hangars and a collection of stored and retired airliners which can usually be seen from aircraft windows or the departure lounge at a distance.

Unfortunately there are no good viewing locations at Sabiha Gokcen unless you have a ticket to go airside, where you can view aircraft from the gates. The streets to the west of the airport can be a place to watch arrivals.

Izmir Adnan Menderes

ADB | LTBJ

The fifth busiest airport in Turkey in terms of passengers, with modern new domestic and international terminals opened in 2014 and 2006 respectively. Izmir is a hub for Corendon Airlines, Pegasus, and SunExpress, with a lot of seasonal holiday traffic from across Europe during the summer.

This airport has two runways, although one is mostly used as a taxiway. It has a small military base on the south-eastern side, with the passenger terminals on the western side.

To the north of the airport there is a spot near Sarnıç train station which is good for watching and photographing arrivals from the north. You can catch the train from the airport terminal which is one stop away. Walk from the station towards a small go-kart track.

Similarly, if aircraft are arriving from the south you can spot near Cumaovasi train station, which is one stop south from the airport.

UNITED ARAB EMIRATES

Abu Dhabi International

AUH | OMAA

This is the capital of the UAE, and the home base of Etihad Airways. The airport has two parallel runways. The long overdue new Midfield Terminal is still expected to open in the coming years. This will replace the three current smaller terminals which are not up to standard for the growth prospects of Etihad and other carriers.

As with elsewhere in the country, spotting is not understood nor encouraged, and extreme caution must be taken when viewing or taking pictures of aircraft. It is highly likely that you will be questioned, and may be arrested.

The Yas Marina Formula 1 racing track sits under the approach to runways 13R/L and photography is possible from here. Alternatively, there are spots at the opposite 31R/L end of the runway off the E11 motorway, but you are more likely to attract attention here.

Spotting Hotel

Premier Inn Abu Dhabi Airport
Opposite Terminals 1 & 3 - Abu Dhabi International Airport - Abu Dhabi | +971 600 500503 This hotel is linked via a walkway to the terminal at Abu Dhabi (soon to be replaced by the new midefield terminal). It has a rooftop pool area with good views over the nearby taxiways, runway and some parking areas. Try for an odd-numbered room in the x13-x19 range for a similar view on the upper floors. Photography is not permitted on the rooftop, and discretion is advised when spotting.

Dubai Al Maktoum International

DWC | OMDW

Dubai World Central / Al Maktoum is a growing hub, but still relatively quiet. You'll find it around 45km from Dubai.

Eventually it will have five runways and three passenger terminals. Today it is growing as a freight hub, and handles passenger flights by some Middle East and low cost airlines such as Aeroflot, flydubai, Pobeda and Wizz Air, plus seasonal summer charters.

The Dubai Air Show is now held here every other year, which makes it easier to visit the airport. Otherwise spotting is quite difficult, with the large cargo aprons spread far apart and a long distance from the small (at present) passenger terminal. If you have a car, you can explore the roads leading to the different areas, but must not stop and draw attention to yourself. With expansion happening at a steady pace, the situation will change a lot over the coming years.

Dubai International

DXB | OMDB

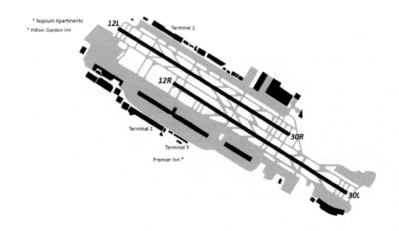

Dubai has grown into one of the busiest aviation hubs in the world in a very short time, thanks mainly to the phenomenal growth of based carrier Emirates Airline. Its far-reaching route network uses Dubai as a transit point between the east and west.

There are three terminals – Terminal 1 on the south/west side with concourses C and D. Emirates and most of the main airlines at Dubai use this terminal.

Terminal 2 is on the north/east side of the site and is home to flydubai and many Middle Eastern, low-cost and charter airlines. There is also an executive terminal next to Terminal 2.

Terminal 3 is alongside Terminal 1 and uses concourses A, B and C. It is home to Emirates and Qantas.

Dubai International has a pair of parallel runways, 12L/30R and 12R/30L.

Spotting at Dubai has always been fairly difficult due to the lack of specific locations around the airport and perimeter, and the general security presence which exists at Middle East airports. Anyone caught waving cameras and binoculars at aircraft will likely be asked to stop or taken for questioning. Therefore, when plane spotting in Dubai it is best to be discrete and use the safety of a hotel with views. You can also spot discretely from certain airside areas within the terminals.

The best locations are either the spotting hotels nearby (see later), or the airside departure lounges for those with flight tickets.

Spotting Hotels
Hilton Garden Inn Dubai Al Muraqabat
Abu Baker Al Siddique Rd - Dubai | +971 4 609 7000 | www.hilton. com Located in the Deira district a mile or so from Terminal 1. It is in a similar place to the old Sheraton Deira, with similar views of aircraft on approach to the 12L/R runways, but slightly more to

the side which makes photography easier (with a 300mm lens). There is a rooftop pool area, and rooms facing north will have a similar view. Aim for rooms 501-503, 601-603 or 701-703.

Nojoum Hotel Apartments

Abubaker Al Siddique Road, Dubai, United Arab Emirates | +971 4 265 8888 | www.nojoumsuites.com The Nojoum has rooms facing the approach to the airport at a more side-on angle, similar to the Hilton Garden Inn. Ask for a room on at least the fifth floor for the best views. Rooms have balconies, which are useful for private spotting without worrying about equipment. The hotel also has a rooftop pool area which can be used for spotting.

Premier Inn Dubai Airport

Opposite Terminal 3 - Dubai | +971 600 500503 | www.premierinn. com The Premier Inn is alongside Terminal 3 and has a rooftop terrace which overlooks the airport terminal area and many of the gates. If you get a good room, you have similar views. Try for even-numbered rooms in the range 402-414 (or on the floor below). The runways are distant beyond, but with flight tracking websites you can tie up most movements. Photography is possible of aircraft around the terminals, providing guests are discreet. Room windows open to allow lenses out.

Sharjah International

SHJ | OMSJ

This airport was once a draw for any enthusiasts visiting Dubai. It is only a short drive away, and would usually be crammed full of old Russian and classic Western workhorses such as the IL-76, IL-18 and Boeing 707. What's more, airside photography tours were easy to organise. Today, Sharjah has grown up into more of a passenger hub and is a major base for Air Arabia. Other airlines also fly from across the Middle East, and cargo flights are very common from most of the big players and some local companies.

It is still worth a visit since some of these carriers are pretty unusual to enthusiasts, and are different to those seen at Dubai. There are also still some stored aircraft at the airport. However, most interesting movements are at night and the airside tours are now a thing of the past.

Spotting Locations:

1. Sharjah National Park
Just off the main road as it passes the airport is the Sharjah National Park, which is opposite the end of runway 30. You can park up here (there is a small fee) and climb up the grass mound for good photography opportunities.

2. Gas Station
A gas (petrol) station just north of the airport entrance on the main road is next to the airport fence, and a small wall allows you to look over at part of the cargo aprons. Be discrete here.

UNITED KINGDOM

Birmingham Airport

BHX | EGBB

The airport gateway to England's second city has a number of based low cost airlines, and ever more long-haul links. Aside from the heavy presence of Jet2, Ryanair and TUI, other carriers of note include Emirates with at least one daily Airbus A380, Qatar Airways, Air India, Pakistan International, Turkish, Turkmenistan Airlines and Wizz Air. Europe's full service carriers are also well represented, including Aer Lingus, Air France, Brussels Airlines, KLM, Lufthansa, Swiss and Scandinavian Airlines.

Birmingham's modern terminal occupies the south western portion of the site, with two piers. Across the runway is the former Elmdon Airport and its historic terminal. Today biz jets and cargo airliners park here, alongside maintenance hangars.

The airport provides an official viewing area in the Long Stay Car Park alongside the runway 33 threshold and taxiway. There are benches and a good view of aircraft movements through the fence, and shortly before touchdown. Follow signs from the terminal.

Bristol Airport

BRS | EGGD

Bristol is the UK's tenth busiest airport. It has a single runway and a modern passenger terminal which is a hub for easyJet, Loganair, Ryanair and TUI Airways.

A dedicated spotting area exists at the Bristol and Wessex Aeroplane Club on the south side of the airport. Following the perimeter road from the terminal to the 'Silver Zone Car Park' and then find the club signposted. Views from the café here look across the runway to the terminal area.

East Midlands Airport

EMA | EGNX

East Midlands is probably the UK's most notable cargo airport. It successfully transitioned from a quiet regional airport into a hub for cargo airlines such as DHL and UPS. These now serve the airport daily alongside their partners, such as West Atlantic and Star Air. This is not to belittle the airport as a passenger base, with airlines such as Ryanair, Jet2, and TUI all offering services.

Cargo flights operate mostly at night between 2100-0200 from Sunday to Friday. During the daytime you will only likely see a few DHL aircraft parked up, although there are usually more evident on Saturdays. UPS and Star Air aircraft usually park on the eastern cargo ramp, whilst others use the large dedicated DHL ramp at the western end of the airport.

Spotting Locations

1. Castle Donington Crash Gate

Most spotters congregate at the crash gate on the northern side of the airfield as it is an accepted place to spot and offers the best views of all movements. To reach the gate, head to the village of Castle Donington. Close to the Aeropark museum (see later), there's a pub with a small road next to it (Diseworth Road, postcode DE74 2PS). This road leads to the crash gate. You can see the passenger terminal and DHL apron, and all runway movements. It is good for photography through holes in the fence and once aircraft are above the fence line. You can also

293

wander along the path which extends along the airport's northern boundary from here.

2. Hangar Area
From the airport's long stay car parks and access roads near DHL, you can drive to an area among the hangars which will yield any aircraft receiving maintenance, as well as some executive and light aircraft. You can photograph them through the fence, but don't stay too long in this area. Head for Dakota Road (postcode DE74 2TL).

Edinburgh Airport

EDI | EGPH

Scotland's busiest airport. Edinburgh Airport has grown significantly in recent years, managing to grow its full service, low cost and cargo services. Key operators of interest to the enthusiast include Air Canada Rouge, American Airlines, Atlantic Airways, Delta, Emirates, Etihad Airways, Norwegian, Qatar Airways, Turkish Airlines, United Airlines and Vueling.

A busy cargo operation is in action at night, with early morning the busiest time for the airport as waves of night-stopping aircraft depart.

The passenger terminal occupies a central position on the airport site, with the main runway to the north. The secondary runway 12/30 was closed in 2018. There is a busy cargo base to the east.

A 15 minute walk west of the passenger terminal is a large open air car park which fronts the perimeter fence alongside the taxiway and runway 06 threshold. Head for the Holiday Inn Express hotel and continue past it.

Farnborough Airport

FAB | EGLF

Most famous for its biennial air show, Farnborough has been the cradle for aviation development and testing in Britain for a long time. The airport is a busy hub for biz jets bringing their owners to London and the South East, making it particularly attractive to enthusiasts.

The cul-de-sac alongside the FAST Museum, Rae Road (postcode GU14 6XE) is more or less in line with runway 24. You can look along its length, and approaching aircraft will pass very low overhead. Walk a little along the main road to get a good vantage point, or read off (with strong binoculars) aircraft parked up on the north side.

At the 06 end of the runway is a distinctive iron bridge off the main A323 Fleet Road. It is technically on Laffan's Road (postcode GU11 2HL) and has a small area for parking. This location has great views of aircraft arriving and departing runway 06, and of departures off 24. You can see aircraft parked on some of the ramps, but not all.

Glasgow Airport

GLA | EGPF

Glasgow's main airport is a busy gateway to Scotland, with many domestic, European and long-haul links. Interesting island hopping services to the extremes of Scotland are a regular feature here.

The passenger terminal sits to the south of the single runway and has three piers. There are no real views from the terminal unless you have a flight ticket, so it's best to head to one of the locations around the perimeter.

From the terminal head under the M8 and then turn left onto Abbotsinch Road. This passes the Loganair hangars, cargo area and FBOs on the eastern side, so it's worth exploring before continuing along the road until you find a layby on the left which looks out to the threshold of runway 23. Aircraft can be photographed landing but you may wish to walk back along the road to find a better view of aircraft on the ground.

Also from the terminal head west for Barnsford Road/A726 (postcode PA3 2TQ) which loops around the end of runway 05. A crash gate adjacent to the threshold is popular, but there's only space for one car to park. A footpath along the road helps you find a good spot to view and photograph through the fence.

Kemble Cotswold

GBA | EGBP

Kemble Cotswold Airport is a few miles to the south west of Cirencester in Gloucestershire. It is a busy general aviation airport, and well known to enthusiasts as one of the UK's main storage airports. At any point there may be 20 or more airliners up to Boeing 747 size in storage or being slowly parted out. You will also see a preserved Bristol Britannia and some Hawker Hunter aircraft, with a VFW-614 sometimes visible inside a hangar.

All aircraft are visible from the café/restaurant near the control tower, however it's easier to identify and photograph airliners on the different ramps if you have a car and can explore the perimeter. In particular, the A429 has places to stop and look through the fence.

Liverpool John Lennon

LPL | EGGP

Too close to Manchester to become a major airport, Liverpool competes well in the low cost market as a base for both easyJet and Ryanair. It also handles summer leisure flights, regional flights and some cargo flights.

Dungeon Lane and the flying school car park at the eastern end of the airport are the best places to watch aircraft, especially if approaching from this direction.

The old Speke airport site to the north west of the current airport still has its preserved terminal building (now a hotel) and a section of apron upon which some heritage airliners are being preserved.

London City

LCY | EGLC

At the heart of London's Docklands is the tiny London City Airport. Despite its size and short runway (which necessitates a steep approach) this is a busy hub and even has daily transatlantic services using British Airways' dedicated Airbus A318 aircraft. Other carriers include Aer Lingus, Alitalia, Eastern Airways, KLM Cityhopper, LOT Polish Airlines, Lufthansa, Luxair, Swiss International and TAP Air Portugal. A biz jet apron is to the west of the terminal.

The airport is currently expanding its terminal and airside infrastructure.

Opposite the airport there is a walkway running the length of the runway with great views. From here you will see every movement, and be able to read off aircraft parked at the terminal. Head for Royal Albert Way, off the A1020, or walk 20 minutes across the

Connaught Bridge from the terminal; it is also the Royal Albert stop on the DLR.

London Gatwick

LGW | EGKK

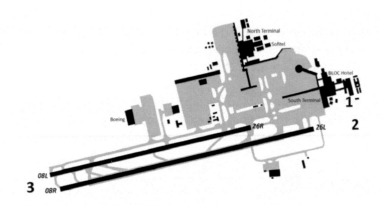

Gatwick is the country's second busiest airport. It is situated to the south of London at Crawley. Whilst it is the world's busiest single-runway airport operation, you'll note that a second runway (08L/26R) does exist, albeit acting as a taxiway except when the main strip is out of operation. There are plans to bring this into use as a main runway.

British Airways retains a healthy presence at Gatwick, operating short, medium and long-haul services with a dedicated fleet that will not usually be seen on an average visit to Heathrow. Additionally, many leisure and low-cost airlines operate from here, with a few airlines not seen at Heathrow.

Gatwick has two terminals – North and South. The North Terminal is home to easyJet and Virgin Atlantic, and has a unique passenger bridge over the taxiway with airliners passing below. British Airways is based in the South Terminal.

A new facility at the western side of the airport is operated by Boeing Flight Services handling maintenance on airliners. A smaller British Airways maintenance hangar is on the south side of the runways.

Sadly Gatwick lost its excellent viewing terrace long ago. Gatwick has since proved a very frustrating airport for the enthusiast. For those with a flight ticket, the sports bar in the South Terminal is an excellent place to watch the movements, as is a suitable room at the BLOC Hotel.

Spotting Locations

1. Multi-Storey Car Park
The top level of the Blue Multi-Storey car park 1 outside the South Terminal is a nice spot for logging aircraft on short finals to Runway 26L. Facing into the sun is not ideal, however. Signs at this location indicate that spotters are not welcome to loiter, and security will often move you on. A similar view exists from the platforms of the railway station.

2. Runway 26L Approach
From the Multi-Storey Car Park, spotters are often encouraged to go downstairs to a perimeter road/path running past the runway 26 approach lights. Previously you could go through the doors to Concorde House, down the stairs, through the door and then walk along the path. However, some recent reports state going through Concorde House is not possible, so you need to make your way downstairs in the terminal, following signs for Lost Property, then out through the tunnel leading to the path. From here you can see all movements approaching runway 26 or departing 08, but can see little of aircraft on the ground.

3. Runway 08R

Following Charlwood Road and Lowfield Heath Road (postcode RH11 0QB) around the end of Runway 08R leads to a crash gate which is close to aircraft lining up on the runway. It is possible to photograph or log aircraft, including those on short final to land. This is the most popular spot for spotters these days, however parking is not allowed near the gate itself so you will need to walk to reach it. You can also get the free bus to Purple Parking and walk the remaining distance.

4. Spotting Hotels
For a somewhat easier time spotting at Gatwick, try one of the hotels and their best rooms for views. See below.

Hotels

BLOC Hotel
South Terminal Gatwick Airport, RH6 0NP | +44 20 3051 0101 | www.blochotels.com Situated atop the South Terminal, the BLOC Hotel is a great place to spot if you have a room facing the airport. It has similar views to the old viewing terrace. Depending on the room you will usually have a view of both terminals and much of the runway.

Sofitel London Gatwick Airport
North Terminal, Gatwick Airport RH6 0PH | +44 1293 567070 | www.sofitel.com Smart hotel situated at the North Terminal, and linked via monorail from the South Terminal. Rooms on the higher floors facing the airport, such as 898, have unrivalled views of aircraft movements to both terminals.

Travel Between London Airports

National Express coaches run between Heathrow and Gatwick airports multiple times per hour. This is cheaper and quicker than going into the city and taking a train.

London City Airport can be reached on the Docklands Light Railway (DLR) which connects to a number of London Underground stations.

London Stansted has a rail link from London Liverpool Street Station, which is connected to the Underground.

London Heathrow

LHR | EGLL

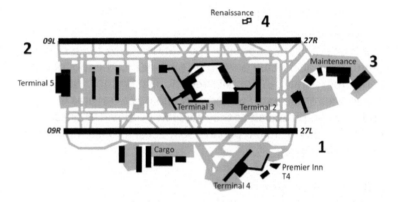

Heathrow is Europe's busiest airport. It offers fantastic variety of airliners and steady stream of movements from all corners of the globe. It is the operating and maintenance base for both British Airways and Virgin Atlantic, and features as a destination for many world carriers.

Heathrow has two parallel runways, 09L/27R and 09R/27L. Patterns of runway assignment between landing and departing switch at 3pm every day. In the central area is Terminal 2, which opened in 2014 for Star Alliance carriers, Terminal 3 which is the oldest and due for redevelopment. Terminal 5, for British Airways and Iberia flights, is to the west, whilst Terminal 4 is located to the

south east of the runways. Cargo aircraft park to the south, and maintenance areas are to the east.

Heathrow sees large numbers of Airbus A380s, A350s and Boeing 787s amongst the airlines flying in. Cargo carriers are quite limited, with relatively few movements compared to other European hubs.

Free buses run around the perimeter roads and between terminals. You can reach spotting locations 3 and 4 using bus #285 from the central terminal area, or bus #423 from Terminal 5.

Spotting Locations

1. Myrtle Avenue
This is one of the most popular spots at Heathrow, but is only useful when aircraft are landing on runway 27L. The spot gets its name from a small residential street close to Hatton Cross, with a grass area at the end. Spotters congregate on this area to log and photograph aircraft as they pass low overhead. There are no facilities and very limited parking, so it's best to walk from Hatton Cross Tube Station.

2. Runway 09L Approach
Stanwell Moor Road runs the length of the western perimeter of the airport, behind Terminal 5. At its northern end. Park by the side of the road at your own risk. Aircraft pass low overhead on approach to runway 09L, and are also visible approaching 09R (but it's hard to photograph these).

3. Runway 27R Approach
A walk along the Eastern Perimeter Road can help you find a good spot to watch arrivals on 27R. Security patrols regularly monitor this area and ask spotters to stay a few metres from the fence. You can take good photographs here of arrivals, but can't see any other parts of the airport.

4. Academy/Renaissance Hotel

Even if you're not staying in the Renaissance Hotel, the car park next to it was formerly the home of the Heathrow Visitors Centre. Today it is the Heathrow Academy and has an enthusiast's shop. From here you can get good views of all movements on the northern runway (09L/27R) from a small grandstand. It is not the best place for photographs. This spot is located off the Northern Perimeter Road (postcode TW6 2AP).

Spotting Hotels

Renaissance London Heathrow
140 Bath Road, Hounslow TW6 2AQ | +44 20 88 97 63 63 | www.marriott.com This is one of the best spotting hotels in the world. Request a room overlooking the airport (you sometimes have to pay more). All movements on the northern runway can be read off and photographed easily, but lower floors have lamp posts and the fence in the way. Movements around the terminals are easy to spot. Those using flight tracking websites can continue to spot throughout the night. Although this hotel is not the cheapest at Heathrow, the quality of spotting makes up for it and it offers special spotter packages through its website.

Premier Inn Terminal 4
Sheffield Rod, Heathrow TW6 3AF | +44 (0) 333 234 6600 | www.premierinn.com A relatively new hotel, situated near the entrance to Terminal 4 on the south eastern corner of the airport, close to Hatton Cross and the Myrtle Avenue spotting location. Rooms on the 6th and 7th floor facing the runway have excellent views of aircraft using runway 27L, with Terminal 2 and runway 27R in the distance. Photography possible through two sets of double glazing. You won't miss much here.

London Luton

LTN | EGGW

Luton is London's fourth largest airport, and is situated some 30 miles north of the capital near the main M1 motorway. It is a busy gateway for low cost carriers and holiday charter airlines, and the home base of easyJet and TUI. Ryanair and Wizz Air also have a heavy presence. A number of cargo airliners pass through each day.

Luton is perhaps best known amongst enthusiasts for the large variety of business jets which pass through on a regular basis. The airport has many ramps and hangars dedicated to this traffic, which can be a little difficult to navigate around and see everything, but there are always plenty to see including some unusual visitors.

Luton has a cramped and confusing central area which includes the terminals, car parks, roads, hotels and administration buildings.

Driving around the access roads to the hangars, cargo centre and other parts of the central complex gives a glimpse of many business jets and other aircraft parked around the various aprons. Signs discourage spotters from parking in these areas, so make only quick stops to log what you can see. You can park at the Holiday Inn for the nearer ramps and walk around the central area.

The newer multi-storey car park near the terminal has views from the top level. This is a useful place for seeing airliners at the terminal, and aircraft on the runway. There is also a crash gate on the southern perimeter with good views of the runway.

Spotting Hotel

Holiday Inn Express Luton Airport
2 Percival Way, Luton LU2 9GP | +44 871 902 1622 | www.ihg.com
Rooms facing the airport are all great for logging aircraft on the

runway and some taxiways, and also have plenty of opportunities for good photographs. If you're facing the other direction you have a view of part of the passenger and corporate parking areas.

London Southend

SEN | EGMC

Southend Airport is fast becoming a major London airport. In recent years, under new management, the airport has focussed more on passenger services having attracted the likes of easyJet to boost the number of passengers passing through its new terminal building and runway extension. However, the companies focusing on aircraft maintenance and storage still exist and exploring the north side service roads usually uncovers a few interesting airframes.

The southern part of the passenger terminal car parks have views across the ramp and of some of the stored airliners, as does the access road if you walk along it.

London Stansted

STN | EGSS

Stansted is a fairly busy airport 30 miles north east of London. It is a hub for easyJet, Jet2 and Ryanair, and a number of other low-cost airlines have a decent presence, including Eurowings. Many charter and cargo airlines can also be found operating through Stansted on a daily basis.

Stansted has a single runway, with passenger terminal and cargo centre on the eastern side, and the area to the north west used extensively for a private jets and corporate visitors. There's usually a lot of interesting aircraft parked here, however recently the decision has been made to ban spotters from using this area to log aircraft. This is frustrating, as many of the aircraft parked in this area are worth seeing, and the majority of spotters would not cause any obstruction or danger by quickly logging there. Fines are likely to be issued if you do use this area.

There are two good spotting hotels near the terminal (the Hampton by Hilton and the Radisson Blu) which have good views of the aprons and action.

On the north side of the airfield is a viewing area alongside the fence along Belmer Road. To reach it use postcode CM24 8UL). It gives distant views of the passenger and cargo terminals, but all runway movements are easy to see, with photography through the fence.

Manchester Airport

MAN | EGCC

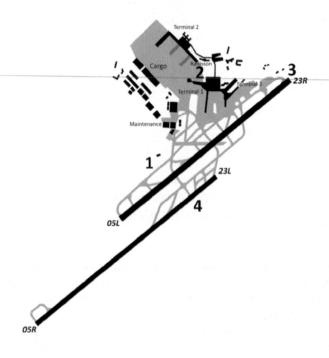

Manchester is one of the favourite airports in the UK for aviation enthusiasts thanks to its excellent viewing facilities and varied mix of movements. The airport can be busy at certain times of the day, particularly in the summer months.

Although traditionally the domain of charter airlines, Manchester has now become very busy with low cost airlines and a growing stable of long-haul flights with American Airlines, Cathay Pacific, Delta, Emirates, Ethiopian Airlines, Etihad, Hainan Airlines, PIA, Qatar Airways, United and Virgin Atlantic.

Manchester Airport has three passenger terminals and a cargo terminal, along with an extensive maintenance area comprising large hangars and bays. Terminal 2 is currently being expanded into a 'mega terminal', with parts of Terminal 1 to be demolished eventually. The airport has two parallel runways, with the newer 05R/23L used only in peak periods.

Spotting Locations

1. Runway Visitor Park
What was one of the best official viewing facilities in the UK, the Runway Visitor Park, is located on the north side of Runway 05L/23R at Manchester. Until recently purpose-built mounds to raise the enthusiast over the height of the fence allowed better photography, but these have recently been lost thanks to a new private terminal being built alongside. Aircraft pass very close by this park, however you are facing into the sun much of the day. Also at the RVP is an aviation shop, café, toilets and various preserved airliners – some of which are open to the public. These include a DC-10 section, British Airways Concorde, Trident, Nimrod and Avro RJX. The park is open daily (except 25/26 December) from 8am till dusk (4pm in winter, 6pm in spring/autumn, 8pm in summer). The entrance fee is for cars, depending on how long you stay. Bus #200 links the RVP with the terminals. Those on foot/bike enter free. www.runwayvisitorpark.co.uk

2. Multi-Storey Car Park

For many years the top level of the Short Stay Car Park outside Terminal 1 was one of the main spotting locations. It is still a popular stop off as it offers fantastic views over the cargo and maintenance ramps, as well as Terminal 2, parts of Terminal 1 – much of which can not be seen from other spotting locations. Spotting and photography are still good from the car park's open roof. It can be expensive to park here for long.

3. The Airport Pub

Located at the threshold of Runway 23R. The beer garden here backs up to the taxiway and holding point for the runway and is ideal for landing shots. A very pleasant summer afternoon can be held here, with food and refreshments on tap. This is a 15 minute walk from terminals 1/3. See www.airport.pub

4. South Side

A favourite for the photographers is a spot on the south side of the airport, alongside runway 23L/05R. Instead of turning into the Runway Visitor Park, continue along Wilmslow Road (A538) and through the tunnels underneath the runways. Immediately afterwards, turn left at the roundabout onto Altrincham Road. Park here, or in the adjacent hotel car park, then follow the footpath towards the perimeter fence. The sun is in a good position and the airliners are very close for fantastic photographs!

Spotting Hotel

Radisson Blu Manchester Airport
Chicago Avenue, Manchester M90 3RA | +44 161 490 5000 | www. radissonhotels.com The best hotel for spotting at Manchester. Located behind Terminal 2, rooms on high floors overlook the aprons and the runways in the distance. The restaurant also offers the same view. Some good opportunities for photographs with a long lens.

UNITED STATES OF AMERICA
ALABAMA

Birmingham-Shuttlesworth International

BHM | KBHM

Alabama's busiest airport, Birmingham-Shuttlesworth can be found a few miles to the north-east of the downtown area. It has two runways, and is a joint civil-military base, with the Birmingham Air National Guard Base occupying the area north of the main runway 06/24.

Air traffic is dominated by Delta and Southwest Airlines mainline aircraft, with Delta Connection, American Eagle and United Express regional jets also prevalent. The central passenger terminal consists of three main concourses. Both FedEx Express and UPS send daily freighter aircraft in, which park on a ramp to the south-west of the terminal. The ANG base is home to a KC-135 tanker wing.

FBOs occupy small ramps and hangars along the northern and eastern sides of the airport, and the Southern Museum of Flight (www.southernmuseumofflight.org) is also on the eastern side.

The terminal has views in the central area once you've passed through security.

Outside you can get a good view from the top level of the parking garage. East Lake Road, which runs along the northern perimeter, is also a useful spot to watch movements and see some of the biz jets parked nearby.

Huntsville International

HSV | KHSV

Huntsville is a busy cargo hub for Atlas Air and its partners, plus carriers such as FedEx Express, Cargolux, Panalpina and UPS. The cargo apron is on the eastern side of the airport.

The top level of the car park behind the terminal is good for watching movements on the runways and around the terminal. You'll need a strong lens for photography.

ALASKA

Anchorage Lake Hood Seaplane Base

LHD | PALH

The world's busiest seaplane base. It is located a stone's throw from Ted Stevens International, so can easily be combined in a spotting trip. The seaplane base comprises a central lake, with aircraft parking ramps all around and easily explored by walking around.

A small gravel strip exists to the north east, and a taxiway links Lake Hood to Ted Stevens airport on its western side.

Fairbanks International

FAI | PAFA

Fairbanks is not as busy as Anchorage for airliner movements, but it is a gateway to the vast Alaskan interior and sees a mouth-watering mix of aircraft movements. In particular, there are still a good number of old piston airliners here, many in storage in the southern part of the airport. Everts Air is based here and always provides an interesting aircraft movement.

On the eastern side of the airport is a large general aviation parking ramp. Drive along University Ave S and stop to log what you can see. Follow the road south to pass the end of the 02L/R runways and then loop back past the Everts Air propliner storage areas towards the terminal. In the centre of the airport are lines of seaplanes which use the lake situated between the regular runways.

Ted Stevens International Anchorage

ANC | PANC

ALASKA

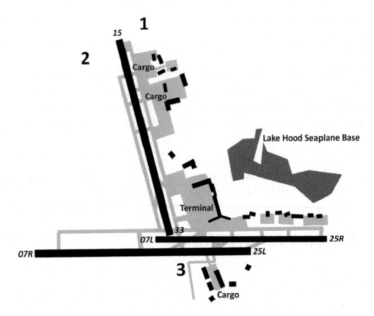

Anchorage Airport is the busiest in Alaska and a major cargo hub. FedEx and UPS base operations here, with many other cargo airlines from Asia, Europe and the USA passing through on their trans-Pacific journeys. Photographers enjoy Point Woronzof on a clear day as their shots have a dramatic backdrop of the city skyline and mountains beyond. This is really special when an Everts Air DC-6 passes in front of the lens!

In addition to the big carriers, Anchorage is a gateway to many of the smaller airfields throughout Alaska, with opportunities to explore one of the last frontiers of aviation. Local carriers like PenAir and Ravn, plus Everts Air Cargo, come and go on local flights each day. For enthusiasts who love light aircraft and seaplanes, the neighbouring Lake Hood seaplane base (see later) is home to hundreds of based light aircraft.

Spotting Locations

1. Cargo Apron
At the northern end of the airport is a spot on rough ground which overlooks a cargo apron. It is also good for photographing aircraft landing on runway 14 or departing from runway 32. You will need to park your car alongside the road and walk along the track to the hill.

2. Point Woronzof
This is the most popular spot for photographers at Anchorage. It overlooks the airport and runway 14/32 with the snow-capped mountains as a backdrop. Follow Northern Lights Blvd along the northern perimeter, and then through the gate with a warning sign if it is open, and park on the dirt. Then walk up the hill for a better view.

3. South Airpark
Driving along Raspberry Road, turn onto South Airpark Pl, follow it as far as possible and park. You can then climb a hill overlooking the southern part of the airport, alongside runways 7L/25R and 7R/25L. You will also be underneath any arrivals on runway 33.

ARIZONA

Davis-Monthan Air Force Base

DMA | KDMA

Davis-Monthan AFB and its associated scrap yard and storage areas are a big draw for aviation enthusiasts. There are over 4,000 aircraft here across a variety of types, from military fighter jets and transports to commercial airliners. The storage site is Aerospace Maintenance And Regeneration Center, or AMARC. Of particular note is the collection of the neighbouring Pima Air and Space Museum (see later). Many spotters choose to take a light aircraft flight over the storage areas from Tucson Airport for the best chance of seeing everything given the vast area and limited access by road.

From the main Valencia Rd artery, turn north onto Wilmot Rd, and then right onto the dirt track Drexel Rd. Along here you will see aircraft on either side of you. Along Wilmot Rd, you will also notice a storage area alongside.

Also from Valencia Rd, turn north on Kolb Rd and you will pass between many more storage areas. On your right, before you reach Irving Rd, are the lines of larger aircraft. Since Kolb is a main road and has embankments on either side, you are best walking along the fence line to see the aircraft. Therefore it's best not to have a car with you. It is a long walk from anywhere.

From the Pima Museum, head west and then turn north on Craycroft Rd. Follow this until Nebraska St. Turn along here and drive to the end. You will come to various areas of aircraft, including DC-3 storage and some airliners. Explore nearby Wyoming St and Rosemont Ave also.

MUSEUM

Pima Air & Space Museum

6000 E Valencia Rd, Tucson, AZ 85706 | +1 520 574 0462 | www.pimaair.org A great museum with hundreds of aircraft preserved, including a Boeing 787 Dreamliner, 777, 707 Air Force One, 737-300, a Sud Caravelle, Douglas DC-7 and lots of military types. Well worth a visit. Open daily 9am to 5pm. Adults $15.50, with concessions for juniors, retired, locals and military. Kids under 6 are free.

Kingman

IGM | KIGM

A storage airport in the Phoenix area which is home to a variety of retired airliners. Most recently it has seen a lot of turboprops and regional airliners in residence, as well as some older Boeing 727s. Kingman is one of the easier storage airports to spot at since you can drive or walk alongside the fence which passes many of the aircraft, hangars and ramps. Flightline Dr is the best place, as it runs the length of the airport.

Marana Pinal Airpark

MZJ | KMZJ

Situated 27 miles to the north of Tucson, off I-10, Marana Pinal Airpark is one of the most significant storage airports in the western United States. Airliners come here for storage and scrapping from all over the world. Although turnover is fairly high, there are some classic airframes which have been here for many years, so it's a good place to catch up with some of the types rarely seen in our skies, like the Boeing 747-200, 767-200, Lockheed TriStar and McDonnell Douglas DC-9/MD-80 series.

For years it was impossible to get close to Marana on the ground as a gatepost refused entry. Today this has been relaxed, so it is possible to drive up to the administration buildings and get some views of the aircraft. Free tours have sometimes been offered to enthusiasts in advance by calling 520-866-6545, subject to availability.

Phoenix Deer Valley

DVT | KDVT

Situated in the north east of the city, this unassuming airport is actually in the top 30 busiest in the world, and claims to be the busiest general aviation airport in the country.

Deer Valley has no airline service, but you don't come here for that. You'll see lots of biz jets and light aircraft. The airport has two parallel runways, and a terminal on the south side. There is an observation deck on top of the terminal and spotting/ photography is fine. Air traffic control is piped through speakers here, but sometimes the haze can make viewing registrations of distant aircraft difficult.

Phoenix Goodyear

GYR | KGYR

Another Arizona storage airport. Goodyear is around 25 miles west of Sky Harbor Airport and the city. It has no airline service, but sees plenty of general aviation activity.

Stored airliners are parked along the northern side of the runway and range in size up to Boeing 747s from carriers around the world. Any aircraft receiving maintenance and attention will be parked around the hangars on the west of the runway. This is a good place to start logging. A little further, the small terminal will have any executive aircraft outside and also has views to the distant storage line.

Bulliard Avenue on the west of the airport is a good place to stop and read the stored airliners off from the fence, but the police will likely question you if they see you.

Phoenix Sky Harbor International

PHX | KPHX

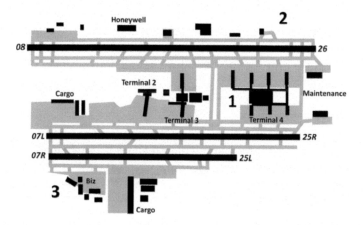

The largest and busiest airport in Arizona, Phoenix Sky Harbor is a sunny hub for the likes of American Airlines and Southwest Airlines. Spotters are generally tolerated here, and it makes an excellent gateway if you're visiting the storage airfields in the state. Views and photographs are fairly easy to come by, and a number of cargo and international airlines pass through the airport (UPS in particular).

Sky Harbor has four parallel runways running east-to-west, with the three passenger terminals in between.

Interesting international carriers include Air Canada Express, British Airways and Volaris. Meanwhile, the south-west corner of the airfield is home to FBOs such as Cutter Aviation, as well as a former FedEx 727 trainer. To the south is the Arizona Air National Guard base, housing the 161st Air Refuelling Wing with KC-135R Stratotankers. Finally, along the northern boundary you'll often see Honeywell's modified Boeing 757 parked up.

Spotting Locations

1. Parking Garage

The top floor of the Terminal 4 parking garage has views over both sides of the airport (although you'll have to walk a fair bit and can't see both at the same time). Photography is possible of aircraft on the ground, and the spot is perfect for noting registrations. Police are usually tolerant of people being here. The garages for terminals 2 and 3 also offer views, and the proximity of the terminals means you can buy food and drink supplies or find air conditioning.

2. North Perimeter

Travelling south on S 40th St from Washington Ave, the road will curve as it reaches the perimeter of the airport. There is an area to park alongside the road, giving you a great view of aircraft landing and departing on runway 26. The area can become a little unsavoury once the sun has set.

3. Old Tower Road

This road leads off from S 24th St near where it passes under I-10. Driving along this road will reveal various ramps on your left, such as the Cutter Ramp and the cargo ramp. Here, you'll log executive aircraft, cargo airliners and some light aircraft. You also have views to the southern runways. It is not advised to loiter here too long.

Tucson International

TUS | KTUS

Tucson International is not as busy as Phoenix for airline service, with mainly commuter flights to various hubs. However, it is also used for airliner storage and maintenance, including a SkyWest Airlines base. The airport also has a wing of the Air National Guard based, with facilities at the northern end of the airport.

The passenger terminal and cargo ramp are on the eastern side of the main runway, 11L/29R. Most stored aircraft are in the north west corner of the airport.

To the north of the passenger terminal is Flightline Drive, which loops past the small executive terminal and parking area. It has some views across the main runway and military side and photography is possible. Similarly, heading south from the terminal along Airport Dr leads past the cargo apron.

To see the aircraft stored on the western side of the airport, head north from the terminal, then turn left onto Valencia Rd. Turn left again onto Nogales Highway, and explore the side streets. Stop to note registrations but don't linger. There are a couple of former FedEx Boeing 727s and a DHC-8 in the on-site Pima Community Aviation College.

CALIFORNIA

Hollywood Burbank Airport

BUR | KBUR

A popular airport for low-cost carrier Southwest Airlines, as well as Alaska, American, Delta, JetBlue and United. Burbank is located north of Los Angeles in the San Fernando Valley, close to Van Nuys Airport. It has two runways and is hemmed in by the city on all sides.

The passenger terminal is in the south-east corner, with FBOs, cargo and general aviation parking stretching around the south-west and western sides of the airport.

Spotting at Burbank is best from the top floor of the car park outside the terminal, from where all movements can be seen. A drive around the perimeter is also useful for picking off parked aircraft.

Long Beach

LGB | KLGB

Formerly the airport at which McDonnell Douglas constructed many of its great airliners. Long Beach, situated to the south of Los Angeles, has flights by Delta, Hawaiian, JetBlue Airways and Southwest Airlines. FedEx and UPS fly in freighters.

The terminal is on the eastern side, with a Gulfstream facility just to its south that usually has a selection of biz jets parked outside. Walking to either side of the entrance to the passenger terminal will yield views of aircraft parked at some of the gates. You can also spot from the restaurant inside.

There's a light aircraft parking area north of the terminal. FBOs, training schools and more general aviation parking are on the western side of the airport, along with the huge Boeing hangars.

A large car park is situated outside the DeVry University building fronts onto the end of runway 30 and one of its taxiways. This is a great spot for aircraft landing or departing on runway 30. The car park is off Kilroy Airport Way. Staff are used to spotters here.

Los Angeles International

LAX | KLAX

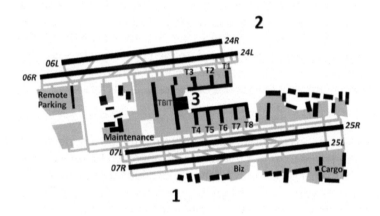

LAX is the busiest airport on the US west coast. It is a major hub for many US and some international carriers, like American, Delta, Southwest and Qantas. In addition to the vast number of overseas airliners arriving from all corners of the globe, it is also busy with smaller regional and commuter airliners, executive aircraft, and cargo airliners, making it an ideal place to spend a few days spotting.

There are four parallel runways, and nine terminals, all situated in the central area between the runways; the Tom Bradley International Terminal is the largest and handles most of the international airlines. To the south and east are cargo and maintenance ramps, whilst additional maintenance and remote parking areas are to the west of the terminals.

There are some great spots for watching aircraft around the perimeter, and the weather is great for most of the year. What's more, LAX makes a great base for exploring the many other airports in the Los Angeles Basin and beyond (such as the desert storage airports).

Spotting Locations

1. Imperial Hill Jim Clutter Park

Situated on the south side of the airport off Imperial Highway, this hill overlooks LAX from a height which offers unobstructed photography of aircraft, and the ability to log all movements on the south side with good binoculars. Movements on the northern runways can be read with a pole, or tied up later with SBS or flight tracking sites. The park provides benches and the shade of trees, and a number of food concessions are located close by.

2. In-N-Our Burger

This fast food restaurant has gained a reputation amongst spotters due to its position under the approach to runways 24L/R. From the car park, this is a fantastic location for photographs; however, viewing aircraft on the ground is nearly impossible. It is also recommended that you purchase food if staying here for any length of time. The In-N-Out Burger is at Sepulveda Blvd and 92nd Street.

3. Tom Bradley Terminal Parking

The top level of the parking garage outside the Tom Bradley International terminal has views over much of the action, particularly aircraft on the north side. Departures on the southern runways are also visible. Police are usually accepting of spotters here, but ask that you stay a good distance from the edge so as not to alarm anyone below.

Spotting Hotels

Crowne Plaza
5985 Century Blvd, Los Angeles, CA 90045 | +1 310 642 7500 |
www.ihg.com This tall hotel to the east of the terminals has views
over the southern part of the airport and its runways and cargo
area. Ask for a room facing the airport and you'll be able to log
registrations easy. It is not a great hotel for photography. The
hotel's multi-storey car park also has good views.

Embassy Suites LAX South
1440 E Imperial Ave, El Segundo, CA 92045 | +1 310 640 3600 |
www.hilton.com A favourite at LAX. Rooms on the 5th (top) floor
looking towards the southern runways and nearby cargo and biz
jet aprons can be requested. Photography can be difficult due
to obstructions outside, but viewing is fine. You'll need tracking
software for aircraft visible on the northern runways. Suites
580 and 581 are reportedly good, but a new building partially
obscures views of the biz jet ramp. It's a short walk to Imperial Hill
from here. Be careful not to book the other Embassy Suites, which
doesn't have views.

Mojave Air and Space Port

MHV | KMHV

Mojave, in the desert north of Los Angeles, is well known as
a storage airport and is worth a visit to see the lines of retired
airliners parked up for scrapping. Mojave has also reinvented itself
as an air and space port and is home to development and testing
programmes.

Driving around the perimeter roads will usually ensure you can
see everything stored at Mojave. Heading away from the airport
buildings on Route 58, turn right onto Route 14 and then explore
the streets on your right. Some have views over the airfield,
allowing you to log what's in with a good pair of binoculars or
scope. Note, it is possible to drive around the dirt tracks which
follow the perimeter fence, although the condition of these is

not guaranteed to be good, and your presence may alert security fairly quickly.

From the access roads leading to the various hangars and offices, it is possible to pull up and note aircraft parked on the main apron and flight line. It is also possible to see across to some of the distant storage areas.

Oakland International

OAK | KOAK

The second busiest airport in the San Francisco Bay area, Oakland is located on the east shore and almost directly across from San Francisco International. It caters much more for low-cost and business aviation than its neighbour, with Southwest Airlines and Allegiant Air as the main operators. It handles some international flights, and there are a number of cargo carriers using the site opposite the terminal, dominated by FedEx. The north complex - away from the terminals and main runway - has many resident biz jets and light aircraft, with three runways of its own. The Oakland Aviation Museum (www.oaklandaviationmuseum.org) is also situated on the north of the airport site.

The small San Leandro Shoreline and Marina has a park with pathways around the shore. This is a good spot for watching aircraft on final approach to runway 30, and you can view some aircraft parked at the terminal. The nearby marina offers similar views, but is a bit distant for photography.

Earhart Road runs the length of the north airfield's complex of hangars and parking areas. Driving slowly along the length of it should give you the opportunity to log most aircraft parked here. You can reach the road at either end from Doolittle Drive

Ontario International

ONT | KONT

Ontario Airport is one of the main Los Angeles airports, and handles over 5 million passengers per year. Although it has two parallel runways, they are situated very close together.

There are two passenger terminals, with Southwest Airlines being the most prominent airline although other major US carriers all have a presence, and China Airlines offers a long-haul link to Asia. UPS also has a strong cargo presence at the airport.

Spotting at Ontario Airport is more difficult as there are no obvious locations. However, the best views can be had on the southern perimeter near the UPS ramp, were views of aircraft approaching the runways can be had from Haven Ave.

San Bernardino International

SBD | KSBD

San Bernardino is a smaller airport in the north east corner of Los Angeles. It has one runway and a passenger terminal, although no scheduled flights exist at present, aside from regular UPS Airlines cargo services. It is primarily a general aviation airport, although spotters will be interested in the scrapping activity that goes on.

A number of airliners have ended their days here (or are currently stored awaiting scrapping), including Boeing 727s, 737s, 747s, 777s and McDonnell Douglas MD-11s. There are also some Boeing 727s used by the fire training college, and one in long-term storage, all on the northern perimeter of the airport. Exploring the roads near the terminal is the best way to see aircraft parked on the various ramps, whilst 3rd St has some roads leading off as it passes the northern perimeter of the airport.

San Diego International

SAN | KSAN

San Diego is a compact but relatively busy airport hemmed in by water, hills and urban development close to the heart of the city. Watching aircraft from the east can be quite spectacular as they swoop low over houses, but few spots are available to the west.

There are two terminals on the south-western side of the airport. Cargo and biz jet aircraft use facilities to the east, on the north side of the runway.

Most US airlines are represented here, as well as a variable mix of international carriers, including British Airways, Japan Airlines and Lufthansa. The weather makes it a pleasant place to enjoy the hobby.

For spotting, Laurel Street has a car park alongside the airport perimeter where it meets Harbor Dr. This is the official place to watch aircraft. It allows you to see aircraft landing and departing runway 27 at close quarters, with the sun behind you. The fence prohibits shots on the ground unless you have a ladder, but allows logging and final approach shots. Be sure not to leave your car unattended.

Next to the parking lot is the Aladdin Parking Garage. You'll have to pay to park here, but the views over the runway and final approach are fantastic (albeit sometimes affected by heat haze). You may be moved on by staff.

Continuing up Laurel Street, you will eventually reach Balboa Park, which overlooks downtown San Diego, and the final approach path to runway 27 around a mile from touchdown. Wander through the park to find a spot that suits you. The bridge over the freeway is a good choice.

MUSEUM

San Diego Air & Space Museum

2001 Pan American Plaza, Balboa Park, San Diego, CA 92101 | +1 619 234 8291 | www.aerospacemuseum.org The official air and space museum for California, situated in Balboa Park - a good viewing location for San Diego Airport. Exhibits here include a SR-71 Blackbird, Ford Tri-Motor, Douglas DC-3 and Catalina. Open daily, 10am to 4pm.

San Francisco International

SFO | KSFO

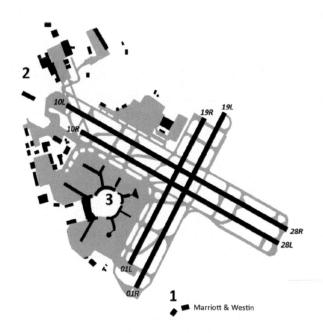

San Francisco is a large airport south of the city with a nice Bay-side location. It has four runways which extend out into the water and cross in the middle. Flights are handled from all major US carriers as well as a lot of intercontinental flights from Asia and Europe.

The airport's large four-terminal complex sits on the western side of the field, linked closely to Hwy 101. On the northern and eastern side you'll find the cargo and maintenance areas.

Spotting Locations

1. Bayfront Park
A small park alongside the Bay on the southern side of the airport provides good views of aircraft on the runways and taxiways. Bayfront Park can be reached on Bayshore Highway which links to freeway 101. Aircraft landing on runways 28L/R can be photographed, and aircraft using runways 1L/R can also be logged easily.

2. Freeway Overpass
At the northern end of the airport San Bruno Ave passes over freeway 101 a short distance from the end of the 10/28 runways. If you leave 101 at the San Bruno exit and park up to the west in the residential area, you can walk across the freeway to get a better view. Low-flying aircraft shots are possible here.

3. SkyTerrace
You'll find the outdoor SkyTerrace on top of Terminal 2. Head into the terminal and upstairs, where you'll pass through a security screening and out onto the terrace. It has views of the gate areas around the terminal. Photography is through glass, but acceptable. Open daily 7am-10pm.

Spotting Hotels

Marriott San Francisco Waterfront Airport
1800 Old Bayshore, Burlingame, CA 94010 | +1 650 692 9100 | www.marriott.com The best-known hotel for spotting at SFO, with higher rooms facing the airport offer views over runways 1L/R and

28L/R. Ask for a Waterfront room to get the views you need, and explain that you want to take pictures of aircraft. Bayview rooms only face part of the approach path. You'll need a long lens for photography.

Westin San Francisco Airport Hotel
1 Old Bayshore Highway, Millbrae, CA 94030 | +1 650 692 3500 | www.marriott.com Next door to the Marriott, so a good alternative. Rooms facing the airport have views of part of the terminals, as well as the runways.

San Jose International

SJO | KSJO

San Jose is the third largest airport in the San Francisco Bay area, serving Silicon Valley. Today it is a hub for Alaska Airlines and Southwest Airlines. Aeromexico, Air Canada, All Nippon Airways, British Airways, Hainan Airlines and Volaris provide daily international links, and UPS Airlines has a decent cargo presence.

The two passenger terminals are hemmed in along the northeastern side of the airport's two runways. The Guadeloupe River restricts growth somewhat. FBOs and general aviation can be found on the opposite side of the runways. Although too restricted for photography, you can at least see most movements from the top floor of the parking garage outside Terminal A.

On the opposite side of the airport to the terminals, Airport Ave runs off Coleman Ave and leads to a free car park alongside various hangars and parking aprons for light and executive aircraft. A quick look through the fence will yield many parked aircraft. Photography is possible, including of movements on the runway.

To the southeast of the airport is a park running next to the river. It has various paths running through and any aircraft landing from the south will pass overhead. Find a gap in the trees for photographs.

Van Nuys

VNY | KVNY

Van Nuys is one of America's best and busiest airports for biz jets and general aviation. It doesn't currently have any airline flights. You will find the airport in the San Fernando Valley north of Hollywood, and operated by the owners of LAX airport. On a visit you are likely to see numerous light and executive aircraft parked up, and occasionally military aircraft can also be seen here.

The airport has one main runway, with a smaller parallel strip to its east. Aircraft parking and hangars are location down both sides of these runways.

Van Nuys offers free guided tours of the airport every weekday and Saturday which delve into its history and its current contribution to Southern California and use in Hollywood films over the years. Tours last 90 minutes and run at 9.30am and 11am (only 9.30am in the summer months). Reservations are required by calling +1 818 442-6526.

Spotting Locations

1. Waterman Drive

This official parking area offers a place for enthusiasts to watch movements from alongside the taxiway and both runways, with ATC communications played through speakers. It is perfect for photographs on mornings. The spot is reached by turning onto Waterman Drive, off Woodley Ave.

2. Hayvenhurst Ave

For afternoon photography, or an alternative place to spot, Havenhurst Ave runs part-way along the length of the runways on the airport's western perimeter. There are various spots to look through the fence.

3. 94th Aero Squadron Restaurant

Situated on Raymer Street on the airport's the northern perimeter. This is a nice place to eat and has views of aircraft traffic at Van Nuys.

Spotting Hotel

Airtel Plaza Hotel

7277 Valjean Ave, Van Nuys, CA 91406 | +1 818 997 7676 | www. airtelplaza.com The nearest hotel to Van Nuys Airport, but it is not cheap. The rear of the hotel faces the airport runway and some parking stands.

Victorville Southern California Logistics Airport

VCV | KVCV

Victorville is a public airport around 85 miles into the desert from Los Angeles. It has carved a niche in the storage and scrapping of airliners. Southern California Logistics are the company behind this operation. A number of airliners spend long periods of time here before the scrap man moves in, giving the enthusiast time to come and catch up on gaps in their logs. Residents include retired fleets of many of the world's major airlines.

The logistics side of the airport has a large apron and a number of aircraft will be parked here undergoing maintenance or part-out. To the north and west sides of the airport are the long-term storage locations, with lines of aircraft parked up on the desert floor.

As many enthusiasts have found out with US desert storage airports, hiring a light aircraft to take an overflight is often the best way to get close to parked aircraft, taking pictures as you go to identify later.

Spotting Locations

1. Phantom Way
Phantom Way runs from Air Expressway past the various central aprons or the logistics side. There are various places to stop and note visible aircraft, but do not loiter too long in this area. At the end, turn left past the power station and follow the road to the end to get a view of some more stored aircraft.

2. Adelanto Road
Driving north from Adelanto on Adelanto Rd. On your right, you will see aircraft parked on the disused runway. Pull over to note these down.

3. Eastern Perimeter

Continuing north on Adelanto Rd you will come across three successive dirt roads leading off to the right. Each leads to the perimeter fence alongside runway 17/35. From here, you can see the remote storage area across the runway. It is hard to take good photographs, however.

COLORADO

Aspen-Pitkin County

ASE | KASE

Popular with the rich and famous and consequently a hub for executive aircraft. Some airliner traffic in the form of regional turboprops and jets connect Aspen to Atlanta, Denver and Los Angeles, but otherwise it's fairly quiet in this respect apart from a surge in seasonal flights to other destinations during the winter ski period. The airport has a single runway nestled high in the Rockies alongside steep mountains, making it a real challenge for pilots. A walk or drive along Airport Rd, which passes the terminal entrance, should reveal most of the parked bizjets and any other airliners. Light aircraft and another executive ramp are not as easy to see at the very north end of the airport.

Denver International

DEN | KDEN

Denver is the largest airport in the USA by area, covering 53 square miles of flat land to the east of the city. It was built to replace the crowded Stapleton Airport, and opened in 1995. It is known for having six runways, all of them 12,000ft (3,658m) long, apart from the 16,000ft (4,877m) 16R/34L. Given the airport's altitude, long take-off runs are often required, necessitating these long runways.

The main terminal building has a distinctive peaked roof which equally reflects the tepees of Native Americans as well as the nearby peaks of the Rocky Mountains. From this building extends one concourse, with two more remote concourses out on the main apron.

Principal carriers operating here are Frontier Airlines, Southwest Airlines and United Airlines/Express.

Spotting is fairly difficult given the spread of the airport in an area, with few roads. Valley Head St
at the southern end of the airport has a small parking area is close to aircraft shortly before landing on runway 35L, and has (more distant) views of aircraft approaching 35R. To reach the spot, turn off Pena Blvd before it turns towards the terminals, onto Jackson Gap Rd. Follow this and take the first right then keep going until you reach a T-junction and turn left onto Valley Head St. The parking area is on your right.

Also, when on Pena Blvd heading towards the airport, turn off onto Tower Road heading north. Follow this to 96th Ave East and turn right. The road will turn left, then right before reaching the approach path to runways 34L/R. Aircraft will pass you at close quarters when arriving or departing.

Spotting Hotel

Westin Denver Airport
8300 Peña Blvd, Denver, CO 80249 | +1 303 317 1800 | www.marriott.com A new hotel near the main terminal building. High floor rooms at either end of the building look out over the nearer parking stands and runways, and you can see movements elsewhere at a distance. This is a large airport, so it's hard to catch everything.

CONNECTICUT

CONNECTICUT

Bradley International Airport, Hartford

BDL | KBDL

After Boston Logan, this is the busiest airport in the New England region, and offers quite an interesting mix of traffic. Bradley International is located at Windsor Locks, about half-way between Hartford and Springfield, MA, giving it a good catchment area.

The airport has three runways in a triangular pattern. The passenger terminal and the smaller international building with its single gate (at present) are on the southern side of the airport. On the eastern side are FBOs, a Bombardier executive jet service centre, a US Army base, and the UPS cargo ramp. On the western side you'll find the DHL/FedEx cargo ramp, Signature Flight Support, and the Connecticut Air National Guard base, with a fleet of C-130 Hercules usually present.

If arrivals are on runway 24 you can park along Marketing Dr (off South St/Route 75, which links to I-91 just to the south of the airport) and walk to a position where you get a good view of aircraft. Be careful not to park in the business car parks unless it is a weekend.

Running along the northern boundary of the airport, close to the fence and the ends of runways 15 and 24, is Perimeter Rd. This has no official places to park or pull over, but offers a good view of movements and some parked aircraft.

Spotting Hotel
Sheraton Hartford Hotel at Bradley Airport
1 Bradley International Airport, Windsor Locks, CT 06096 | +1 860 627 5311 | www.marriott.com Located right outside the main terminal. Upper floor rooms have a great view over the parking gates and the main runway. You can take photographs easily. There are also views from some of the public areas.

FLORIDA

Fort Lauderdale Executive

FXE | KFXE

Probably the premier biz jet airport in Florida, 13 miles to the north of Fort Lauderdale – Hollywood International.

It has two runways, with a maze of hangars and parking aprons strung along the northern, eastern and southern boundaries. Over 900 aircraft were based at the last count, including many stored aircraft, so it's worthwhile visiting.

A car is essential to explore all of the parking areas through the perimeter fence. A friendly request to look inside a hangar will often be granted. The airport provides a small viewing area off Perimeter Road/NW 56th St close to the end of runway 09. It has piped ATC broadcasts and picnic benches.

Another good location is the Jet Runway Café (www.jetrunwaycafe.com) off NW 55th Ct. With good food and drink, it has views and photography opportunities across the runway and neighbouring parking areas.

Fort Lauderdale – Hollywood International

FLL | KFLL

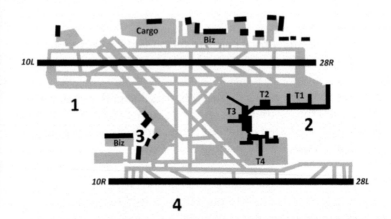

Fort Lauderdale – Hollywood Airport is a major domestic and international gateway to southern Florida. It has four passenger terminals in a central area, alongside a cargo terminal. Executive and light aircraft us ramps on the western and northern portions of the airport.

The biggest carriers here are Allegiant Air, Spirit Airlines, Southwest Airlines, Delta and JetBlue, and it is home to some smaller carriers like IBC Airways and Tropic Ocean Airways. All major US airlines fly here, along with leisure airlines and some international carriers. It is also heavily used by executive aircraft. FedEx and UPS are the main cargo carriers.

Many spotters come here to photograph airliners due to some good locations and the regular sunshine conditions. Given its proximity to Miami, it is also a good place to combine with trips to other airports in the area.

Spotting Locations

1. Ron Gardner Aircraft Observation Area

The official spotting location at Fort Lauderdale is situated alongside the threshold of runway 10L. It is excellent for landing and taxying shots. The fence here is possible to shoot through, or over. To reach the signposted park, exit I-95 onto Griffin Rd, heading west. Turn right onto Anglers Ave, then turn right again onto SW 42nd St. Take the first left after crossing the interstate.

2. Terminal 1 Parking Garage

The top floor of this parking garage, outside the terminal, has excellent views over runway 10L/28R and spotters are welcome here. This is good for photography if you have a longer lens. You will see most movements from here, although aircraft on the Signature Ramp are a little distant.

3. General Aviation Area

From the first location, continue past the road leading to the viewing park and head towards the control tower. There are various areas around here to log the parked light aircraft and biz jets.

4. Southwest Park

A long park runs along the south western portion of the airport perimeter alongside runway 10R/28L. There is a car park and paths lead to the fence, and also rise up small hills to elevate your camera angle above obstructions. The park is accessed off Griffin Rd, which is easy to get to from US Hwy 1 near where it passes underneath the runway.

Miami International

MIA | KMIA

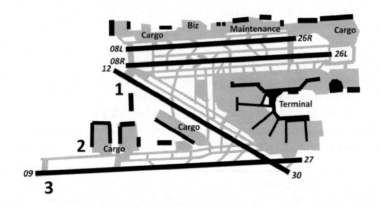

Miami is a major hub airport, and has long been the primary US entry for flights from Latin America, which traditionally brought in a variety of exotic airlines. Whilst older types and prop airliners are rarer these days, Miami still presents and interesting mix of carriers, and has a large cargo operation which also brings in airlines aside from the usual FedEx, DHL and UPS seen at most other US airports. Miami is a major hub for American Airlines.

The airport has four runways – three parallel, and another (12/30) running diagonally across the field. A large a complex passenger terminal occupies the central eastern side of the airport, split into North, Central and South concourses. Also in this area is a maintenance base for American Airlines, which is the airport's dominant carrier.

Along the northern perimeter of Miami Airport is a series of FBOs, aircraft maintenance and storage areas, and the cargo centres of FedEx Express and UPS Airlines at either end. Additional cargo facilities can be found in the western side of the airport.

Airlines from all over the world fly into Miami daily, covering the full spectrum from air taxi and executive aircraft, to regional jets and long haul widebodies. Cargo is also a massive part of daily life, and so spotters can expect to see a good range of aircraft.

Spotting Locations

1. Western Boundary

A spot on the western side of the airport is popular with photographers, and the airport authorities have even created holes in the fence to make photography a little easier. This spot is ideal for arrivals on runways 08L/R and runway 30 departures. To reach it from the 826N Expressway, exit onto NW 25th St and drive towards the airport fence.

2. Cargo Area

Following the steps for position 1, turn right onto NW 68th Ave and follow it south to the fence, next to some of the cargo buildings where cargo aircraft and the southern runway can be seen.

3. Southern Boundary

There's a spot on the southern perimeter close to the threshold of runway 09. It is good for arrival shots, and watching aircraft depart this runway, which is often used by cargo carriers and arrivals from South America. To reach the spot, head south on Millam Dairy Rd which passes close to the spot above. Turn east onto NW12th St. At the next lights, turn left onto NW 72nd Ave near the El Dorado furniture store and follow to the end.

Spotting Hotels

Hilton Miami Airport

5101 Blue Lagoon Drive, Miami, FL 33126 | +1 305 262 1000 | www.hilton.com A good hotel for views over the southern half of the airport, particularly when runways 27 or 30 are in use. Aircraft on the northern runways are a little difficult to see. Ask for a high room facing the airport. Executive double rooms with balconies offer the best views, however all now have mesh which hinders the views and photography.

Clarion Inn & Suites Miami Airport
5301 NW 36th St, Miami Springs, FL 33166 | +1 305 871 6000 | www.comfortinn.com The best hotel for in-room spotting at Miami. High rooms facing the airport overlook the 08/26 runways and northern side of the field. All movements can be seen, but those on the southern part of the airport may need a flight tracking site to tie up. Avoid even-numbered rooms and ask staff for an airport view.

Miami Opa Locka Executive

OPF | KOPF

Opa Locka is an airport which has a mixed civil and military role. It is seven miles north of Miami International. A Coast Guard Air Station is based here, and the airport also handles plenty of GA and executive aircraft. For the enthusiast, the main reason to visit is for the many airliners and props to be found stored here, either awaiting scrapping, restoration, or a return to service. This business has highs and lows, but it's always worth checking what is here.

For those with a car, enter the airport on Curtiss St and make your way along the various side roads which lead to the different parking areas and hangars. The stored airliners can be found in the north-eastern part of the airport, whilst general aviation is generally in the southern part. Executive aircraft and maintenance areas are in the south and north of the airport. It is possible to walk around, but allow a couple of hours.

Orlando International

MCO | KMCO

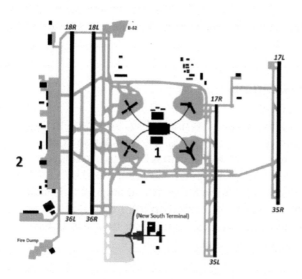

Because of the popularity of the area for leisure travellers, Orlando International has become a very busy airport with links from across the country and many other countries.

Leisure airlines dominate – especially Frontier Airlines, JetBlue, Southwest Airlines and Spirit Airlines. However, all US carriers are present along with charter and mainline airlines from Canada, Europe, Central and South America.

The terminal is a central building linked via monorail to four remote concourses. However, a new South Terminal Complex and associated infrastructure is being constructed to the south of the existing site, due to open in 2021.

Orlando has four runways, all parallel in a north-south orientation. Along the western boundary are a series of cargo centres served by FedEx Express, DHL and UPS Airlines, plus various FBOs.

Classic aircraft enthusiasts should make a point of seeing a retired BAC One-Eleven and a couple of Boeing 727 aircraft in the extreme south-western corner of the airport. A B-52 bomber is preserved in a memorial park close to the airport entrance.

Spotting Locations

1. Parking Garage

The MSCP parking garage has good views from the 9th floor. From this spot you can see most of the runways and gates. You are required to sign a Use of Facilities Form to use this spot. The form must be completed in person, accompanied by a valid photo ID, between 8am-5pm, Mon-Friday (excluding public holidays), at the Public Affairs office, located on the 3rd level of Terminal A in the Aviation Authority Executive Offices (to the left of the East Security Checkpoint for Gates 70-129).

2. Tradeport Drive

Tradeport Drive runs down the western side of the airport, and passes the executive jet parking areas, maintenance areas, and the cargo ramp. The best thing is to drive along and pull in to read aircraft off, then move on. At the end of the road, you can make a left onto County Road 530 which should give you views of the BAC 1-11 and Boeing 727 on the fire dump to your left.

Spotting Hotels

Holiday Inn Express Orlando Airport
7900 S Conway Road, Orlando, FL 32812 | +1 407 581 7900 | www. hiexpress.com This hotel has excellent views over the airport from the top floor. You will see most movements, and those on the nearby runways will be within range of decent camera lenses. Movements on the far runway can be tied up if you use flight tracking websites or SBS.

Hyatt Regency
9300 Jeff Fuqua Blvd, Orlando, FL 32827 | +1 407 825 1234 | www.
hyatt.com By far the best hotel at Orlando Airport, and situated
within the central terminal complex. If you ask for a room facing
the runways, you will see most movements. The hotel's car park
and pool area also have views of movements.

Orlando Sanford International

SFB | KSFB

Sanford Airport is 28 miles north of Orlando and acts as a
secondary gateway to the city used by Allegiant Air and leisure
operators from Europe like TUI.

In recent years Sanford has become a storage location for airliners
being refitted, maintained or scrapped. This is an additional draw
for enthusiasts who may be lucky to see something classic or
rare. The two areas used for this purpose are on the north of the
airfield, off E 25th St, and on the east, which is not easily accessible
but visible at a distance from the passenger terminal.

The top floor of the parking garage outside the terminal has
views. You can also explore the access roads around the terminal
which give views through the fence onto different ramps and
parking gates.

Palm Beach International

PBI | KPBI

A busy airport in the shadow of Fort Lauderdale and Miami,
but still handling over 6 million passengers per year. Primary
operators include American Airlines, Delta, Frontier, JetBlue, Silver
Airways, Southwest and United. The two-pier terminal is on the
northern side of the field.

The airport has two main runways, and a smaller parallel runway to the south which is used by light aircraft. There are always lots of corporate jets parked up at the various FBOs around the airport.

A car park fronting the fence has great views of aircraft on the main runway 10L/28R, as well as anything landing on 32, and is great for photography. To reach this point, driving west along Southern Blvd, which passes the south side of the airport, turn right at the lights onto Kirk Rd (you'll see the Atlantic hangar in front of you). Turn right onto Perimeter Rd and follow it past the end of runway 32. You'll see the viewing area on your left.

At the passenger terminal, the 7th floor of the Short-Term Parking has views over most of the terminal gates, and the runways in the distance.

Tampa International

TPE | KTPE

Handling a fair share of domestic and international traffic, Tampa is one of the busiest in Florida. It is a focus city for Southwest Airlines, Spirit Airlines and Silver Airways. American, Delta and United are also dominant carriers. The airport has three runways and a single terminal with multiple concourses spread in all directions as satellites, located between the parallel runways. To the east are FBO ramps, general aviation facilities and the cargo terminal (Atlas Air, FedEx and UPS mainly).

The top level of both the Short Stay and Long Stay multi-storey parking garages have some good views over the satellite terminal gates, with photography possible for those with longer lenses.

Another good location is the large International Plaza retail centre on the south-east corner of the airport. Its car park and surrounding roads are within sight of two of the runways, and you can log in relative peace, but are a bit distant for photographs.

Spotting Hotel

Tampa Airport Marriott

4200 George J Bean Pkwy, Tampa, FL 33607 | +1 813 879 5151 | www.marriott.com A large hotel at the northern end of the central terminal complex at Tampa. Rooms are spread over three wings, each facing different directions, so what you end up seeing may differ depending on where you are, since there are runways and terminals on either side of the hotel. A higher room is important nevertheless.

GEORGIA

DeKalb-Peachtree Airport

PDK | KPDK

DeKalb Peachtree, located a short distance north of Atlanta, is the second busiest airport in Georgia, despite only handling a small number of airline passengers. The reason is that much of Atlanta's general aviation and executive traffic uses this airport as an alternative to the crowded Hartsfield-Jackson International.

An outdoor recreation area, named Doc Manget Memorial Aviation Park, can be found near the control tower on Airport Rd. It has an elevated grandstand as is very popular with locals and spotters alike, particularly at weekends. Another good option is the 57th Fighter Group Restaurant on Clairmont Rd, which has views over the southern part of the airport.

Hartsfield-Jackson Atlanta International

ATL | KATL

Atlanta Hartsfield is the busiest airport in the world in terms of the number of passengers handled, with over 101 million passing through in 2016. Naturally, this the one of the best airports in the US for sheer numbers of aircraft operating. Variation is perhaps slightly lacking, given that the vast majority of movements are by Delta Air Lines, but if these are what you need then a couple of days here would yield hundreds of entries to your logbook. In addition to Delta, Atlanta is a base for Southwest Airlines and has a large number of cargo carriers. It is also home to one of the best spotting hotels in the world. It should be on the list of number crunchers at least once in their life.

Atlanta has five parallel runways and two central terminal with six parallel concourses. All of them are used by Delta. There are also large maintenance and cargo areas, and the excellent Delta Flight Museum to visit.

Spotting Locations

1. Renaissance Concourse Hotel
One of the best-known spotting hotels in the world, with excellent views over the airport. The best option for any dedicated spotting trips to Atlanta. See Hotels section.

2. Terminal Parking Lots
The top floor of the parking lots to the north and south of the terminal have great views over the northern and southern runways and taxiways respectively. Photography here can be excellent, although the sun is worse on the southern lot. Contact Department of Aviation for a photography permission slip to avoid hassle with security.

Spotting Hotel

Renaissance Concourse Hotel Atlanta Airport
1 Hartsfield Center Parkway, Atlanta, GA 30354 | +1 404 209 9999 | www.marriott.com Many rooms at this fairly luxurious hotel overlook the entire airport, and many have private balconies,

which give spotters the chance to spend all day and night watching the action. Aircraft on the furthest runways can be seen with good telescope, but are hard to read off; everything else is seen with a good pair of binoculars. Photography is possible on the closer runways too. The hotel offers spotter packages on request. It is cheaper at weekends. Rooms on higher floors are better, with 819, 933, 1016, 1022, 1024 and 1025 singled out as excellent.

MUSEUM

Delta Flight Museum

1060 Delta Blvd, Building B, Atlanta, GA 30354 | +1 404 715 7886 | www.deltamuseum.org A heritage centre on the northern perimeter of the airport full of Delta (and now Northwest) memorabilia, including some heritage aircraft from the Delta fleet, such as a L1011 section, DC-3, DC-7, DC-9, 747-400, 757-200, and 767-200. Open daily except Wednesday, 10am-4.30pm (12pm-4.30pm Sunday). Tickets are $12.50 for adults, with discounts for concessions.

HAWAII

Honolulu Daniel K. Inouye International

HNL | PHNL

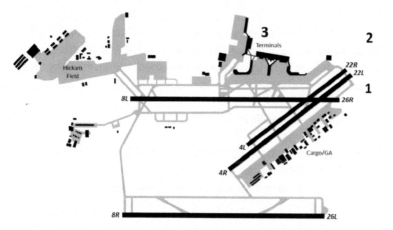

Honolulu is the busiest airport in the island chain and has a healthy inter-island commuter and cargo network. Naturally Hawaiian Air and Mokulele Airlines are principal operators, along with carriers such as All Nippon, American Airlines, Delta, Japan Airlines, Southwest and United. Some other interesting carriers include AirAsia X, China Airlines, Fiji Airways, Jin Air, Korean Air, Qantas and Scoot.

Honolulu International shares its runways with Hickam Air Force Base, situated to the west. It is home to various Air National Guard and other operational wings.

The airport has four main runways, with a couple of water runways. Most departures use the Reef Runway, 08R/26L, and pass close to the city and Waikiki Beach after departure. For passengers, once through security there are open walkways looking out over the aprons in a few places, which are good for photographs and spotting.

Spotting Locations

1. Lagoon Drive
The best place for spotting aircraft at Honolulu is undoubtedly Lagoon Dr. This road runs past the end of runways 22L/R and 26R. It is also good for observing (and photographing) departures on runway 08R. Beware, however, that the police have been known to turn people away from this road. To reach the spot, drive along Aolele St from the airport access road, then turn right onto Lagoon Dr.

2. Ke'ehi Lagoon Beach Park
This is a public park a short distance east of the airport and right underneath the departure path for runway 8L. The park has a car park from which good photographs of aircraft can be taken. You can also observe movements on runway 08R, 04L/26R and 04R/26L. The park can be reached from Nimitz Hwy or Lagoon Dr.

3. Inter-island Car Park
The top floor of the parking garage outside the Inter-Island Terminal is good for viewing aircraft parked on this ramp and the adjacent maintenance areas which are often used by Hawaiian Air. Photography is possible from here, but beware that security may move you on.

ILLINOIS

Chicago Midway

MDW | KMDW

Midway is Chicago's low-cost airport, with the vast majority of services provided by Southwest Airlines, supported by Delta, Porter Airlines and Volaris. There are many biz jet movements here also. Midway is Chicago's original airport, replaced by O'Hare in 1955 largely because it is crammed in amongst residential streets and couldn't be expanded any further.

Sadly, a high wall surrounds the airport making viewing aircraft from neighbouring streets difficult. Once airside, the terminal's piers have plenty of large windows looking out onto the aprons and taxiways.

Outside departures where the Southwest Airlines check-in is located, walk opposite to a position where you can see the end of runway 22L. It is possible to take shots of aircraft landing and lining up for take-off here.

A 15 minute walk south from the terminal leads to the corner of W 63rd St and S Cicero Ave underneath the approach path to the 31 runways. There are footpaths by the road, and a few places to park discretely. Photographs can be good at the right time of day.

The corner of Central Avenue and 63rd Street is also good for aircraft arriving on runways 04L/R. Good for photos until mid-afternoon, this spot is a 20-30 minute walk from the terminal, or a short ride on public bus 63W.

Chicago O'Hare

ORD | KORD

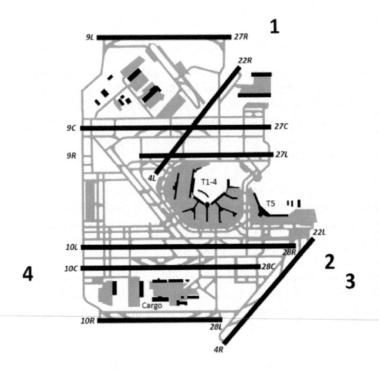

Chicago O'Hare is an incredibly busy and complicated airport. It currently has eight runways and a complex of four passenger terminals and various cargo aprons.

The airport is a great place to put a dent into your American Airlines and United Airlines fleets, along with their regional partners, as well as observing international carriers. Spotting is not very well catered for, but there are some opportunities for those with a car to get views from the surrounding roads.

A large dedicated cargo area exists at O'Hare to the south of the terminals, between runways 28L/10R and 28C/10C. UPS,

FedEx and Lufthansa Cargo have large facilities, however most international cargo airlines and many regional and US carriers visit regularly.

Spotting Locations

1 Allstate Arena
This large sports venue is situated just off Mannheim Rd with a large parking lot underneath the approach path to runway 27R. In winter, however, the parking lot is closed but you can use the alternative lot across Mannheim Road.

2 Scott St
Formerly one of the best spots at O'Hare is around the USG Corp building on Scott St close to its intersection with Mannheim Rd and Lawrence Ave, on the east side of the airport. However, since runway 10C/28C opened the location has fallen out of favour as aircraft tend to land on 28C now, meaning they are backlit and not good for photographs. If they do land on 28R you can get good shots, however.

3 Schiller Park Metra Station
A good public location for watching and photographing aircraft land on runway 28C. The Metra station is off Ruby St and has a large car park. It is one of the most popular places for spotting now.

4 Gateway Rd
A good location for spotting on the west side of O'Hare providing arrivals are on runway 10C (and 10L a little further away). Make sure you do not block the road or any driveways and you should be left alone here.

Spotting Hotel

Hilton Chicago O'Hare

O'Hare International Airport, Chicago, Illinois 60666 | +1 773 686 8000 | www.hilton.com Perfectly situated within Terminal 2 at the heart of O'Hare, this Hilton has rooms overlooking the American Airlines gates and southern runways. Ask for an even-numbered, high-floor room. Good photographs are possible of aircraft around the terminal. Unfortunately, the hotel is quite expensive, and charges a premium for a guaranteed airport view room.

INDIANA

Indianapolis International

IND | KIND

Indianapolis is the largest airport in the state and one of the main hubs in the country for FedEx Express. It is also served by all major US airlines, with Allegiant Air, Delta and Southwest focussing large numbers of flights here. The huge FedEx Ship Center ramp is on the eastern side of the airfield, whilst other cargo carriers operate from ramps to the north west.

The new Col. H. Weir Cook terminal is situated in the middle of the field, replacing the now demolished original terminal on the north side. It has two piers for aircraft parking, and sits between the two main, parallel 05/23 runways; a third runway, 14/32, is to the north.

FBO Million Air uses a ramp on the north-west corner of the airport, whilst Republic Airways has a maintenance facility to the south-west. As well as its own regional jets, it also services aircraft from other airlines.

Most of the FedEx movements occur at night. You might like to spend the night at the Clarion Hotel in order to catch these when they move, as they are difficult to log when parked up.

Spotting Locations

1. Terminal Car Park
The top floor of the multi-storey car park has views over some of the gates and across to the FedEx ramp, but the views aren't extensive or ideal.

2. Washington Street

W Washington St runs along the north-western side of the airport. A number of old, empty residential streets run off it, leading to positions under the approach to runway 23R.

Security are known to move spotters on from the perimeter roads which can seem tempting to explore. If you do try them, try to avoid stopping.

KENTUCKY

Louisville International Airport

SDF | KSDF

Louisville's passenger offering is meagre compared to its status as a worldwide cargo hub, and the home of UPS Airlines. Many of the carrier's aircraft pass through every day (except Sundays). The airport is also home to the Kentucky Air National Guard's C-130 transport aircraft. Passenger operations are mostly by regional jets, alongside Allegiant Air and Southwest Airlines low-cost operations.

The UPS facilities occupies the centre of the airport, between the two parallel runways. Aircraft park in bays and it's difficult to see them until they depart. The passenger terminal is at the north of the airport.

The short-term Cell Phone Lot car park designated for people waiting to pick up passengers is very close to runway 17L, near the passenger terminal. Most passenger airlines use this runway, and photography is good here in the afternoons. You will not usually be bothered if you keep a low profile.

Alternatively, if you have a car you can try parking at the northern end of the southern portion of Crittenden Dr, which culminates at the fence on the western side of the airport. You have a view across to one side of the UPS area. To find it, take exit 128 (Fern Valley Rd) off I-65 towards the UPS facility. Turn left onto Grade Ln, and then right onto Crittenden Dr, which will pass the end of runway 35L.

Spotting Hotel

Crowne Plaza Louisville Airport Expo Center
830 Phillips Ln, Louisville KY 40209 | +1 502 367 2251 | www.
ihg.com A short distance north of the passenger terminal. High
level rooms facing the airport have views of movements on both
runways. Photography is not possible, and during the night time
UPS rush you will need SBS or flight tracking websites to tie up
movements. Some UPS stands can be seen.

MARYLAND

Baltimore – Washington International

BWI | KBWI

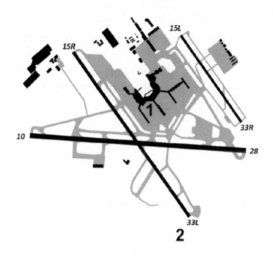

Situated 30 miles north of Washington, BWI Airport (as it is commonly known) attracts large numbers of passengers through its association with the nation's capital, and also serves a wider population in the surrounding area. The airport has become a busy hub for Southwest Airlines, its principal carrier, with all other mainline and low-cost carriers present. International flights are provided by Air Canada Express, British Airways and Condor.

The large, five-concourse terminal area sits between the airport's three runways. To the north of the terminal, partially visible from the access roads, is the cargo area. It is dominated by FedEx Express/Feeder, UPS Airlines and Amazon Air.

Spotting Locations

1. Terminal Observation Deck
Unusually for a US airport, BWI has a dedicated viewing park and observation deck. The observation deck is within the terminal between concourses B and C. It is not airside, so anyone can go there. This spot is best for logging aircraft, but photography is possible through glass.

2. Thomas A. Dixon, Jr. Aircraft Observation Area
The dedicated viewing park on the south side of the airport is close to the threshold of runway 33L. It is reached by taking Aviation Blvd around the perimeter from the terminal, and then Dorsey Road which acts as the southern perimeter road. The spot is good for photography throughout the day when arrivals are on 33L (as they mostly are). It has plenty of parking space and is free.

MASSACHUSETTS

Boston Logan

BOS | KBOS

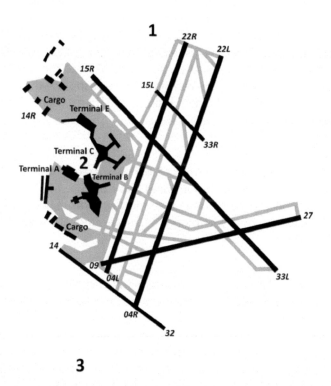

Logan Airport has one of the most unique settings of all major US airports, being sat on a peninsula in Boston Harbor, with the downtown skyscrapers as a backdrop. The airport is well served by all US airlines, and handles a lot of transatlantic flights given its relative proximity to Europe. Delta and JetBlue have hubs here alongside Cape Air which has a fleet of commuter prop aircraft linking to all of the outlying communities in New England.

The airport has four main runways in a crossing pattern, with four terminals together at the western side, closest to the city. Cargo and executive aircraft use ramps on either side of the terminal.

Spotting Locations

1. Constitution Beach
If the weather is right, then sitting on this beach watching aircraft is excellent. It is a great spot for arrivals on runways 22L/R, or departures from 04L/R. From I-90 heading away from the terminals (north), take the first exit onto Bennington St. After half a mile, turn right onto Wordsworth St. and follow to the end. There is parking at the beach. You can also reach this spot via the Metro's Blue Line by alighting at Orient Heights and then walking south along Barnes Ave.

2. Parking Garages
The Central Parking and Terminal B parking garages have good views over traffic on the ground, and traffic on runway 15L/33R. The local police are known to move spotters on from here, so it is best to advise them if you intend to hang around. At the very least be compliant.

3. Castle Island
To the south of the airport is Castle Island, and Fort Independence, which is a tourist attraction. The area has a family park, boardwalk and beach. It is also under the approach path to runways 04L/R. There is free parking here. To reach the spot, take I-90 south (through the tunnel). Take exit as you exit the tunnel and turn left onto Haul Rd, then right to reach Summer St. Follow this to 1st St and turn left. This turns into Shore Rd just before the beach and parking.

Spotting Hotels

Hilton Boston Logan
One Hotel Drive, Boston, MA 02128 | +1 617 568 6700 | www.hilton.com The closest hotel to the terminal, and connected via a bridge. High rooms look out over most aircraft movements if you request an airport-facing room. Good photography is not possible. The windows next to the elevators look out over the Delta Airlines terminal.

MICHIGAN

Detroit Metropolitan Wayne County

DTW | KDTW

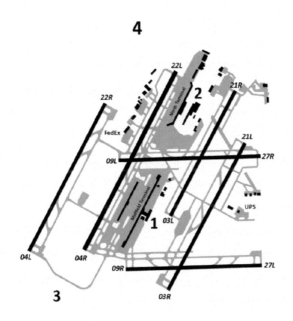

Detroit Metro is one of the country's top 20 busiest airports. It grew up as a major Northwest Airlines hub – a legacy which continues today with Delta Air Lines and its regional partners. Spirit Airlines also has a base here.

The airport has six runways, four of which are in one direction and the other two running across east to west. This gives the large site a complicated feel.

There are two passenger terminals, both built in the 2000s to replace the original ageing structures and cope with growing demand. The modern midfield Edward H. McNamara Terminal is home to Delta and its Skyteam partners. Spirit and other non-Skyteam airlines use the North Terminal.

The airport is very busy and has a number of intercontinental links, making it a good entry point to the country.

Spotting Locations

1. Midfield Terminal Parking
The top level of the Midfield Terminal Parking garage has views over some of the parking gates at this terminal, and excellent views over runway 03L/21R. This is one of the main runways, so in good conditions you will see most traffic from here and be able to photograph many aircraft.

2. North Terminal Parking
The large, blue-topped parking lot alongside the North Terminal has great views of runways 04R/22L and 03L/21R and is good for photography.

3. McNamara Cell Lot
The Cell Phone Lot at the southern side of the airport sits under the approach to runway 04R and has views of traffic on other runways at a distance. You can park here, but don't obstruct anyone. Accessed off Eureka Rd.

4. Wick Road
To the north of the airport is Wick Rd, accessed via Merriman Rd and Wickham Rd, off I-94 where the airport hotels are. The road runs under the approach path from the north to runways 22L/R and is good for photography. Avoid the FAA building on this road.

MINNESOTA

Minneapolis St. Paul International

MSP | KMSP

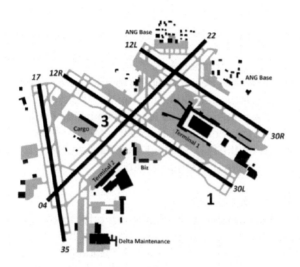

Serving the twin cities on the Mississippi River, this large joint
civil and military airport has grown to become one of the busiest
airports in the USA. It is a major hub for Delta Air Lines, whose
aircraft make up most of the movements. It can be incredibly cold
in the winter.

The majority of travellers will be passing through MSP between
flights, in which case you have ample viewing opportunities
from within the main terminal. Similar in layout to Amsterdam
Schiphol, it is possible to walk from one end to the other, logging
aircraft as you go.

The smaller Terminal 2 is located to the south-west of Terminal
1 and handles low-cost and leisure flights, such as Southwest

Airlines and Sun Country. You can see some of the gates from Terminal 1, but not vice versa.

MSP has a confusing layout of four runways. A cargo centre and parking apron is on the western side of the airport, whilst the military base is on the northern side; you can usually log some of its C-130 Hercules aircraft from Terminal 1. The base is also home to the Minnesota ANG Museum.

Spotting Locations

1. Cell Phone Lot Observation Area
A small parking lot has been providing for those wishing to watch aircraft at MSP. It is located alongside the threshold of runway 30L, which is the primary runway for long haul airliners, and also commonly used for departures. The spot is off Post Road, and situated alongside the Fort Snelling National Cemetery. The spot is easily reached from the terminal with a car.

2. Concourse D Observation Deck
An indoors observation area is located just prior to entering the Concourse D departure lounge and signposted. It has views of runway 12/30 and concourses C and E. Photography is possible, albeit through glass, and most movements will be seen.

3. MSP Aircraft Viewing Area
A recent and welcome addition to the official spotting locations at MSP, opened in 2015. This viewing area is in the centre of the airfield, behind the FedEx cargo buildings. There are parking spaces and views across runways 12R/30L and 04/22, as well as part of Terminal 1 and most of Terminal 2. Access to the viewing area is from the west side of the airport. To get there from Richfield or Cedar Avenue, travel on 66th St. east to Longfellow Avenue and follow Longfellow south to Cargo Road. Follow Cargo Road to its end at the new viewing area. From Bloomington or I-494, take 24th Ave. north to 77th St. Take 77th St. west to Longfellow Road, and follow Longfellow north to Cargo Road. Turn right on Cargo Road and follow it to the new viewing area, located just past and the FedEx facility. It is free to enter.

Spotting Hotel

SpringHill Suites Minneapolis-St. Paul Airport/Mall of America
2870 Metro Dr, Bloomington, MN 55425 | +1 952 854 0300 | www.
marriott.com Minneapolis St. Paul is a complex airport with
runways and parking areas in all directions. The choice of hotels is
also quite limited. However, the SpringHill Suites at the southern
end of the airport, near the Mall of America, is acceptable for
viewing some movements. The few north-facing rooms look
directly into the Delta maintenance hangars, with an awkward
view along runway 17/35. Rooms facing west have a good view of
aircraft landing on runway 35, but little else.

NEVADA

Boulder City Municipal Airport

BLD | KBVU

Boulder City is around 26 miles from Las Vegas, close to the Hoover Dam and Lake Mead. It has become one of the main locations for boarding scenic Grand Canyon flights.

The airport car park and access roads are good for logging resident light aircraft through the fence, whilst the Southern Nevada Veterans Memorial and Buchanan Blvd sit under the eastern runway approach path.

Henderson Executive

HSH | KHND

Some 13 miles south of Las Vegas is Henderson Executive. It is a small airport which has grown to become a popular place for biz jet aircraft to use, as well as light aircraft.

The airport has two parallel runways, with aircraft parking areas on the western side. There are views from the main car park through the fence.

Las Vegas McCarran

LAS | KLAS

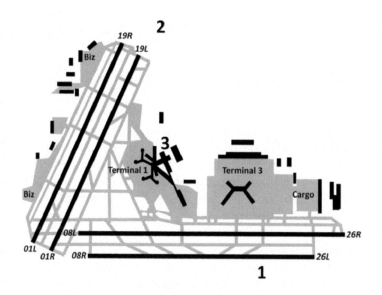

Las Vegas McCarran is one of the busiest airports in America due to the popularity of the city as a leisure destination. The warm weather throughout the year adds to the appeal for the enthusiast, and various spots around the airport allow movements to be seen. Traffic is dominated by Allegiant Air, Southwest Airlines and Spirit Airlines, but most US carriers have a presence and many international leisure airlines arrive from Asia, Europe and Mexico.

A lot of executive aircraft use McCarran Airport and park on the north east side of the field. This area is also home to the special Boeing 737 fleet which shuttle employees to and from secret facilities in the desert throughout the day.

Due to the growth of The Strip, McCarran Airport is now very close to the city and its large hotels. So it's quite easy to get to by public transport and taxi, or even by walking if you can stand the heat.

NEVADA

Spotting Locations

1. Viewing Area

On the southern perimeter of the airport is a designated
viewing area off Sunset Road. The spot has parking for a number
of vehicles, and fairly good views across the 08/26 runways,
terminals and cargo apron. Fairly good photographs can be taken
of anything on these runways, and all movements can be logged.
Aircraft on the 01/19 runways and parked on the executive ramps
are difficult to see from here. The viewing area does not have any
shade.

2. Tropicana Ave and Paradise Rd

The best location for viewing aircraft using the 01/19 runways.
When landing from the north, aircraft pass low over the road here.
There are various places to spot, but it is best to step away from
the busy roads to avoid arousing suspicion. It is possible to take
good landing shots here.

3. Parking Garage

The top floor of the parking garage outside the terminals has
views over different gates depending on which corner you are
standing. This spot occasionally brings about a visit from security
officers, so it is best to avoid spending long here.

Spotting Hotels

La Quinta Inn & Suites by Wyndham Las Vegas South
6560 Surrey Street, Las Vegas, NV 89119 | +1 702 518 5955 | www.
wyndhamhotels.com This hotel is quite far from the pleasures of
The Strip and the big hotels, but it's close to the official spotting
area and higher rooms facing the airport see aircraft pass close by.
Aircraft using the north-south runways are visible in the distance
and can be tracked online.

Tropicana Las Vegas
4520 Paradise Rd, Las Vegas, NV 89169 | +1 702 739 2222 | www.
troplv.com Of the big Strip hotels, the Tropicana is probably the
best for spotting as it's the closest to the airport. Be warned,

however, that many rooms have privacy mesh over the windows which means photography is no good and you have to work to note registrations. But with flight trackers you can work out everything, and see most movements. Runways 19L/R and the executive ramps are the nearest. Ask for high floor even-numbered rooms in the Club Tower (1670 to 1692 are known to be good).

NEW JERSEY

Newark Liberty International

EWR | KEWR

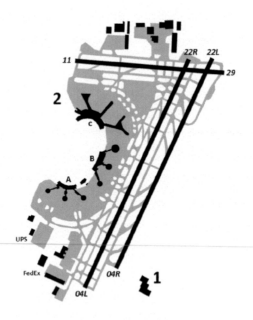

Newark is the second-busiest of New York's airports, located across the state border in New Jersey. It is a major hub for United Airlines, with many aircraft from its mainline and Express fleets operating through here in waves throughout the day. The airport also handles a lot of international traffic from Africa, Asia, Europe, the Middle East and South America, although the diversity is not as enticing as at JFK.

Newark has a large central terminal area, split into A, B and C areas, on the western side of the two parallel runways (there is also another east-west runway to its north). The main cargo hub for FedEx Express and DHL are on the southern side of the airport, whilst maintenance, biz jets and other cargo operators are located on the northern boundary.

Sadly, Newark is known as a difficult airport to spot at with few obvious locations, and authorities who usually move on spotters using cameras and binoculars.

You can reach Newark easily from New York City by taking the Amtrak train from Penn Station.

Spotting Locations

1. IKEA Parking Lot
An IKEA store on the southeast side of the airport has a parking lot from where it is possible to take great shots of aircraft approach runways 04L/R or departing from 22L/R. IKEA staff and the police have been known to move spotters on from here. From I-95, IKEA is off North Ave, which is exit 13A.

2. Airport Monorail
Riding the monorail which links all three terminals and the airport train station will give various opportunities to view aircraft parked at gates.

Spotting Hotel

Marriott Hotel Newark Airport
1 Hotel Road, Newark, NJ 07114 | +1 973 623 0006 | www.marriott. com This hotel is situated in the middle of the terminal complex and has views across the airport from certain rooms, including views of all runways. Rooms reported as excellent are 832, 932, 1032 and 1050. Weekend rates are quite affordable.

Teterboro

TEB | KTEB

Teterboro Airport provides convenient access to New York City for users of executive aircraft avoiding the congestion of JFK, La Guardia or Newark airports. Thus, this is the place to come to spot biz jets when in the New York area. The airport also handles a lot of general aviation traffic.

The airport has two runways, 01/19 and 06/24, with aircraft parking areas scattered all around the airport. Security is often a problem for spotters at Teterboro, but are usually familiar with the hobby at least. It is beneficial to have the use of a car at this airport, as the most fruitful spotting is done by driving a tour of the perimeter roads.

Biz jets from all over the country and world are often present, with over 400 movements on an average day. The Aviation Hall of Fame of New Jersey museum is also based here.

Teterboro is linked from Manhattan by bus routes 144, 161 and 165. Wood Ridge rail station is a short walk from the airport, too.

Industrial Ave leads from Route 46 along the length of the airport's western parking aprons, which are the main areas for biz jets. Walking or driving along this road should allow you to log plenty of parked aircraft. There is a car park outside the Walmart and Costco superstores. Take care when taking photographs through the fence as security are likely to question you.

The corner of Redneck Ave and Moonachie Ave also has views to the biz jet parking area at the southern side of the airport, and is also underneath the approach to runway 01. It is best to find somewhere to park your car nearby and walk to this spot, but try not to loiter too long.

Spotting Hotel

Hilton Hasbrouck Heights/Meadowlands
650 Terrace Ave, Hasbrouck Heights, NJ 07604 | +1 201 288 6100
| www.hilton.com If you ask for a room on a high floor facing
Manhattan, you can get views of aircraft approaching Teterboro
from the north. Distant traffic from LaGuardia and Newark can be
seen in good weather, too.

NEW MEXICO

NEW MEXICO

Roswell International Air Center

ROW | KROW

Quiet in terms of air service (Roswell is served by American Eagle), and few flying saucers have been spotted lately. However, enthusiasts are drawn to Roswell as one of the main desert storage airports in the Western USA. It seems to be the airport of choice for American Airlines who have retired their McDonnell Douglas MD-80 (and other aircraft) fleets here over the recent years.

Roswell has two runways. Most aircraft are stored on a disused runway in the centre of the airfield, and another at the southern side of the field. Recent arrivals park up on the large apron at the north of the site around the administration buildings and hangars. It's difficult to see everything, and ideal to have a car to explore the roads around the airport, such as Earl Cummings Loop which runs from E Hobson Rd past all of the administration buildings and the airport terminal. By driving along this road, you will find various opportunities to stop and log aircraft stored on the adjacent ramps. Photographs are possible through the fence, although the angles are not ideal and heat haze can be a problem.

NEW YORK

New York John F Kennedy International

JFK | KJFK

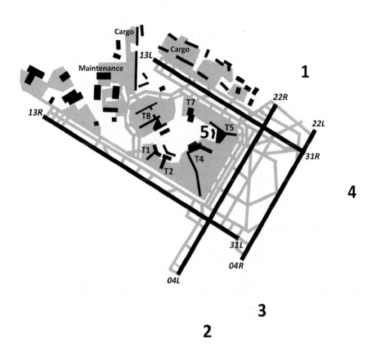

JFK airport is a large and confusing jumble of terminals, runways and parking areas located on Long Island. It is difficult to keep an eye on everything, or find a spot where all movements can be monitored.

The main carriers at JFK are American Airlines, British Airways, Delta Air Lines, JetBlue Airways and United Airlines. Together, these airlines handle nearly 70% of the passengers that fly though the airport each year. If you're a registration spotter, these are the airlines you're going to see the most aircraft of.

Spotters may also be interested in the good mix of airlines from elsewhere in the world. In addition to the main carriers of Europe and Asia, JFK is also a hub for South American and Caribbean flights, with Aeroflot, Aerolineas Argentinas, Aeromexico, Avianca, Cayman Airways, Copa Airlines, LATAM Airlines and Volaris.

Cargo airlines are also very prevalent, with very large freighters to be seen regularly. The main carriers are China Airlines, FedEx Express, Korean Air Cargo and Lufthansa Cargo. In all, around 100 cargo carriers use JFK and a new cargo centre is being constructed.

There are various ways to reach JFK from Manhattan, including taxis, shuttle buses and the AirTrain which links to the New York Subway. Allow up to an hour for the journey.

Spotting Locations

1. Brookville Park Mounds

This position offers an elevated mound to the side of a school football field near Brookville Park where you can see arrivals on runway 22L or departures from 04R. It is good for photography and you won't usually get any attention from the police by being here. To get to this spot, head for 230th Place and follow it to the end where you'll see the school and field.

2. Bayswater Park

A good place to monitor and photograph aircraft arrivals and departures on runways 04L, 04R and 31L. To find this spot, head for Mott Avenue in the residential district to the south of the airport. Head as far west as you can go, and you will reach Bayswater Park on the edge of Jamaica Bay. Simply park up, and then walk until you find a spot that suits you.

3. Inwood Park

A good afternoon spot for photography is Inwood Park, where you can watch and photograph runway 31L arrivals. You need to drive to Bayview Avenue and park at the end (it is signposted Inwood Park), then walk along the shore to get closer to the action.

4. North Woodmere Park

A public park to the north east of the airport which is good for runway 22L and 31R arrivals logging, and photography with a long lens. The park is at the end of Hungry Harbor Road, and has a car park. You can then walk towards the path and find a spot.

5. TWA Hotel

This new hotel has an observation deck on the roof. (see later)

Spotting Hotel

TWA Hotel

One Idlewild Drive JFK International Airport, NY 11430 | +1 212 806 9000 | www.twahotel.com A recent addition to the hotels at JFK, and the only one in the central terminal area. This hotel makes use of the former TWA Terminal which had lain vacant for many years. Two large house the rooms, many of which have views over the gates at terminals 4 and 5, plus runways 13L/31R and 04L/22R. The hotel also has a rooftop pool area and observation deck which has excellent views (when weather permits!) and is good for photography. Outside the hotel is a preserved Lockheed Constellation airliner which is used as a cocktail lounge.

New York LaGuardia

LGA | KLGA

LaGuardia is a very busy airport which primarily handles domestic and regional flights, including some into Canada. It is the closest airport to Manhattan and served by all of the big airlines, with American Airlines and Delta operating the majority of flights. Frontier, JetBlue, Southwest and WestJet operate low-cost flights.

The terminals are currently being redeveloped to improve congestion and cramped spaces. An AirTrain connection will also be built to connect the airport with Manhattan.

Getting to La Guardia from Manhattan can take an hour or more depending on traffic. Private buses are more comfortable and direct, however the cheapest way is to take the MTA bus or subway.

Planeview Park is a great spot for watching arrivals on runway 4 and departures from runway 22. The park has benches and partial views of aircraft on the ground. You can find it on 23rd Ave a short walk west from the terminals, or east from the Metro station at Astoria Blvd.

The boardwalk at the World's Fair Marina in Flushing is also a good place for photographing runway 13 departures. You can reach this spot from the Grand Central Parkway, following signs for the World's Fair Marina or Shea Stadium, and then park up. Walk to find the best position. Public transport can also get you as close as Shea Stadium.

Spotting Hotel

Ibis Styles New York LaGuardia
100-33 Ditmars Blvd, East Elmhurst, NY 11369 | +1 718 606 7400 | www.accor.com Quite a small, circular hotel situated behind the terminals and Grand Central Pkwy. From rooms on the top floors which face the airport you have views of some aircraft stands and the runways beyond. Only a long lens might yield acceptable photography, but logging is fine.

NORTH CAROLINA

Charlotte Douglas International

CLT | KCLT

Charlotte Douglas is the busiest airport in North Carolina, and one of the top ten busiest in the world based on aircraft movements. It is a hub for American Airlines, and is also a busy military base of the Air National Guard and Air Mobility Command, with Hercules aircraft in residence.

American sends most of its mainline and Eagle regional fleets through, including Airbus A330s serving destinations in Europe, and a widespread domestic network.

The airport has three long parallel runways in a north-south direction, and a shorter cross runway. The passenger terminal and its six concourses is at the north of the airport, whilst the Air National Guard facility is to the east. Cargo and maintenance areas are to the south of the cross runway, served by Ameriflight, Amazon Air, FedEx Express and UPS Airlines.

When here, be sure to visit the Carolinas Aviation Museum (see later). The outdoor parts of this museum have a good view of runway 18L/36R and the eastern part of the passenger terminal.

The airport's official viewing location is The Overlook. It is situated alongside the threshold of runway 18C and close to the taxiway linking runway 18R/36L. The location has plenty of parking spaces, and excellent elevated views for both logging and photography when aircraft are landing from the north on 18C. Movements on 18L/36R are a little distant to see. The Overlook is located off Old Dowd Rd, which links to the terminal area.

MUSEUM

Carolinas Aviation Museum

4672 First Flight Drive, Charlotte, NC 28208 | +1 704 359 8442 | www.carolinasaviation.org Tucked away in the north east corner of the airport, this is a great little museum charting the history of aviation here in the Carolinas, where the Wright Brothers made the world's first powered flight. The collection here includes a Piedmont DC-3, USAF C-47, many military jets and helicopters, and the US Airways A320 which landed on the Hudson River in New York. Open daily from 10am (1pm on Sunday). Admission is $12.87 for adults, $10.73 for seniors and $8.58 for students/military. Under 5's are free.

OREGON

Portland International

PDX | KPDX

Portland is the largest and busiest airport in Oregon, and a major hub for Alaska Airlines and its partner Horizon Air, which make up the bulk of the movements. All other major operators fly here, plus their regional partners and some international carriers, including Aeromexico, Air Canada, Condor, Icelandair and Volaris.

The airport has one passenger terminal which is split into five concourses, surrounded on all sides by the airport's three runways – two parallel and one cross runway. There are two large cargo areas – one to the south, and the other to the south-east. On the south side of the airfield is the Oregon Air National Guard base which operates F-15 Eagle fighters.

Cargo airlines are quite prominent, with Ameriflight operating a base here.

The best place to view aircraft movement is on Level 7 of the Short Term Parking Garage (follow the signs as you approach the terminal while driving on Airport Way just before coming up to the main terminal). This vantage point offers a full view of the north runway (10L/28R) with a fantastic backdrop of the Columbia River, and ramp area around Concourse E. This location also offers a partial view of the south runway (10R/28L) and the Air National Guard Base as well as the Alaska Airlines/Horizon Air ramp area at Concourses A & B.

Spotting Hotels

Sheraton Portland Airport Hotel
8235 NE Airport Way, Portland, OR 97220 | +1 503 281 2500 | www.sheraton.com Like the neighbouring Hampton Inn, the Sheraton has great views (particularly from top floor rooms) overlooking runway 10L/28R, as well as some FBO parking areas. Photography is possible. Ask for a room facing the runway.

PENNSYLVANIA

Philadelphia International

PHL | KPHL

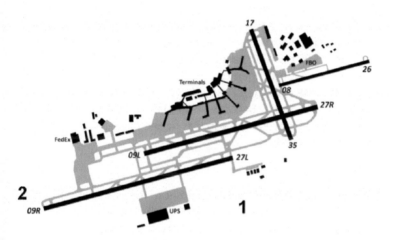

Philadelphia is one of the busiest airports in the USA. It is a large hub for American Airlines, and Frontier and Southwest Airlines also have a decent presence. The airport is served by a number of international airlines such as Aer Lingus, British Airways, Icelandair, Lufthansa and Qatar Airways.

There are four runways, but most aircraft will use the two parallel 09L/R and 27L/R runways. The terminal is split into seven main areas, each with concourses of gates serving different airlines. To its west is a large cargo terminal dominated by UPS Airlines, and also served by FedEx and DHL. The FBO area is to the east.

The airport has plenty of locations for photography and registration spotting.

Spotting Locations

1. Fort Miffin Road/Hog Island Road
This road runs the length of the airport's south side, giving many opportunities to see aircraft landing and departing on the 09/27 runways, and also the 08/26 runway at a distance. Depending on the runway directions in use, you'll want to move your position for the best views, particularly if photographing. You may also have runway 35 arrivals passing closely over you. To reach the spot, from I-95 heading past the airport, take exit 13 for Valley Forge Island Avenue, then turn south onto Island Ave. This turns into Enterprise Ave. Then turn onto Fort Miffin Road and follow it round (it eventually becomes Hog Island Rd). You may get questioned or moved on if you stay in one place too long, or cause an obstruction.

2. Runway 9R
Following Fort Miffin/Hog Island Rd from the first spots, above, you will round the end of runway 09R, which offers some exhilarating close-up action when aircraft are arriving on this runway. A little further around, you will pass an apron on your right often used for de-icing and cargo aircraft.

Spotting Hotel

Marriott Philadelphia Airport
One Arrivals Road, Philadelphia, PA 19153 | +1 215 492 9000 | www.marriott.com Asking for a high room facing the airport should give you a great position looking over aircraft movements at the terminals, and on the runways in the distance. The opportunities for photography are not as good, but will a long lens you can get some acceptable shots. The hotel is linked to Terminal B by a walkway.

Pittsburgh International

PIT | KPIT

This is a joint civil-military airport 20 miles west of the city. It is fairly busy, but has lost hub status from the days of US Airways. Today Southwest Airlines and American are the busiest carriers and the airport is hoping to attract more with the redevelopment of the present terminal structure.

The Air Force Reserve and Air National Guard have regular flights of transport and other military aircraft out of their facility on the eastern and southern sides of the airport.

There are four runways at Pittsburgh, three of which are parallel in the 10/28 direction, with a shorter 14/32 cross runway. The cargo terminal is on the north side of the airport, served by FedEx and UPS mainly.

The top floor of the Horizon Drive Parking Garage is great for viewing aircraft on the ground - both civil and military. They will pass here after landing on runway 32, or before departing runway 14. It is perfect for photographing these aircraft, but views of other parts of the airport and terminals are not good. The car park is reached off Penn Lincoln Pkwy, at Air Side Business Park.
If arrivals are on runway 32 due to winds, a nearby cemetery is a popular place to photograph and log arrivals. You can use the cemetery during daylight hours. It is located at 100 Resurrection Rd, off Penn Lincoln Pkwy and Ewing Rd.

SOUTH CAROLINA

Charleston International

CHS | KCHS

Charleston is not a hub of any airline, but sees all major US carriers flying through with their mainline fleets, as well as regional counterparts. In addition, cargo carriers Atlas Air, FedEx Express and Mountain Air Cargo serve the airport daily.

The recently-modified passenger terminal has two concourses and occupies a central position within the airport. Once airside you have some views across the runways to the military areas.

A big draw for Charleston is the Boeing 787 Dreamliner production hall to the south-east of the passenger terminal, which was opened in 2011 and rolls out the completed airliners at a steady rate. These aircraft can regularly be seen test-flying.

The huge Charleston Air Force Base occupies the western side of the airport. It is home to various air wings and a Civil Air Patrol Coastal squadron. Many C-17 Globemaster aircraft are based on site, and there is an outdoor air park along Arthur Dr with a few preserved transport aircraft which, sadly, you need permission to go and see. They can often be seen when departing in an aircraft, however.

Aviation Ave runs from the main access road to the terminal at the southern end of the airport (just off I-526) all the way along the eastern boundary until it reaches the air base checkpoint. Driving along will give you some views over the Dreamliner ramp, and also across the airport's runways. Sadly any obvious places to park have been blocked off, so this isn't a good road to stop along.

A little further north of the airport is Ashley-Phosphate Rd, which has several parking lots for stores. Aircraft will pass overhead here either departing or arriving on the main 15/33 runway.

TENNESSEE

Memphis International

MEM | KMEM

Memphis International ranks as one of the world's main cargo airports as it is the worldwide hub for FedEx Express. This is a major draw to enthusiasts, despite how relatively quiet the passenger aspect of the airport is (served by a usual mix of the main carriers and their regional fleets). The airport endures a couple of waves of FedEx movements every day, with most of these movements happening until late at night.

The airport is split into two sections, with the regular terminal situated in the southern half between the three 18/36 parallel runways. The other section is the huge FedEx facility stretching along the north and south of the 09/27 runway. Don't miss the small UPS and DHL cargo facilities, too!

A small Air National Guard base with transporter aircraft is located in the south-east corner of the airport.

The best on-airport location for watching aircraft is on the top level of the parking garage outside the passenger terminal. It is only three storeys high, but has views over all runways and taxiways, and you can see most of the aircraft parked on the FedEx ramps with good binoculars. Good photographs of aircraft on taxiways and runways can also be had. It is best to inform Memphis Airport Police if you intent spending time here. The newer six-storey car park is not as good for viewing.

Tchulahoma Road runs along the eastern perimeter of the airport and is a good place to watch FedEx aircraft arriving on runway 27 if this direction is in use. You can try parking in the flying school car park, near the retired FedEx Boeing 727-100, but may be moved on. Another option is Airport Center Ln. Photography will not be good, and you'll probably be spotting at night anyway. So having SBS or flight tracking apps would be useful.

Spotting Hotel

Holiday Inn Memphis Airport – Conference Center
2240 Democrat Rd, Memphis, TN 38132 | +1 901-332-1130 | www.ihg.com Located to the north west of the airport, close to the vast FedEx World Hub aprons. Odd number rooms on the top floor, such as 551, 553, 555 offer distant views of the northern runways and FedEx movements, which can easily be tied up using flight tracking websites or SBS.

TEXAS

Austin Bergstrom International

AUS | KAUS

Austin has significantly grown in stature over the past decade, growing into a true international airport with flights not only from Canada and Mexico, but from Europe too. It is a hub for Allegiant Air, Frontier Airlines and Southwest Airlines.

The airport has two parallel runways, with one main passenger terminal stretching between them at the north side of the site, along with a cargo centre near Hwy 71. A smaller low-cost terminal used by Allegiant Air and some charter airlines is to the south.

The Family Viewing Area is located on the eastern side of the airport. To reach it, drive east past the airport exit off Hwy 71, and turn right onto Golf Course Rd. Follow it to the end. You have views of runway 17L/35R, and part of the passenger terminal in the distance. Photography is good on the morning.

Dallas Fort Worth International

DFW | KDFW

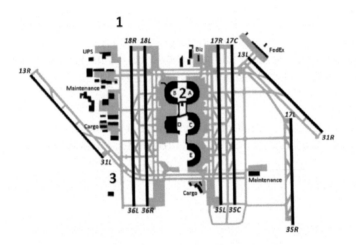

This huge airport is one of the busiest in the world. It has an impressive seven runways and five terminals, and is the country's second largest airport (after Denver) in terms of area.

Dallas Fort Worth is the main hub for American Airlines, and any spotting trip here must surely be to make inroads into their fleet, and that of their partner American Eagle. The airport Is also well served by international airlines and cargo carriers, including Aeromexico, Avianca, British Airways, Emirates, Etihad, Interjet, Korean Air, Lufthansa, Qantas, Qatar Airways and Volaris.

Ameriflight and UPS Airlines have cargo hubs at Dallas, operating from the western side of the main parallel runways.

Spotting Locations

1. Founders Plaza

This official spotting location is excellent for photography and logging movements. It has car parking, seating, canopies and a live ATC feed. The spot is best for movements on the western side of the airport. Movements on the eastern side are difficult to log due to heat haze. The spot is excellent for photography, and is close to the eastern cargo aprons. The Plaza is easily reached from Airfield Drive or John W. Carpenter Fwy.

2. Airport Monorail

Although this monorail is airside and used for transferring between terminals, it is one of the best ways to log aircraft at all of the gates. You can hop on and off as much as you like and complete a circuit, with views at each spot. You can see cargo aircraft parked on the remote ramps from some stops.

3. Minters Chapel & Cemetery

This small chapel and cemetery is a public place with shade and great views over the 36L/R and 31L runways and associated taxiways. This location is accessed of W Airfield Drive or E Glade Rd, and is a short distance from the freeway. A short drive further along the road from here is the fire training centre with various Boeing 727 and MD-80 airframes.

Spotting Hotels

Grand Hyatt DFW

2337 South International Pkwy, DFW Airport, TX 75261-9045 | +1 972 973 1234 | www.hyatt.com This is the best hotel for spotting at DFW, and is located right within the airport complex above Terminal D. If requested, you should be able to obtain a higher room facing the runways. Unfortunately, you'll only be able to see either the east side or west side of the airport, and not both. There is also a rooftop pool with views.

Hyatt Regency DFW Airport
2334 N International Pkwy, Dallas, TX 75261 | +1 972 453 1234
| www.hyatt.com On the opposite side of the central terminal
area to the Grand Hyatt. This hotel also has excellent views and
spotting/photography opportunities from its rooms, but only of
the eastern side of the airport.

Dallas Love Field

DAL | KDAL

Love Field is a busy secondary airport for Dallas, situated a few
miles from downtown. It is the home base of Southwest Airlines,
which is the busiest operator. The terminal was recently updated
and, along with the relaxation of restrictions on destinations, it
now handles flights from across the country. This airport is also
particularly good for spotting biz jets, as many choose it over DFW
for access to the city. The Frontiers of Flight Museum is located at
Love Field.

Shorecrest Drive runs along Bachman Lake through parkland, to
the north of the airport. It passes both runways 13L and 13R. If
arrivals are on these runways, this is an excellent spot to watch the
action and take photographs.

The top floor of the main terminal's car park is also a good spot for
watching all movements. From here you can log and photograph
aircraft on the ground, and also using runway 13R/31L. This is
also a good spot for noting aircraft parked on the remoter ramps
alongside runway 13L/31R.

MUSEUM

Frontiers of Flight Museum

6911 Lemmon Ave, Dallas, TX 75209 | +1 214 350 3600 | www. flightmuseum.com A small museum charting the story of flight from the earliest days, situated on the southeast corner of Love Field. It has exhibits including Tiger Moth, Learjet 24D, Northrop T-38, Sopwith Pup, Boeing 737-200 nose, complete 737-300 and Apollo 7 Command Module, amongst others. Open daily from 10am to 5pm (from 1pm on Sundays).

Houston George Bush Intercontinental

IAH | KIAH

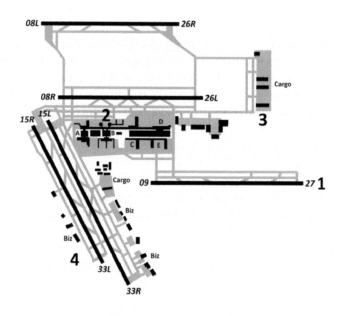

George Bush Intercontinental is the second largest airport in Texas (after Dallas/Fort Worth). It is the main hub for United Airlines, and the airport has long-haul connections to Africa, Asia, Europe, the Middle East and South America, as well as cargo links worldwide.

There are five terminals in a central loop, and five runways spread around the airport in a confusing pattern. Many cargo operators use the airport, with facilities both to the south and east of the passenger terminals.

Spotting Locations

1. Lee Road
The official spotting location at IAH. It is very close to the end of runway 27 and great for photography when the sun is right. To reach the spot, follow Clayton Pkwy from Hwy 59 as it passes the east of the airport. Pass Lee Rd, then U-turn and come back to Lee Rd, where you turn right and follow to the runway lights. A small car park is on your left.

2. Parking Garages
The A/B and D/E parking garages in between the terminals are excellent spots to log and photograph aircraft from. Head for the 7th or 8th levels for the best views. Each garage has its own advantages, and has different views depending on whether you are facing north or south. Runway movements are visible in most cases. You should inform Houston Airport System Security on +1 281 230 1300 before spotting here.

3. Cargo Parking Lot
Alongside the parking lot for the cargo companies, there is a car park that is open for anyone to drive in (although it remains private property). From here you can see and photograph arrivals on runway 26L. Around the corner you can see all of the parked cargo aircraft. Security is not usually a problem here, but you may wish to contact them. The spot is reached along Lee Rd in the opposite direction to location 1.

4. Rankin Road

On the western side of the airport is Rankin Rd. To reach, follow John F Kennedy Blvd south from the terminals and turn right onto Greens Rd. After a mile turn right onto Aldine Westfield Rd, then right onto Rankin Rd after another mile. At the end is a turning circle with views through the fence of the 15/33 runways in particular.

Spotting Hotel

Marriott Houston IAH
18700 John F. Kennedy Blvd, Houston, TX 77032 | +1 281 443 2310 | www.marriott.com This centrally-located hotel can be expensive, but has some great views. Ask for a high-floor room facing the airport and you shouldn't be disappointed. However, most rooms will only have a view of part of the huge airport. The windows at the eastern end of the corridors look out towards the cargo apron.

Houston William P Hobby International

HOU | KHOU

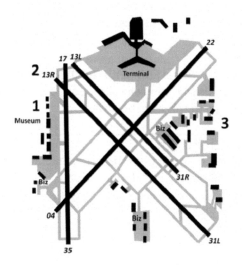

Houston Hobby was the original air terminal for the city until George Bush Intercontinental opened in 1969. Despite this, Hobby Airport still handles over 14 million passengers per year, and acts as a hub for Southwest Airlines. It also has regional flights with other carriers such as American Eagle, and Delta. One of the airport's main attractions is its 1940 Air Terminal Museum on the airport's western side, in among the various FBOs. More FBOs and the Southwest maintenance facility are situated on the eastern side.

Spotting Locations

1. 1940 Air Terminal Museum
The on-site museum is actually the best place to watch aircraft at Hobby. There is an admission fee, but the views are worth it. You will see all aircraft movements from here, but the fence is a problem for photography. On special events days you can gain ramp access here.

2. Northwest Spotters Park
An area is available at the northwest corner of the airfield which has excellent views of aircraft on final approach to runways 12L/R and 17. Photographic possibilities are good here. Views over the rest of the field are not good, however. It is reached from Telephone Rd, close to the 1940 Museum.

3. W Monroe Rd
This road passes many of the FBO ramps on the eastern side of the airfield. Driving slowly along will allow you to note down most aircraft. Do not linger in this area, however.

4. Southeast Spotters Park
This new area allows for great photographs of aircraft landing on runways 30L/R. Easily reached off Monroe Road.

Spotting Hotel

Hampton Inn Houston Hobby
8620 Airport Blvd, Houston, TX 77061 | +1 713 641 6400 | www.
hamptoninn.com An affordable hotel on the edge of the airport.
If you request a north-facing room, you will have a view of any
aircraft landing on runway 22, and photography is possible. No
other parts of the airport are visible.

UTAH

Salt Lake City International

SLC | KSLC

A fairly large civil-military airport close to the city centre. It is a base for Delta Air Lines and its partners, and thus most of the movements are by these carriers. Other airlines of interest include Aeromexico, Alaska Airlines, American Airlines, Frontier Airlines, JetBlue, Southwest Airlines and United Airlines.

A decent-size UPS hub to the north of the passenger terminal (and out of sight unless on board an aircraft) usually has aircraft from various partner airlines. FedEx and Ameriflight use distribution centres and parking ramps to the south-east of the terminal.

The eastern side of the airport is essentially a separate facility, with its own runways (albeit with taxiway links to the civil side). Here, the Utah Air National Guard's 151st Air Refuelling Wing has a base of KC-135R tankers, and some FBOs handle executive jets.

Spotting is possible from the top level of the car park, and also from a walking/biking trail which runs from the Hyatt Place hotel along the southern perimeter of the airport, which is good for photographing arrivals. Once airside in the terminal you have good views, but it's hard to see the cargo and maintenance areas.

VIRGINIA

Washington Dulles International

IAD | KIAD

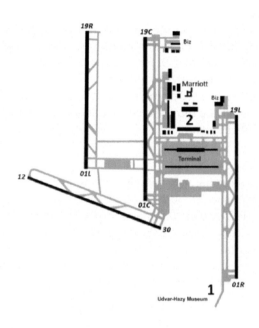

Dulles is the main international gateway to the American capital. It is a hub for United Airlines and United Express and is served by all major mainline and low-cost carriers, plus airlines from around the world. Being the primary gateway to the nation's capital gives the airport importance, but it is not as busy as airports in New York in terms of passenger numbers.

Dulles has three parallel north-south runways and an additional east-west runway. All movements are handled through a main terminal, with two long remote concourses of parking gates for aircraft, and a smaller commuter concourse nearer the main building. Cargo facilities are to the north of the terminal, alongside runway 01C/19C.

Enthusiasts are advised to visit the on-site Udvar-Hazy Museum and its wonderful collection of aircraft.

Spotting Locations

1. Udvar-Hazy Museum
There is an observation tower at the museum which is good for viewing arrivals onto the 01 runways from the south. The car park for this museum is also a great spot for photographing arrivals onto runway 01R as they pass by at low altitude. The museum is easily accessed and signposted from the Lee Jackson Memorial Hwy. You will not usually be moved on from this spot given the aviation theme of the museum.

2. Parking Garages
The multi-storey parking garages outside the terminal are great for watching the action. From both garage 1 and 2 you can see arrivals on runway 19C, and aircraft manoeuvring around the nearer parking gates and taxiways. Photography is possible, particularly with a good lens and in the afternoon. You will also be able to see the cargo apron quite easily. It is advisable to warn the airport police of your intentions to spot from here.

Spotting Hotel

Marriott Dulles Airport
45020 Aviation Drive, Dulles, VA 20166 | +1 703 471 9500 | www.marriott.com Situated in the central airport area, this hotel is probably your best bet for any aircraft views. If you request a room facing the adjacent lake, you will see arrivals on runway 19L from a distance.

MUSEUM

National Air & Space Udvar-Hazy Museum

14390 Air & Space Museum Pkwy, Chantilly, VA 20151 | (202) 633-1000 | www.nasm.si.edu Along with the Museum of Flight in Seattle, this is the greatest aviation museum in the USA, linked with its sister National Mall Building in downtown Washington. Exhibits include SR-71 Blackbird, Space Shuttle Enterprise, Boeing Dash 80 (707 prototype), Air France Concorde, B-29 "Enola Gay", and many more on display. The museum is linked via taxiway to Dulles, situated just to the south of the airport. Open daily (except Christmas Day) from 10am to 5.30pm, admission free.

Washington Reagan National

DCA | KDCA

National Airport is situated very close to downtown Washington DC, in close proximity to the Washington Monument, Lincoln and Jefferson Memorials and the White House. Due to its location, aircraft approaching from the north fly an unusual pattern along the Potomac River, with a late turn onto final.

Movements are mainly regional jet aircraft, with American Airlines operating a hub here. Alaska Airlines, Delta, Frontier, JetBlue, Southwest, United are the other airlines which currently hold slots. A particular emphasis is on the Washington-New York shuttle operation.

Gravelly Point is the best spotting location at the airport, situated a stone's throw from the runway 15 and 19 thresholds. This is a great spot for watching the River Visual Approach, and is perfect for arrival photographs. Aircraft on the ground can also be seen. This spot is just off the George Washington Memorial Pkwy to the north of the terminals, and has parking. You can also walk from the terminals in 15 minutes.

Spotting Hotel

Residence Inn by Marriott Arlington Capital View

2850 S Potomac Ave, Arlington, VA 22202 | +1 703 415 1300 | www.marriott.com Upper floor corner rooms at this hotel (one of many in Crystal City, but probably the best for aircraft views) have limited views across to the southern end of the airport and its passenger terminals. Aircraft arriving from or departing to the south can be seen, but you'll need flight tracking to help you tie them up.

WASHINGTON

Paine Field Everett

PAE | KPAE

One of the three main Boeing production and testing airports in the Seattle area. Paine Field is located 30 miles north of the city and exclusively produces the manufacturer's widebody jets – namely the 747, 767, 777 and 787. The flight line is often full of examples that are undergoing testing and pre-delivery work, and the facility itself is the world's largest building by area.

The airport has a complex layout, with aircraft parked everywhere. Yet despite Boeing's activity is also used by general aviation and regional airlines flights. It has one main runway, with a smaller parallel runway off to the east used by light aircraft from the neighbouring parking garages.

The best spotting location is the roof of the Future of Flight building in the north-west corner of the airport. It has a rooftop balcony which overlooks the runway 16R threshold and is perfect for photography. You can see the production lines at a distance. It holds a museum of Boeing, various aircraft exhibits, and a fantastic Boeing store selling all sorts of merchandise. The Future of Flight is also the place where 90 minute tours of the Boeing Production Facility begin. Open daily 8.30am to 5.30pm. See www.futureofflight.org

There are a number of historic aircraft stored and under preservation at Paine Field. From the access road (or the observation deck with binoculars) you might see a de Havilland Comet 4B, a Learjet, and a B-52. There's also a retired FedEx Boeing 727 hidden among the Everett Community College buildings.

Spotting Hotel

Hilton Garden Inn Seattle North/Everett
8401 Paine Field Blvd, Mukilteo, Washington, 98275 | +1 425 423 9000 | www.hilton.com The Hilton Garden Inn Seattle North/Everett is situated alongside the Future of Flight. Any east-facing room should have views of the runway and part of the flight line. Photography is possible, and the viewing area at Future of Flight is a short walk away.

Renton Municipal

RNT | KRNT

Located 12 miles from downtown Seattle, and only six miles from Boeing Field, this is another Boeing production facility and also a busy seaplane and general aviation base. Over 50 Boeing 737s are produced here every month, so there's always something interesting to see. Most aircraft are initially tested here, then flown off to Boeing Field for finishing.

The airport has a single runway, which ends abruptly at Lake Washington. The production halls are in the north-east corner of the airfield. Aircraft are then lined up around the edges of the airfield for finishing work, intermixed with aprons for light aircraft parking. New 737 fuselages arrive by train alongside Logan Ave.

A parking spot on W Perimeter Rd, off Rainier Ave, is great for looking over the airfield and Boeing 737 ramps. You can take pictures of movements, and you're right alongside the seaplane base for views of action on the lake.

At the southern and of Rainier Ave is a parking lot alongside a clothes bank. It has a fantastic, elevated view of the runway and part of the flight line. Spotters are often parked here, but be aware that it is a car park for the business's use.

On the eastern side of the airport, if you're driving along Logan Ave, turn along N 6th St. At the end is the Cedar River Trail. The road runs alongside the runway, with a car park at the end. Follow the trail in either direction to get a view through the trees of aircraft movements and aircraft parked up. At the northern end you can see some of the freshly built 737s at the factory. Photography of the factory is not permitted, however.

Seattle King County/Boeing Field

BFI | KBFI

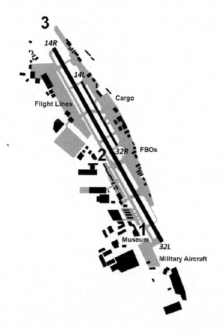

Boeing's primary finishing and testing facility for its 737 aircraft is at King County International, just five miles from downtown Seattle. It is a historic airfield, one of the busiest in the country for movements, and is home to the Museum of Flight (see later). There are two runways and no airline service, but plenty of biz jet movements along with general aviation and cargo flights.

Spotting Locations

1. Museum of Flight

The museum is located in the southern corner of the airport alongside the threshold of runway 31L. Arriving at the museum passes Boeing aircraft destined for military operators, which can also be read off from the museum car park. The observation room in the museum looks over the runway, so you'll see any aircraft being tested.

2. Midfield Viewing Area

A small fenced-in viewing area exists at E Marginal Way and S 86th Pl, with parking for a few cars and excellent views of all movements. The fence gets in the way of any ground shots, so you'll need a step ladder. It's a ten minute walk north of the museum.

3. Ruby Chow Park

At the northern end of the airport where Albro Pl and Hardy St meet is a small park. It sits under the approach to runway 13R and has some benches. Photography is possible, but usually into the sun.

MUSEUM

Museum of Flight

9404 E Marginal Way S, Seattle WA 98108 | +1 206 764 5720 | www.museumofflight.org A giant museum taking in many of the original Boeing factory buildings, and a huge collection of aircraft from the earliest days of flight to the present day, both civil and military. The airliner collection includes the prototype Boeing 737-100, 747-100 and 787-8, plus an Air Force One 707, Canadian Lockheed Constellation, a Boeing 727, and British Airways Concorde. The 'air traffic control tower' part of the museum and the area outside the entrance are good places to spot aircraft movements on the runway. Open daily 10am to 5pm (9pm first Thursday of the month). Adults $20. Cheaper for concessions and under 5's are free.

Seattle-Tacoma International

SEA | KSEA

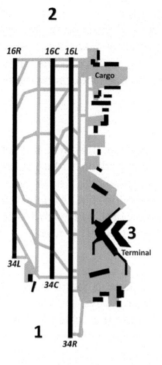

The Pacific Northwest's busiest airport. Sea-Tac, as the locals call it, is a major hub for Alaska Airlines/Horizon Air and Delta. It is also well served by other legacy carriers and sees international services from Asia and Europe. It is a perfect gateway for exploring the nearby Boeing airfields and Pacific Northwest.

The airport has three parallel north-south runways, with a large terminal on the south-eastern side which has two satellites linked via an underground people mover. To the north of the terminal complex is the cargo apron served by FedEx, Amazon Air, and a variety of Asian carriers.

Spotting Locations

1. S 192nd Street

This spot is good for spotting and photographing aircraft on approach to all three runways from the south. You can also quite easily spot aircraft departing these runways in either direction from this spot. Simply move along the road to suit your needs. From the terminal head south on Pacific Hwy S. Turn right onto S 188th St. After the tunnel take the first left onto S 16th Ave and follow it round until you pass over the lights of Des Moines Memorial Dr. You can park your car by the side of the road where it rises.

2. Water Tower

If aircraft are landing from the north, this spot is great for photographs. You can park on S 146th St near the water tower. Aircraft departing to the north are also within range to see registrations. To reach the spot, from the terminals head north on Pacific Hwy (route 99) until you reach S 146th St, then turn left and follow until the water tower (1.5 miles).

3. Parking Garage

The top floor of the parking garage outside the terminal offers good views over the runways, and you can see most movements as they travel to or from their gates. Police will often question you unless you pay them a visit in the terminal to request permission to stay there.

Spotting Hotels

Coast Gateway Hotel
18415 Pacific Highway South, Seattle, WA 98158 | +1 206 248 8200 | www.coasthotels.com Situated just across the road from gate A14. Rooms on floor 5 and higher have views of the approach from the south and parts of the ramp (when large aircraft don't obscure the view), however a new monorail has now ruined the view from many rooms. Reasonable prices.

DoubleTree Hotel Seattle Airport

18740 International Blvd, Seattle, WA 98188 | +1 206 246 8600 | www.hilton.com This hotel has 12 floors and rooms facing the airport on the higher floors have partial views of the parking apron and runways beyond. You can usually see most movements, and closer aircraft can easily be read off. Still a little distant for photography.

WISCONSIN

Milwaukee General Mitchell International

MKE | KMKE

The largest airport in Wisconsin, Milwaukee has a complex layout of five runways and a single passenger terminal with three concourses on the western side of the airfield, with a large cargo apron nearby. To the north and south are areas for private operators, whilst on the eastern side of the field is the General Mitchell Air National Guard base. Primary airline operators are Delta Air Lines and Southwest Airlines.

The airport provides an observation area and parking on the northern perimeter of the airport, off Layton Ave and close to the end of runway 19R. It is a little distant, but you can see most movements from here, and photograph arrivals onto this runway.

A second observation area is off S 6th St which has great views of aircraft arriving on runway 07R and is suitable for photography. It has car parking.

Additionally, the top floor of the multi-storey car park offers views of aircraft at the terminal and on the cargo ramp.

Oshkosh Wittman Regional

OSH | KOSH

Wittman Regional Airport is for most of the year a quiet airport and has no passenger flights. However, during the annual EAA AirVenture show, Oshkosh becomes the busiest airport in the world due to the sheer number of movements and aircraft visiting. AirVenture is organised by the Experimental Aircraft

Association and heavily features this type of aircraft. However, it is also visited each year by teams of historic, homebuilt, restored, ultralight, helicopter, airliner and executive aircraft. Each day has a showcase and flying display of aircraft. AirVenture takes place each July or August. Find details at www.airventure.org

The rest of the year, this airport is used by general aviation, some corporate jets, and some freight feeder flights. There is also the excellent EAA AirVenture Museum on site, which offers flights in classic aircraft. It uses the small 'Pioneer Airport' site to the west of the main airport, with its own grass runway. The roads around here are good for watching any movements at Oshkosh.

VIETNAM

Hanoi Noi Bai International

HAN | VVNB

Vietnam's second major gateway, after Ho Chi Minh City, is located in the north of the country and acts as a hub for international traffic and regional flights, with many long-haul links and connections around Asia. It has two terminals.

On the northern side is a small military base where fighter jets are housed under shelters. There are views airside in both terminals, with those in Terminal 1 being better.

Landside in Terminal 2 you'll find a food court with seating and views over the nearby gates and the runway. You can also see the military area in the distance. The domestic terminal is not visible from here. The glass is clean and good for taking pictures through, but the area can get crowded at times.

Ho Chi Minh City Tan Son Nhat International

SGN | VVTS

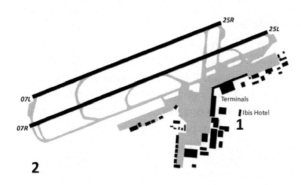

Tan Son Nhat International is Vietnam's busiest airport and the main home base of Vietnam Airlines. Despite adding a modern international terminal in 2007, the airport is overcrowded and in need of further expansion and upgrade. A new airport is due to open in the coming decade.

Alongside the international terminal is a domestic terminal, a busy cargo hub, and areas of parking for local and executive aircraft. The airport has a pair of parallel runways.

Spotting is difficult at this airport, however the Ibis hotel is perfect for some views. The terminal buildings have plenty of windows, and there are some views when approaching the airport by road.

Spotting Locations

1. Ibis Hotel
An easier way to spot at Ho Chi Minh city than by tackling the roads. (see later)

2. Cong Hoa

This street is to the west of the terminal area and passes close to the end of the runway. A café on the high floors of 602 Cong Hoa has an outdoor terrace and good views of aircraft on approach if coming from the west.

Spotting Hotels

Ibis Ho Chi Minh City Airport
2 Hong Ha Street, Ho Chi Minh, Ho Chi Minh City 700000 | +84 8 3848 5556 | www.ibis.com A fairly new hotel. King rooms on floors 7 and up in the *18-*26 range have views of aircraft landing and departing, but not on the ground as the airport terminal is in the way. There is also a rooftop pool bar area. A strong camera lens will give you some good shots.

INDEX

Kathmandu Tribhuvan International, Nepal, 186
Keflavik International, Iceland, 128
Kemble Cotswold, United Kingdom, 296
Khon Kaen, Thailand, 281
Kingman, USA, 315
Koh Samui, Thailand, 281
Kraków John Paul II International, Poland, 213
Kuala Lumpur International, Malaysia, 174
Kuala Lumpur Sultan Abdul Aziz Shah (Subang), Malaysia, 176
Kuwait International, Kuwait, 168
Lanseria, South Africa, 240
Lanzarote Arrecife Airport, Spain, 248
Larnaca International, Cyprus, 67
Las Palmas Gran Canaria, Spain, 249
Las Vegas McCarran, USA, 371
Leipzig/Halle Airport, Germany, 111
Lelystad Airport, Netherlands, 191
Liège Airport, Belgium, 32
Lima Jorge Chávez, Peru, 207
Lisbon Airport, Portugal, 218
Liverpool John Lennon, United Kingdom, 297
Ljubljana Jože Pučnik Airport, Slovenia, 236
London City, United Kingdom, 297
London Gatwick, United Kingdom, 298
London Heathrow, United Kingdom, 301
London Luton, United Kingdom, 304
London Southend, United Kingdom, 305
London Stansted, United Kingdom, 305
Long Beach, USA, 320
Longreach, Australia, 12
Los Angeles International, USA, 321
Louisville International Airport, USA, 359
Lukla Tenzing-Hillary Airport, Nepal, 186
Luxembourg Findel Airport, Luxembourg, 172

Got some feedback?

The spotting situation at airports around the world is constantly changing and it is hard to keep abreast of changes at every airport.

If you have spotted an inaccuracy in this book, would like to suggest a great spotting location, or would like to tell us about an update to the spotting situation at one of the airports listed, please send us an e-mail to info@destinworld.com.

Airport Spotting Blog

The author of this book maintains a website which delivers regular news and updates from airports around the world, including new or updated spotting locations, news about airlines, and inspiration to go out and make the most of your hobby. Visit today at **www.airportspotting.com**

ALSO FROM MATT FALCUS

Other spotting guide book available from the same author now:

Airport Spotting Hotels
ISBN 9781999647094
Updated in 2020. Our popular guide to the best spotting hotels
at airports around the world. Find out where to continue spotting
after dark. Includes addresses, contact details and suggestions of
the best rooms at hundreds of hotels around the world!

Airport Spotting Guides Europe
ISBN 9781999647032
Airport Spotting Guides Europe is the most concise and detailed
book available on spotting at European airports. Includes spotting
details at over 330 of Europe's most notable and worthwhile
airports to visit across 44 countries.

Featured airports incude maps and detailed descriptions of
spotting and photographic locations, plus information on airlines,
runways, and important contact details. Other recommended
airports and spotting details are covered in each country, plus tips
on aviation museums and spotting hotels.

Airport Spotting Guides Asia & Far East
ISBN 9781999647001
Written with the travelling aviation enthusiast and photographer
in mind, the book covers essential details at hundreds of the most
notable and worthwhile airports to visit in the Far East.

Many featured airports include a map and detailed descriptions of
spotting and photographic locations, plus information on airlines,
runways, and important contact details.

Airport Spotting Guides USA
ISBN 9781999717551
This book covers essential spotting details at over 400 of America's most notable airports, including locations, hotels, attractions, airlines and statistics.

In each of the 50 states we feature the most important airports, with a map and detailed descriptions of spotting and photographic locations, plus information on airlines, runways, and spotting hotels. We also cover the other noteworthy airports and airfields in each state.